Integral Humanism

Integral Humanism:

Perspectives of Deendayal Upadhyay and Jacques Maritain

Editor

Sonu Trivedi

India Foundation

Motilal Banarsidass Publications

MOTILAL BANARSIDASS
PUBLICATIONS
4741/23, Ansari Road, Daryaganj, New Delhi - 110002 (India)
Email: mlbd@mlbd.com | sales@mlbd.com
exports@mlbd.com | publications@mlbd.com
Website: www.mlbd.com

Integral Humanism
by
Ed. Sonu Trivedi

First Edition Published in 2025

Published in India by
Motilal Banarsidass Publications
and
India Foundation

ISBN : 978-81-979177-9-0 (PB)
978-81-979177-8-3 (HB)

Printed and bound in India

About the Book

Integral Humanism, as a philosophical and political concept, finds expression in the works of thinkers from diverse cultural and ideological backgrounds. This book aims to compare the integral humanism articulated by Deendayal Upadhyay, a prominent figure in Indian political thought, and Jacques Maritain, a French Catholic philosopher. Despite the contextual and cultural differences between their perspectives, both thinkers share a commitment to the holistic development of human beings within the framework of a fair and balanced society. The comparative analysis of Integral Humanism as articulated by Upadhyay and Maritain reveals the universality of certain principles despite the cultural and religious diversity of their contexts offering valuable insights into the promotion of human dignity, ethical governance, and the integration of material and spiritual dimensions in the pursuit of a just social order. In this book, the contributors provide diverse perspective and offer deep insight into the ideas of Deendayal Upadhyay and Jacques Maritain who based on their shared values continue to inspire and guide humanity towards a more integral and harmonious future.

Contents

About the Editor

Sonu Trivedi teaches Political Science at Zakir Husain Delhi College, University of Delhi and is a Distinguished Fellow at the India Foundation, New Delhi. She was on deputation as Director, Swami Vivekananda Cultural Centre, Embassy of India, Seoul from Sept. 2019–March 2023. Before moving to the diplomatic assignment at Seoul, she was a Fellow at Nehru Memorial Museum and Library, New Delhi (April 2018–Sept 2019). She was also a Visiting Fellow at Institute of Asia Pacific Studies, Chinese Academy of Social Sciences, Beijing (2011); Member of Myanmar Core Group at Indian Council of World Affairs (2014); Visiting faculty at Indian Institute of Management, Indore (2015–16); Convenor, Southeast Asia Research Group at Department of Political Science, University of Delhi and Founder Director, Centre for Vietnam Studies, New Delhi. She was the recipient of 'Medal of Friendship' conferred by the President of the Socialist Republic of Vietnam in 2021 and Award from Embassy of Vietnam, New Delhi in 2018 for her contributions in promoting relations between India and Vietnam. She has several publications to her credit, most significant being book titled 'Transition from Authoritarianism to Democracy: Comparative Study of Indonesia and Myanmar' and 'Democratisation in Myanmar: Progress and Prospects.' She has also co-edited a book titled 'Emerging Horizons in India-Vietnam Relations.'

Contributors

1. **Ram Madhav** is the President, India Foundation and Member, National Executive, Rashtriya Swayamsevak Sangh.

2. **R. C. Sinha** is the former Chairman, Indian Council of Philosophical Research, New Delhi and former Head of the Department of Philosophy at Patna University.

3. **Claude Vishnu Spaak** is the Head of the Department of Philosophy and Sociology at Sorbonne University Abu Dhabi and a member of its Research Institute (SAFIR). He also has scientific affiliations with the Husserl Archives in Paris and the Centre of Philosophy at the University of Lisbon.

4. **Côme Carpentier de Gourdon** is a Distinguished Fellow of the India Foundation and the convener of the International Editorial Board of World Affairs: The Journal of International Issues.

5. **Felix Machado** was the Archbishop of the diocese of Vasai from 2009-2024.

6. **Lal Ji Pal** is Assistant Professor at the Department of Political Science, Banaras Hindu University (BHU) and **Sandeep E** is Assistant Professor at the Department of Political Science, Central University of Andhra Pradesh.

7. **Krishna Mohan Upadhyay** is a Doctoral Fellow at the Department of Political Science, BHU.

8. **Alexis Rostand** is a French financier, economist, author and a lecturer in economy and philosophy at Sorbonne University Abu Dhabi.

9. **Sanjay K. Jha** is Dean, School of National Security Studies and Professor at Centre for Security Studies at Central University of Gujarat, Gandhinagar.
10. **Sonu Trivedi** is a Distinguished Fellow of the India Foundation and teaches Political Science at Zakir Husain Delhi College, University of Delhi.
11. **Shameem C C.** is Assistant Professor, Department of Arts, Koneru Lakshmaiah Education Foundation (Deemed to be University), Vaddeswaram, Guntur, Andhra Pradesh.
12. **Pratibha Poonia** is a Research Scholar at School of International Studies, Jawaharlal Nehru University.
13. **Shweta** is a Research Scholar at the Department of Philosophy, University of Delhi.
14. **Yashowardhan Tiwari** is the Program Manager of Public Policy in the Office of the Vice Chancellor at Rishihood University.
15. **Nidhi Singh** is a Research Scholar at the Pt. Pandit Deendayal Upadhyay Chair, BHU.
16. **Ranjana Singh** is a Doctoral Fellow at the Department of Political Science, BHU.
17. **Timothy Samuel Shah** is a Distinguished Research Scholar in Politics at University of Dallas.
18. **Divyapani Dwivedi** is a Doctoral Fellow at the Department of Political Science, BHU.

Acknowledgements

This edited volume on "Integral Humanism: Perspectives of Deendayal Upadhyay and Jacques Maritain" is the culmination of a collaborative effort inspired by the ideas and philosophies of two towering intellectuals. It brings together carefully selected papers, offering diverse insights into Integral Humanism as articulated by Deendayal Upadhyay and Jacques Maritain at the International Conference on "Integral Humanism: Perspectives of Deendayal Upadhyay and Jacques Maritain" held on March 4-5, 2024.

I extend my heartfelt gratitude to the India Foundation for taking the initiative to organise the conference that served as the genesis of this volume. The team at the Foundation has been instrumental in bringing this project to fruition. I also express my sincere thanks to the Pt. Deendayal Upadhyay Chair at Banaras Hindu University for the partnership and academic collaboration. The Chair's commitment to exploring and promoting the legacy of Deendayal Upadhyay has enriched this endeavour immensely. I also take this opportunity to thank the Indian Council of Social Science Research for its generous support of this initiative.

My deepest appreciation goes to the contributors of this volume for their insights and well researched papers which forms the core of this book. Their thought-provoking and meticulously researched papers reflect the richness of the conference discussions and deepen our understanding of Integral Humanism in both Indian and global contexts.

The editorial and publishing team of Motilal Banarsidass Publications deserve special thanks. Their long-standing reputation for excellence in academic publishing has ensured that this work reaches a wider audience.

It is hoped that this volume serves as a meaningful contribution to the study of Integral Humanism and inspires deeper engagement with the ideas of Deendayal Upadhyay and Jacques Maritain.

Sonu Trivedi

Preface

The concept of Integral Humanism, as articulated by Deendayal Upadhyay and Jacques Maritain, represents a profound exploration of the human condition, emphasising the integration of material and spiritual dimensions within a just and harmonious society. Despite emerging from vastly different cultural, political, and historical contexts, their philosophies converge in their commitment to holistic human development, ethical governance, and the universal principles of dignity and harmony.

This volume, Integral Humanism: Perspectives of Deendayal Upadhyay and Jacques Maritain, is a compilation of selected papers presented at the international conference jointly organised by India Foundation and the Pt. Deendayal Upadhyay Chair at Banaras Hindu University. Supported by the Indian Council of Social Science Research, the conference sought to facilitate dialogue and deeper understanding of the comparative dimensions of Integral Humanism as envisioned by these two great thinkers.

This edited volume is divided into thematic sections, encompassing philosophical, social, economic, and political dimensions of Integral Humanism. The contributors provide nuanced analyses of the subject, offering fresh insights into the relevance of these ideas in addressing contemporary global challenges. From discussions on ethical frameworks and inter-religious spirituality to reflections on governance, digital age paradigms, and sustainable development, this volume serves as a significant academic resource.

The introduction by Ram Madhav elaborates the concept of integral humanism as developed by two scholars from different contexts: Jacques Maritain, a French catholic philosopher, and Pandit Deendayal Upadhyay, an Indian political thinker. Although separated by time and geography, both scholars articulated similar philosophies that sought to harmonise social, political, and religious dimensions of human life, offering a third way beyond the dominant ideologies of capitalism, communism, and fascism.

Under the theme of philosophical perspectives on Integral Humanism, the chapter "Integral Humanism: A Paradigm Shift in Ethical Framework" by R. C. Sinha delves into the philosophy of integral humanism of Deendayal Upadhyay rooted in vedantic philosophy. He also explores the similarities between Deendayal Upadhyay's integral humanism and Jacques Maritain's humanistic philosophy. Claude Vishnu Spaak in his contribution explores a philosophical dialogue between Jacques Maritain and Deendayal Upadhyay, comparing their concepts of integral humanism. Despite their cultural differences—Maritain rooted in Christian thought and Upadhyay in the Hindu tradition—both thinkers share a commitment to a universal spiritual 'absolute', which they argue should shape integral humanism. Both philosophers seek to reconcile tradition with universality. While Maritain envisions a future where humanism continues to evolve, Upadhyay sees tradition as a dynamic force that guides humanity toward progress. The chapter on "Humanism, Integrity and the Quest for an Inter-Religious Spirituality" by Côme Carpentier de Gourdon, traces the evolution of humanism and its intersection with spirituality, focusing on Jacques Maritain's and Deendayal Upadhyay's concepts of integral humanism. Maritain, emerging from a Catholic tradition, sought to integrate spirituality with modern social institutions, advocating for a form of humanism that balanced individual rights with the common good, rooted in Christian theology. Deendayal Upadhyay, drawing from Indian philosophical traditions, emphasised the organic unity between the material and spiritual realms, advocating for a socio-political order based on dharma. Both thinkers, despite their cultural and religious differences, shared a vision of humanism that integrates spirituality with societal well-being. Felix Machado in his chapter "The Human Person: Perspectives of Jacques Maritain" explores Maritain's philosophy of the human person within his concept of integral humanism. Maritain's vision of integral humanism calls for the integration of material and spiritual dimensions of life, promoting justice and friendship in society. He believes that true Catholics and Hindus, despite their differences, can find common ground in working toward a shared vision of human dignity and a just society. The chapter "Locating the Reflections of 'Self'" in the thoughts of Deendayal Upadhyay and Jacques Maritain by Lal ji Pal and Sandeep E. compares the concepts of "Self" in the philosophies of Deendayal Upadhyay and Jacques Maritain. It explores how their socio-political and cultural backgrounds shaped their thoughts on human identity and self. Krishna Mohan Upadhyay in his chapter "Integral Humanism and Radical Humanism: A Philosophical Inquiry" examines two key strands of Humanist thought: 'Integral humanism' of Deendayal Upadhyay and 'Radical Humanism' as elaborated by M. N. Roy. These philosophies represent distinct approaches to understanding human dignity, rights, and the organisation of society. The chapter compares the two philosophies, highlighting their shared concern for human dignity and social justice.

Elaborating upon the economic dimensions of Integral Humanism, the chapter titled "Integral Humanism and Integral Development" by Alexis Rostand discusses the philosophical and economic foundations of integral humanism through the lens of Jacques Maritain's contributions to the social doctrine of the Catholic Church. He outlines the development of the concept of integral humanism within the context of the neo-Thomist revival in Europe, which sought a balanced approach between extremes like individualism and collectivism. Maritain, a key figure in this movement, influenced the Church's social teachings by integrating spiritual and economic considerations, arguing for an economy embedded in social relations rather than the other way around. Sanjay K. Jha explores the economic philosophy of 'Integral Humanism' that harmonises material progress with spiritual and ethical values, diverging from western capitalist and socialist paradigms. The philosophy critiques the reductionist tendencies, emphasising the need for policies that ensure basic necessities such as food, education, and healthcare for human dignity and societal well-being and advocates for a decentralised economy that fosters local industries, reduces reliance on external resources, and integrates traditional wisdom with modern advancements. The Chapter on "Integral Humanism and Sustainable Development Goals" explores the philosophy of Deendayal Upadhyay and Jacques Maritain particularly in the context of the United Nations' Sustainable Development Goals. Both philosophers underline the interconnectedness of ecological, social, and cultural dimensions, advocating for balanced development and harmony between humans and nature. This synthesis provides a robust foundation for addressing contemporary global challenges while promoting inclusivity, ethical governance, and long-term environmental stewardship. In the chapter "Integral Humanism in the Digital Age", the author discovers how Deendayal Upadhyay's philosophy of Integral Humanism remains relevant in the modern, technology-driven world, while being a powerful tool for human advancement. Upadhyay's vision of technology advocates for its ethical use, ensuring that it enhances human dignity and spiritual well-being. He warns against unchecked materialism and advocates for responsible stewardship of natural resources.

Focussing on "Crisis of Modern Times and Integral Humanism", Sonu Trivedi looks at how Deendayal Upadhyay's philosophy of Integral Humanism answers to the challenges facing modern civilisation. Upadhyay's belief in cultural rootedness and civilisational heritage are essential for meeting up the common challenges of modern world and holistic development of society. His socio-economic model advocates for decentralisation, self-reliance, and sustainable development fostering a more equitable distribution of economic benefits. The chapter outlines on how, Integral humanism also places a strong emphasis on 'dharma', proposing that societal progress should be guided by ethical considerations and a sense of duty towards others. Pratibha Poonia in "Social Welfare and Individual Dignity: A Dialogue Across Cultures" explores the philosophical frameworks of integral humanism by Deendayal Upadhyay and Jacques Maritain, emphasising their similarities and differences. Both thinkers promote the holistic development of individuals within society, focusing on human dignity and the common good, however, their approaches are rooted in distinct cultural traditions.

Discussing political aspects of Integral Humanism, Yashowardhan Tiwari conceptualises an alternative paradigm of sovereignty and explains Upadhyay's political philosophy of integral humanism as an alternative framework of sovereignty rooted in Indian civilisation and values. The chapter contrasts this approach with the western concept of sovereignty, which is centred on the state and its power. In contrast to the western political tradition, where sovereignty resides in the state, Upadhyay's model places sovereignty in 'Dharma', reflecting the cultural and spiritual ethos of Bharat. On the "Effects of

Deendayal Upadhyay's Thought on Modi's Governance", Nidhi Singh discusses the influence of Deendayal Upadhyay's philosophy on Modi's governance and how his philosophy continues to inspire the BJP 's governance model, emphasising on cultural nationalism, economic self-reliance, and a decentralised approach to governance. Ranjana Singh in "Unfolding the Idea of Humanism and Integral Humanism," offers a comparative analysis of the humanist philosophies of Deendayal Upadhyay and Jacques Maritain. Both thinkers, despite coming from different cultural and historical contexts, developed the concept of integral humanism as a response to the socio-political challenges of their times. Both philosophies share a critique of extreme individualism and collectivism, seeking a middle path that integrates personal and collective well-being. However, their approaches differ—Maritain focuses on individual rights and dignity within the framework of natural law, while Upadhyay prioritises cultural rootedness and the holistic development of society. The chapter by Timothy Samuel Shah explores the potential for a confluence rather than a clash between civilisations, particularly through the philosophies of integral humanism as articulated by Deendayal Upadhyay and Jacques Maritain. A key point in the chapter is the convergence between the Thomistic understanding of natural law, central to Maritain's thought, and the Hindu concept of Sanatana Dharma, which underpins Upadhyay's philosophy. Shah argues that these concepts are essentially aligned, providing a strong moral and philosophical basis for cooperation between Hindu and Christian communities. Exploring the "Vision of Global Peace in Integral Humanism of Deendayal Upadhyay" Divyapani Dwivedi discovers Upadhyay's philosophy as a framework for achieving global peace amidst contemporary geopolitical tensions and conflicts. The chapter examines how Dharma can guide states to act ethically, avoiding war and prioritising the welfare of humanity. The conclusion chapter encapsulates the key themes explored in the book, bringing out the similarities and differences between Upadhyay's and Maritain's integral humanism while positioning their thought as relevant for addressing modern global challenges.

In the backdrop of such thought-provoking essays, this volume looks forward to deepen the discourse on Integral Humanism and its practical implications, bridging the timeless wisdom of Deendayal Upadhyay and Jacques Maritain with contemporary aspirations for a balanced and equitable world. This book is intended to inspires further study and dialogue on these transformative ideas and their everlasting impact.

Sonu Trivedi
Editor

Introduction

Integral Humanism: Jacques Maritain and Deendayal Upadhyay

Ram Madhav

Harold Macmillan, the former Prime Minister of the UK, was once asked by someone about his vision for the country. "If you want to have a vision for the UK, consult a saint; I am a politician," Macmillan replied bluntly. Rare exceptions apart, politicians govern, while it is for the saints and scholars to give a vision for national societies. Two such scholars, separated by thirty years and 3000 miles, who articulated the philosophy of integral humanism in the last century, belong to this category of 'visionary saints.' Pandit Deendayal Upadhyay's name is well-known in India. But the other, lesser-known scholar was Jacques Maritain, a French philosopher. Maritain was a devout Catholic, while Deendayal, although entering politics in later years, was primarily a Pracharak—a saintly functionary of the Rashtriya Swayamsevak Sangh (RSS).

Integral Humanism is a profound social-political-religious philosophy that inspired a generation of politicians and social thinkers in both Europe and India. While Deendayal's integral humanist philosophy became the sheet anchor for the Hindu Nationalist Movement in India, Maritain's version of it three decades earlier became the driving ideology for the Christian Democratic Movement in Europe.

Maritain presented his thesis on integral humanism in 1936, which was later published in the quarterly journal of the University of Notre Dame, Indiana, US, in its January 1939 issue. Almost three decades later, in 1965, Deendayal presented his thesis of integral humanism in the form of four lectures in Mumbai. Both were renowned personalities in their respective areas during their lifetime. Maritain played an important role, albeit behind the curtains, in the framing of the Universal Decleration of Human Rights in 1948. His was a renowned name in the intellectual circles by the 1950s, and Notre Dame University established a Jacques Maritain Centre in 1957. Yet, there is no evidence to suggest any interaction between the two scholars during their lifetime. Deendayal met with an untimely death in early 1968, while Maritain passed away in 1972. However, one finds a number of similarities in the theses of both. Interestingly, both called their theses 'Integral Humanism'.

Samuel Huntington, the celebrated American political philosopher, had authored his most talked-about and controversial book, "The Clash of Civilizations," in which he found an inherent clash among the dominant global civilisations of the last century. It could be an interesting rebuttal to Huntington to explore the commonalities in the theses of Maritain and Deendayal in order to understand the scope of civilisational confluence between the East and the West.

India was colonised by the Mughals and the British for many centuries. Colonised people develop a few distinct syndromes. The first one is called the Stockholm Syndrome. It is a form of mental slavery, which is experienced in a hostage situation. Sometimes, the captives start developing a psychological bond with their captors, thinking that the captors have actually done a lot of good for them. We are very well familiar with this syndrome in post-independence India. There is no dearth of scholars in India who see a great virtue in Mughal and British rule. 75 years after independence, a new drive has been launched to end this mental colonisation, which is euphemistically called "decolonizing the Indian mind." Renowned Indian political psychologist Ashis Nandy once observed that "colonialism is, first of all, a matter of consciousness, and needs to be defeated ultimately in the minds of men."

The other syndrome is just the opposite. Colonisers leave such a strong antipathy in the minds of the colonised, that generations of the colonised develop intense hatred for not only the colonisers, but also their present-day progeny. That too is not unfamiliar to us in India. Hating the West, its language, culture, and customs is considered an important element of one's nationalist credentials.

Renowned English poet and novelist Rudyard Kipling authored a famous poem in 1889 called "The Ballad of East and West." In that, he famously mused, "East is East, and West is West, and Never the Twain shall Meet." There are many who firmly believe in this thesis that there is no meeting ground between the East and the West. Kipling had said it in a different context. But is that sentiment really relevant today? Don't there exist many meeting points between the two? Millions of Indians that live in the West are an important bridge that connects the two worlds. Yet the syndrome continues.

But there is also a third syndrome, representatives of which include great statesmen like Swami Vivekananda and Mahatma Gandhi. Both had emphatically highlighted the distinction between the Eastern and Western worldviews in their writings and speeches. But they never rejected the other outrightly. On the contrary, they believed in the synthesis and syncretism of ideas. On a chilly winter evening in Europe, Vivekananda was offered a warm suit, which he happily wore. But when asked to replace his 'Pagdi'—typical Indian headgear—with a European hat, he jocularly replied that he was willing to surrender his body to the West but not his head. "Western body and Eastern mind," Vivekananda exclaimed. Gandhi too was an eloquent critic of Western civilisation. Yet he emphatically declared his openness to ideas, stating that "I do not want my house to be walled in on all sides and my windows to be stuffed. I want the culture of all lands to be blown about my house as freely as possible. But I refuse to be blown off my feet by any."

Both statesmen saw good and evil in both the Western as well as the Indian worldview. "There are two great obstacles in our path in India," Vivekananda said, "the Scylla of old orthodoxy and the Charybdis of modern European civilisation." This is an idiom from Greek mythology that can be identified with the proverb of "devil and deep sea" or "lesser evil." Scylla and Charybdis were the two immortal and irresistible monsters described in Homer's Odyssey. Vivekananda's expression of being between Scylla and Charybdis means being caught between two equally unpleasant alternatives.

During the colonial era, there was doubtless a superiority complex of "White man's burden" in the West that led to an effort to impose Western values on the rest of the world. India too was subjected to that imposition by force and deception. Another renowned British poet and cultural critic of the 19th century, Matthew Arnold, summed up the Indian response to it in a beautiful poem:

"The East bowed low before the blast,
In patient deep disdain,
She let the legions thunder past,
And plunged into deep thought again."

Later on, many in the West too realised the futility of this process of universalisation of the value system on European lines, that had led to severe destruction of countless local cultures and civilisations and unmitigated pain and suffering to communities and societies. Elise Boulding, a distinguished American sociologist, who is also considered the mother of the discipline of "peace and conflict studies," had openly warned that "the dominant Eurocentric concepts are not easily applied to two-thirds of the world." Finally, in 1972, the UNESCO Bellagio Conference report on "Reconstructing the Human Community" admitted that there was a need for "a transcending of 'only a European point of view' in regard to the origins of science, democratic development, nationalism, and the United Nations, as well as transcending of the psychology of dominance, especially in regard to the power of science and technology."

While this cautious distinction is important, it is no statement to shut the doors on the arena of ideas and thinking. For ideas cannot be constrained to geography or boundaries. One drop of ink that takes the shape of a few words in one corner of the world has the potential to revolutionise millions of minds in another corner of the world. That is the power of ideas.

Ideational Churning in Europe

There was massive ideational churning in Europe in the 17th and 18th centuries. Ideas concerning religion, God, reason, freedom, and nature dominated this discourse. It was the period of Enlightenment and the Reformation in the West, which threw a powerful challenge at the dominant Church-centred customs and traditions of the times.

Roman emperor Constantine's decision in the early 4th century to convert to Christianity and his efforts at promoting

Christian theology by calling for councils of clergy and building Christian churches and institutions had given great fillip to the Catholic religion, which never looked back in the next millennium. It's control over not only the religious but temporal life of the believers became absolute by the 12th century in Europe. With the clergy becoming handmaidens for rulers and despots, 'Churchianity', not Christianity, became the dominant creed.

But by the middle of the millennium, the political dominance of Rome and the Church started facing a serious challenge from movements for Reformation and Renaissance. The Reformists had vehemently argued that there was no need for the Church to reach heaven, and thus the road to wisdom and heaven need not pass through Rome. That was the time when Catholic priests were granting remission for a price from divine punishment for sins committed by the high and mighty. Salvation was up for sale, and the riches thus collected were being used by the Catholic establishment to build lavish establishments across Europe.

Martin Luther was one of the first to raise his voice against this outrage. "Why does the Pope, whose wealth today is greater than the wealth of the richest Crassus, build the basilica of St. Peter with the money of poor believers rather than with his own money?" He bluntly questioned the bishop, Albert of Mainz. Enclosed with that letter was a document that came to be known as "The Ninety-Five Theses." In his revolt against the Catholic Church, Luther had set in motion the movement of Reformation, which became the progenitor of Protestantism in Europe and laid the groundwork for the formation of secular nation-states.

Many Western scholars consider the Treaty of Westphalia of 1648, which brought the Thirty-Years War to an end, as the birth date of the Reformation in Europe. Europe was largely under the symbolic control of the Holy Roman emperors until mid-17th century. One of the first actions of the Holy Roman Emperor Ferdinand II, after ascension to power in 1619, was to force the citizens to adhere to Roman Catholicism. Tensions were already simmering between the Catholics and the Protestant sects of Calvinism and Lutheranism. Ferdinand's action led to an open war between the two religious sects, and the kings and royals who were the adherents of those faiths engaged in brutal wars in several places. The Treaty of Westphalia had ended that bloody Thirty Years War between the Protestants and Catholics, fixed boundaries of the territories, and made the kings and rulers the sovereign authority over their respective territories, replacing the Catholic Church's authority. Thus began the journey of churning of ideas in Europe.

The 17th and 18th centuries in Europe are called the Age of Enlightenment. Freedom granted from the Church's stranglehold had led to churning of the European mind over deeper philosophical questions concerning God, reason, nature, and humanity. A new philosophical worldview evolved from this churning, triggering major developments in areas of philosophy and politics. John Locke, Immanuel Kant, Voltaire, Rousseau, and Jeremy Bentham were some of the renowned Enlightenment-era thinkers in Europe.

The Enlightenment era helped European nations like the Germans, French, and British come out of the imposed religious identity and start to affirm their identities in terms of language, ancestry, and culture rather than religion. It culminated in the famous French Revolution from 1789, which became a milestone in European politics in the last two centuries. It was a popular revolution that broke out on the streets of Paris, leading to the deposition of the centuries-old Ancien Régime led by King Louis XVI. This historic event, although it survived only for a decade, established a constitutional government in France and laid strong foundations for the ideology of liberalism based on the famous principles of liberty, equality, and fraternity.

The French Revolution was a clumsy affair. In an effort to unshackle from the clutches of the monarchy on one side and the Catholic religious orthodoxy on the other, the French deputies had revolted and thrown out King Louis XVI, who was eventually executed in 1793, attracting massive protests from all over the world. The Liberal French Revolution in the first decade was a massively violent and unstable period that ended with the rise of Napoleon Bonaparte towards the end of the 18th century. The liberals of his time had hoped that Napoleon would be the new messiah of Liberalism. But soon he turned France into a war machine, and restored some of the policies of the old monarchy by befriending the Catholic Church again.

Early Liberalism had done no good to Europe or mankind. It was namesake liberal. The French Revolution had witnessed massive violence, executions, and killings. Anarchy ruled the roost until Napoleon took over. Edmund Burke, the godfather of European Conservatism, was the first to harshly criticise the French Revolution. He refused to call the French revolutionaries as liberals, branding them 'illiberal' instead. In his pamphlet 'Reflections on the Revolution in France', Burke used harsh language for the leaders of the revolution, the French deputies, for their "presumptuous ignorance" and "savage manner." He bemoaned that the destiny of France had fallen in the hands of a "swinish multitude." Whether it was proper for Burke to use such uncivil language was a hot debate at the time. Many scholars had condemned Burke for his choice of words. But the fact remains that Liberalism as a political idea had not had a hoary entry on the world stage in Europe.

Liberalism's by-product was Capitalism. Freedom from, and rejection of the state and religious control became the hallmarks of early capitalist order. It had resulted in a situation that Thomas Hobbes, the English philosopher, described a hundred years before as a "war of every man against every man." Some capitalist thinkers had argued for a laissez-faire economic system, where there would not be any interference of the government in matters of economy in any form. Laissez-faire and free trader intellectuals were vehemently against the 'socialist' ideas of workers' interests, etc. They were capitalists of the highest order. According to them, the sufferings of the working class were their own providence. Any idea of state intervention to protect the interests of the working class was a crazy one. Giving in to workers' demands would not be charity, but plunder, these intellectuals argued. Government's role should be limited to providing physical protection and justice; the rest should be left to God.

One of the foremost Laissez-Faire intellectuals was a French political economist called Frederic Bastiat. For Bastiat, the poverty and sufferings of the working class were of their own making because they were "lazy, irresponsible, and prone to prodigality." In fact, they were a part of "the providential plan." "Government had nothing to do with their hardship. Nature assigned each person his position in society, and the only way to better one's condition was by improving one's own character," Bastiat argued.

Liberals entered the 20th century with such quixotic ideas bordering on craziness. They were opposed to universal adult suffrage because they did not agree with the maxim that men and women were born equal. The American liberals were even opposed to Abraham Lincoln on the fantastic grounds that

Lincoln had used emergency measures like arrests of suspected traitors, suspension of the writ of habeas corpus, overlooking several constitutional provisions, etc. Liberal campaigns gradually acquired arrogance and superiority complexes. They even defended colonialism in the name of 'civilising the world'. By the time of World War II, liberals were convinced about their greater global mission. The American magazine mogul Henry Luce had declared in 1941 in an editorial to Life magazine that "We (American liberals) are the inheritors of all the great principles of Western civilisation. It now becomes our time to be the powerhouse."

Europe had responded to this Liberal capitalist project in the early 20th century with a twin response. Mass politics of two kinds had erupted: – Fascism and Nazism of the radical nationalist kind, and Communism of the Marxist-Engelsist kind. Fascists had adopted National Socialism, while it was International Socialism for the Communists. Fascism was never an ideology articulated in any coherent manner, whereas Communism was a well-articulated response to the Liberal capitalist order. These responses were shorter-lived than imagined by their preceptors. But they had nonetheless catalysed a major ideological churning in the 20th century. The world was divided into two camps—one led by the Western liberals and the other by the Fascists and Communists in Europe.

Communism had made a grand entry into Europe with the opening statement of the Communist Manifesto of Marx and Angels proclaiming, "A spectre is haunting Europe—the spectre of Communism. All the powers of old Europe have entered into a holy alliance to exorcise this spectre." As an ideology, Communism had envisaged a world split vertically into two—the haves and the have-nots. It was a response to the Liberal capitalist dogma of free markets and less government.

Communism had proposed that there would be a perpetual conflict between the haves and the have-nots, and this conflict would end in the establishment of a "Proletarian dictatorship." Coined by a Socialist revolutionary and a military officer in Prussia, Joseph Weydemeyer, this phrase was adopted by Karl Marx to indicate the intermediate stage between capitalist control and the Communist ideal of the "withering away of the state." Proletariat was the word used by Marx to denote the working-class people who have nothing but their two hands to live. While the liberals wanted the working class to accept their plight as fate, Marx insisted that the working class should rise in revolt against the Liberal capitalist order in order to overthrow the exploitative regimes and establish the rule of the collective working class.

Marx's ideology achieved temporary success in 1871 when Paris was captured by the Socialists and was converted into a Commune. The Commune that controlled Paris from March 18 to May 28, 1871, was a revolutionary Socialist government. During their two-month-long government, the Communards implemented policies of social democracy. Feminist, Socialist and Anarchist currents played important roles in the Commune. The Commune was eventually suppressed by the national French Army during La Semaine Sanglante ("The Bloody Week") beginning on May 21, 1871. Around 20,000 Communards were killed in the battle. In Engels's judgement, the Paris Commune was history's first example of the "Dictatorship of the Proletariat."

Marx had predicted that the Proletarian revolution would occur in industrialised countries like Britain and Germany where the working-class populations were in large numbers. But his predictions did not prove to be right. While the labour in the industrialised West did organise into a political force, democratic polity continued to flourish in the industrialised world. However, the predominantly agrarian economies like Russia and China fell to Communism in the 20th century. It was Vladimir Ilych Ulyanov, popularly known as Lenin, who had succeeded in establishing a Communist government in Russia in 1917 through a revolution famously known as the October Revolution. Interestingly, Lenin was not a part of the Proletariat. He was born into a middle-class, well-to-do family and studied law. Influenced by Marxist ideology, he moved to Europe and became the theoretician for the revolutionaries in Russia. The Tsarist regime in Russia was overthrown by the revolutionary force in February 1917, and a provisional government was established. Soviet history described it as the "Bourgeois Revolution." It was followed by another revolution in October of the same year, which is called the "Great October Socialist Revolution." Lenin was not physically present when the revolution took place and had only returned after the capture of power by the Bolsheviks was complete. The regime put in power by Lenin after the October Revolution in Russia was the first Communist regime in the world.

The Leninist Communism project, which ostensibly came as a response to the bourgeoise exploitation of the capitalist regime of the Tsars like Nicholas II, turned out to be the bloodiest regime in the 20th century, bloodier than its ideological cousins like the Nazis in Germany. As soon as he captured power, Lenin began a violent purge of "class enemies." It began with the brutal execution of the entire family of the Tsarist rulers, including Tsar Nicholas II at Yekaterinburg in July 1918 through shooting and bayoneting. In the ensuing seven years, until the death of Lenin in 1924, thousands perished in brutal executions.

Stalin, who took over the Communist regime of Russia in 1924, had taken this brutality to a new level. American historian Timothy Snyder gathered modern data from the Soviet archives that became available after the collapse of the Soviet regime in the 1990s and concluded that the number of victims of brutal Soviet Communist regimes exceeded 9 million. More than 6 million were targeted by the regime for purging under various pretexts, while another 3 million perished due to man-made famines, harsh imprisonments at Gulags, etc. It became so brutal that historians started parodying the dictum "war is a continuation of politics" by stating that in Communist Russia it was "politics which is the continuation of the war by other means.".

Integral Humanism as the Third Alternative

Both Jacques Maritain and Deendayal studied these developments intensely. Maritain, a Catholic priest, was worried about the absence of God and Christianity in the evolving new world under these ideologies. Deendayal too viewed the growing influence of the European ideas on Indian political and social life and a wilful rejection of the Sanatan wisdom as retrograde with concern. In different geographies and timelines, this common concern encouraged these two scholars to build a third alternative. Thus, was born the philosophy of integral humanism.

Maritain had traversed in his lifetime through Protestantism and Atheism before finally settling down with Catholicism. Although he authored dozens of books, two stand out: Integral Humanism, written in 1936, and Man and State, written in 1951. His 1936 book "Integral Humanism" was an effort to build the intellectual basis for a personalist theory of democracy. Maritain's focus in developing integral humanist philosophy was in the historical context of the rise of totalitarian ideologies like Fascism, Nazism and Communism. Deendayal would add capitalism also to this list of evil challenges. Like Deendayal, Maritain also believed that these challenges were "destructive of human rights and of the family, as well as of a democracy of freedom and responsibility towards the common good."

In his thesis, Maritain rejected both fascism and communism as against "natural law" and as too individual-centric. He argued that man's connection with God is a part of natural law, and family, society, and nature are intermediate agencies of that natural law. Maritain argued that "once the spiritual dimension of human nature is rejected, we no longer have an integral, but merely partial humanism, one which rejects a fundamental aspect of the human person." Accordingly, in Integral Humanism, he explores the prospects for a new Christendom, rooted in his philosophical pluralism, in order to find ways Christianity could inform political discourse and policy in a pluralistic age.

"For a society of free men implies basic tenets, which are at the core of its very existence. A genuine democracy implies a fundamental agreement between minds and wills on the bases of life in common; it is aware of itself and of its principles, and it must be capable of defending and promoting its own conception of social and political life; it must bear within itself a common human creed, the creed of freedom," he opined.

Maritain's critics observe, "When he published Integral Humanism, those ideologies were already at work politically, and about to unleash the Second World War with the fanaticism of a racial and nationalistic imperialism. The 'integral humanism' proposed by Maritain in 1936 aspired to lead the human person towards a full development under the 'primacy of the spiritual' that would eventually be fulfilled in Christ.".

Maritain's philosophy had acquired a prominent place in Catholic theology in the latter half of the 20th century. In a speech in Rio de Janeiro on July 1st, 1980, Pope John Paul II invoked Maritain's 'integral humanism' to explain that "culture must cultivate man and each man along the extension of an integral and full-fledged humanism, through which the whole man and all men are promoted in the fullness of every human dimension. Freedom must be understood in a more substantive sense than mere freedom of choice. The freedom which Christian democracy seeks to promote above all is what St. Augustine called libertas maior, namely freedom in its full development, freedom in a morally adult state, capable of autonomous choices in regard to the temptations coming from every form of disorderly love of self. The integral culture includes the moral formation, the education in values of individual, social and religious life."

Although Deendayal based his initial thoughts in a contemporary historical context like Maritain, he gradually widened his canvas to draw his ideas from the age-old civilizational richness of India. While Maritain's integral humanism revolved around man as the axis, Deendayal made man, society, nature, and the divine as the axis of his thesis. In Maritain's view, democracy and Christ were the guarantee for man's progress; Deendayal's integral humanism proposes that it is the all-encompassing idea of Dharma that should be the basis for universal good.

Deendayal's integral humanism comes three decades after Jacques Maritain's thesis, challenging and discording the Eurocentric socio-political doctrines on the same lines and proposing a civilizational counter-narrative in the form of a socio-political philosophy. In that, Deendayal heavily draws from the wisdom of ancient Indian scriptures and traditions, thus making it more into a philosophical school of thought than any ideology.

Delivering his lecture series in Mumbai on integral humanism in early 1965, Deendayal takes a conciliatory approach towards European ideas, while insisting that India should find answers to its challenges in its own culture. "Independence can be meaningful only if it becomes an instrument for the expression of our culture. Such expression will not only contribute to our progress, but the effort required will also give us the experience of joy. Therefore, both from the national as well as human standpoint, it has become essential that we think of the principles of the Bharatiya culture. If with its help we can reconcile the various ideals of the Western political thought, then it will be an added advantage for us".

While Deendayal's and Maritain's premise for professing a third way was largely identical, Deendayal turns to Indian wisdom for building his distinct philosophy from that of Maritain. He argues that in the Indian view, "society is self-born." "Like an individual, society comes into existence in an organic way. People do not produce society. It is not a sort of club, or some joint stock company, or a registered cooperative society. Society is an entity with its own "SELF", its own life; it is a sovereign being like an individual; it is an organic entity," says Deendayal.

Deendayal takes the concept forward and argues that, like individuals, nations too have a soul. It is acknowledged that nations develop cultures, traditions and even a personality. Deendayal makes a distinction, insisting that those are only the outward manifestations of the core idea that guides the nation. Deendayal calls that core idea of the nation as "*Chiti*"—national soul.

"*Chiti* is the soul of the nation. On the strength of this *Chiti*, a nation arises, strong and virile," says Deendayal, making his original contribution to the idea of nation.

The other unique dimension of Deendayal's integral humanist philosophy is the concept of Dharma. Although not new in the Indian context, Deendayal brought it forward as an alternative to the Capitalist, or Communist or Fascist or Christian idea of capital, state, or religion as the dominant force of a nation to Dharma as the supreme feature of a national society.

"The laws that help manifest and maintain *Chiti* of a nation are termed Dharma of that nation. Hence it is this Dharma that is supreme. Dharma is the repository of the nation's soul. If Dharma is destroyed, the nation perishes. Anyone who abandons Dharma, betrays the nation," Deendayal says. In other words, according to him, Dharma is the legal and constitutional framework around which the *Chiti* of the nation manifests and is protected.

Maritain and Deendayal represented the nativist response to the overpowering European ideologies of the last few centuries. Both emphasized the supremacy of "spiritualism" and "natural law" in their own different contexts. It will be instructive to undertake a comparative study of the two to understand the common human reflexes in the East and the West to onslaughts that occur in the form of modernity and liberalism.

Philosophical Perspectives on Integral Humanism

Chapter One

Integral Humanism: A Paradigm Shift in Ethical Framework

R.C. Sinha

Integral humanism is a philosophy that emphasizes the centrality of the individual in the process of development. It asserts that human welfare and dignity should be the primary focus of progress. This approach advocates for a holistic balance between material, social, and spiritual needs. It ensures that economic growth does not overshadow essential human values and well-being. By emphasizing sustainable development that harmonizes with nature and respects cultural diversity, integral humanism seeks to foster a society where every person can flourish. Deendayal Upadhyay champions comprehensive development, striving to create a just and equitable society where all individuals are empowered to thrive.

Humanism, stemming from the Latin term 'studia humanitatis', encapsulates a philosophical disposition that places paramount importance on humanity, specifically on the individual. It underscores the centrality of 'Man' as the pivotal figure in navigating both societal structures and technological advancements. Within this framework, humanity is not merely a passive participant in the unfolding of events, but rather an active agent capable of shaping its own destiny. It recognizes that human beings possess the capacity to mould their circumstances, both individually and collectively. Thus, humanism advocates for the cultivation of human potential and the realization of individual capabilities. It asserts that man is not merely a product of external forces and factors, but rather the architect of his own fate. Man is capable of self-realization and transcendence through conscious choices and actions. It embraces inclusivity and extends its embrace to those dwelling on margins of society. It champions the dignity and worth of every individual. It also weaves together the diverse strands of humanity into a cohesive tapestry of mutual respect and understanding.

The Philosophy of Integralism is rooted in Vedantic philosophy, which emphasizes the fundamental oneness of all existence. Vedanta teaches that the apparent differences in the world are mere illusions. Integralism promotes harmony and integration over division and fragmentation. It advocates for a holistic approach to life, where all aspects are seen as interconnected and interdependent, reflecting the core Vedantic principle of unity. So, the essence of the philosophy of integral humanism is that all souls are connected, whether they belong to humans, animals or plants. It rejected differences based on race, colour, caste or religion, and instead perceive all human beings as parts of a unified whole. This philosophy emphasized that everyone shares a common consciousness and should be treated equally.

Humanism is more than just a compassionate outlook towards others. It confers upon humanity a unique status amidst all other beings. Unlike humanitarianism, which often involves acts of benevolence, humanism asserts that human beings are endowed with wisdom. It posits that humans occupy the highest position within the cosmic order. Therefore, they cannot simply be objects of compassion or benevolence. Instead, humanism emphasizes the inherent dignity, capability, and significance of the human individual within the broader context of existence. Integral humanism can be comprehended from both metaphysical and ethical standpoints. Metaphysically, it harmonizes the principles of materialism with those of idealism or spiritualism, acknowledging the coexistence and interdependence of both realms. Ethically, integral humanism brings together secular, everyday values with higher, spiritual values, creating a holistic approach that encompasses the full spectrum of human experience.

This integration underscores a balanced perspective of values both the tangible and intangible aspects of life. It aims for a comprehensive understanding of human existence. Deendayal Upadhyay and Jacques Maritain, originating from different cultural and ideological backgrounds, both championed the concept of integral humanism. They emphasized its deep roots in their respective cultural contexts. Deendayal Upadhyay's integral humanism was framed within the philosophical and spiritual traditions of India, advocating for a holistic development that harmonizes material and spiritual well-being. This philosophy reflects the ancient wisdom and values of the country. Maritain, on the other hand, articulated his vision of integral humanism within the Western tradition, influenced by Thomistic philosophy and Christian humanism. He stressed the dignity of the human being and the importance of moral and spiritual dimensions in social and political life. Both thinkers sought to create a societal framework that respects cultural heritage while addressing contemporary challenges. Their ultimate aim was to achieve a balanced and humane development of individuals and societies.

Humanism is more than just a philosophical viewpoint. This embodies a profound exploration of the place of humanity within the intricate fabric of existence. At its core, humanism reflects a collective endeavour by philosophers to illuminate the significance of human beings amidst the complexities of social, moral, spiritual and political realms. Here, I understand that humanism gives rigid parameters to prove challenges of complex society. Instead, it emerges as a dynamic attitude of the mind. It is concerned with inherent human dignity and potential of humanity. It grapples with the complexities of the life and human existence. In fact, it celebrates the highest aspirations of individuals and societies and urges a deeper understanding of our roles and responsibilities within the broader tapestry of life. Thus, humanism emerges not as a fixed ideology but as a guiding ethos, continually evolving to reflect the ever-changing landscape of human experience.

The contribution which we can call the legacy of the people of 'Bharat' is the principle of 'Ekatma Manava Darshan'. This was to be the third way of development discarding the two extremes of capitalism and communism. The third way is purely Bhartiya way. He delved deep into the Vedantic Philosophy. Vedanta is out and out Idealistic and Integral one. Deendayal Upadhyay developed his Integral Humanism based on Vedantic Philosophy.

Deendayal Upadhyay emphasizes the importance of the wellbeing of marginalized people, advocating for an approach he termed 'integral development'. This concept extends beyond mere economic growth to encompass both material and spiritual development. It aims to create a holistic and balanced advancement of human society. By focusing on the comprehensive upliftment of every individual, particularly the underprivileged, his vision promotes a model of development that ensures social equity and fosters an environment where all aspects of human life, including cultural and moral dimensions, are nurtured and respected.

Deendayal Upadhyay's conception of 'Antyodaya' and Jacques Maritain's concern for the good of all people on the margins, despite their different cultural backgrounds, share several common themes. Both philosophers emphasize the intrinsic human dignity that should be afforded to every individual. They advocate for a holistic approach to development that integrates economic, social, and moral dimensions. They also stress the importance of social justice, ensuring that the marginalized and disadvantaged are uplifted and included in the progress of society. Furthermore, both Deendayal Upadhyay and Jacques Maritain underline the moral foundations of human behaviour. They recognize that true development and social well-being must be rooted in ethical principles. This convergence of ideas underscores a universal commitment to fostering a just and humane society where every person can thrive.

Deendayal Upadhyay and Jacques Maritain adhere to common good and social justice of subaltern people. Here, I would like to make the difference between subaltern and proletariat. Karl Marx considered proletariat as economic category whereas subaltern I think is cultural one. Deendayal Upadhyay and Jacques Maritain both emphasize the central role of morality in their philosophical frameworks. Integral Humanism, as developed by Upadhyay, constructs an ethical foundation that integrates the spiritual, social, and economic dimensions of human life. This philosophy advocates for a balanced and holistic approach to human development, where moral values guide socio-economic policies and personal conducts. Similarly, Maritain's Humanism underscores the importance of moral principles derived from a synthesis of Christian theology and humanistic ideals. Both thinkers argue that true human progress cannot be achieved without a moral compass, underscoring the necessity of ethical considerations in both individual and societal growth. Thus, their philosophies converge on the idea that morality is indispensable for achieving a just and harmonious society.

Comparative methodology stipulates creativity. When comparing philosophers and their philosophy, this creativity extends beyond merely identifying similarities; it encompasses recognizing and articulating unique insights that emerge from their differences as well. To clarify the concept of Integral Humanism, it is essential to undertake a comparative analysis with other philosophical frameworks. Integral Humanism, as articulated by Deendayal Upadhyay, emphasizes a holistic approach that integrates the material and spiritual dimensions of human existence. Integral Humanism advocates for a balanced development of the individual and society. In contrast, M.N. Roy's 'New Humanism', while also focused on the comprehensive development of human beings, is rooted in rationalism and scientific humanism. It emphasizes the importance of reason, individual freedom, and scientific progress. By comparing Integral Humanism with New Humanism, we can better understand the distinctive features of each philosophy. Integral Humanism synthesizes tradition and modernity, spirituality and material progress, while New Humanism is committed to rationality, individualism, and secularism. This comparative analysis not only highlights the unique contributions of each thinker but also enriches our understanding of humanism as a multifaceted and evolving concept.

M. N. Roy was more widely known in his life-time for his phenomenal career as a revolutionary and propounder of New Humanism. He was a man of action and a man of thought. As a man of action, he was a devoted and dedicated revolutionary.

As a man of thought, he developed into a profound and original socio-political philosopher. He passed through three phases of political life. He started as an ardent nationalist. He became an equally ardent communist. He ended as a creatively active Radical Humanist. Deendayal Upadhyay called humanism as 'Ekatma manava vada'. He was equally revolutionary but not that of radical as M.N. Roy. He believed in spirituality. His humanism is certainly based on spiritualism.

The rise of cold-war in the post war international politics presented a dilemma for M.N. Roy who was once a member of Comintern and later realizing the limitations of Marxism founded a new socio-political theory called New Humanism. Faced with a choice between Democracy and communism Roy felt distressed because he was earnest advocate of freedom. He was anxious to check communism and free himself from communism. He felt that popular movement against communism could be derived only from the democratic tradition.

Democracy is informed with the norms and ideals of humanistic culture. The most important thing, it deals with, is freedom and dignity of the man. Neither communism nor the existing parliamentary capitalist democracy but the third alternative was necessary for further progress of human existence and civilization. Thus, Deendayal Upadhyay tried to construct a new political theory and economic doctrine based on his Humanism. M.N. Roy observes that the cultural and moral crisis of modern civilization is compelling sensitive and thoughtful men throughout the world to turn towards its humanist tradition. The restoration of moral values in public life is the crying need of the present era. The present era is characterized as full of contradictions and clashes. It is not only overshadowed by technology but violence and hatred. In order to get rid of dissension and clashes we have to cultivate humanism. Deendayal Upadhyay felt that the restoration of moral values in public life could be achieved if we could have a new political and social philosophy deduced from a spiritual interpretation of Humanism.

Every political philosopher based his philosophy, either explicitly or implicitly, upon a view of human nature. Some take man as a spiritual being and some consider him as a mere biological entity. Some philosophers consider man as selfish economic being while others take him as a social animal. Thus, political philosophy must be founded on the correct view of human nature. We must explain man if we are to understand human nature. So, an explanation of man leads to the question of his origin and thereby political philosophy is led into philosophical theory. Deendayal Upadhyay believed that an appropriate approach to individual and social life must be founded on philosophy embracing the totality of human existence. He also contends that in society lowest and downtrodden should be given its due. Vedanta also contemplates that discrimination based on hierarchical caste system must go. His concept of 'Antoydaya' is quite relevant. Integral Humanism is creative and spiritual in nature. It will not be out of place to compare Integral Humanism with New Humanism of M.N. Roy. Integral Humanism of Deendayal Upadhyay is product of Indian ethos and gives emphasis on moral values.

The fundamental problem of philosophy is to define itself. This is so because philosophy, in a sense, happens to be the foundation on which the edifice of a civilization rests. Thus, civilization being a dynamic process, philosophy also evolves with it. This explains the fact that philosophy differs from one age to another, from one civilization to another and requires to be defined a new. Roy's conception of philosophy depends on the basic characteristics of our modern civilization.

Our civilization is unthinkable without any consideration of technology and its all-pervading effects on our life. Indeed, technology is so unique and central to our civilization that it is natural for a great thinker like M.N. Roy to provide a scientific basis of his philosophy.

In modern thought the universal appeal of science and technology is apparent. Scientific enquiry is objective. It rejects authority, faith, prejudice and superstition. It relies on the test of universal evidence and rigorous logic. Such methodological awareness gradually led to that objective body of knowledge which revolutionaries the whole context of our intellectual life. The starting point of M.N. Roy's philosophy can be traced to its acceptance of science as the only form of valid knowledge and its rejection of faith and authority of all forms. Thus, Roy claims to have provided us with an out and out scientific philosophy. Being modern thinker, Roy thought that the fundamental problems of philosophy is its definition. He dealt with this problem in a scientific spirit. Deendayal Upadhyay is not a technical philosopher like M.N. Roy. He has integral vision. In India, the concept of philosophy is often referred to as 'Darshan,' which means vision. In this context, Deendayal Upadhyay can be regarded as a philosopher due to his profound and visionary thoughts. His philosophy presents a holistic vision for society, integrating spiritual and material well-being. His ideas emphasize the importance of a balanced and inclusive approach to development, reflecting a deep understanding of the cultural and philosophical heritage of India.

Hence, his contributions go beyond mere political theory, embodying a comprehensive vision for human progress. M.N. Roy was a materialist but Deendayal Upadhyay was spiritualist from the core of his heart. Roy claimed that man originated from inanimate matter and is the highest product of the process of organic evolution. He maintained that man's intelligence, will and emotions have a physical basis. While charting the Western intellectual tradition Roy found mainly two main assumptions, regarding human nature. In the first place, there is the assumption that man is selfish by nature and so instinctively concerned only with his own interest. Secondly, it is also held by people that human nature is to believe in benevolent supernatural power.

Obviously, this second assumption was historically associated with the religious tradition that believed in man's original sin. This view led to the view of redemption of man by virtue of his readiness to subordinate himself to a supernatural power. Roy also opined that both these assumptions had inspired social philosophies which could conceive of society only as a coercive organization. Either man made laws or providential ordinance were admitted to curb the evil instinct of man. Roy held that on the basis of these views of human nature it was not possible to develop any social philosophy which could allow economic and political theories that guarantee freedom and dignity of man. This resulted in the present crisis of modern civilization. The view that man is a self-interested creature and that the incentive of all economic enterprises is personal gain leads to economic determinism. Thus, Karl Marx gives the economic interpretation of history. Economic determinism therefore cannot be the social philosophy which is required to lead civilized mankind out of the present crisis.

Social philosophies founded on erroneous beliefs about human nature have eroded our self-confidence, leading to a deep spiritual crisis that defines the modern condition. To address this predicament effectively, we must construct a social framework grounded in an accurate and positive conception of human nature, thereby restoring faith in ourselves and fostering genuine social progress.

If man is by nature a believer in some power greater than himself then the idea of human freedom must be abandoned. Hence, the assumptions about super natural power cancels human freedom. The great contribution of Deendayal Upadhyay is that he conceived the third way of development discarding the two western models of capitalism and communism.

Deendayal Upadhyay delved deep into Bhartiya Tattvajnana (Philosophy). The English version of Ekatma Manava Darsan is Integral Humanism. Though he does not subscribe to any 'ism' but the expression 'Integral Humanism' has no overtones of 'ism' used in political arena. Capitalism and communism both believed in conflicts. Integral humanism emphasizes on harmony. The integral humanism is the basis of Ideology of Deendayal Upadhyay. Ekatmata is the central theme of Advaita Vedanta. The Advaita philosophy believes in harmony and integration. Ordinarily, humanism is charged with anthropocentric bias. Here Integral humanism is not concerned only to human being. It is also concerned to the well-being of all living beings. It is cosmo-centric in nature. Indian culture is integral and 'Ekatma Darsan' is true to Indian culture.

According to western humanist, Man is essentially a rational being. Rationality, therefore, is a biological function which can very highly develop in the highest biological form. Rationality can subordinate man's selfishness to enlightened self-interest, which is a social virtue. Though Roy was a materialist, he never accepted the supremacy of the social environment over the nature of man. According to the philosophy of new humanism human nature is mainly determined by physical and biological factors. Though, M.N. Roy was not humanist of Vedantic type. But he had strong leaning towards ethical values of life. In the far end of his life, he left the membership of Comintern, the International Executive Committee of Communist Party. Hence, the main problem before Roy was to find in human nature a basis for a harmonious social order and the incentive to all social progress. Man's urge for freedom is the basic thrust of both Deendayal Upadhyay and M.N. Roy's Philosophy.

Man being the product of evolution, his nature is subject to this rational process. Yet he maintained that there is some common and constant thing in human nature. Thus, the uniqueness of the individual was recognized as well as the fact that the individuals have some factors in common which constitute the foundation of human nature. Two basic features of human nature are emphasized in the philosophy of New Humanism. The first feature is the rationality of man and the second is man's urge for freedom. I have tried to understand 'Ekatmavada' of Deendayal Upadhyay by reading his book in Hindi published by Suruchi Prakashan (Fifth edition, June 2014). Deendayal Upadhyay has tried to decolonize the Indian mind by propounding 'Integral humanism'. Here I pinpoint that Integral humanism believes that man is essentially spiritual in nature. Rationality is an essential component but man goes beyond rationality. In this way man becomes conscious of the law-governed nature of the universe. The mind, Roy maintained, becomes conscious of the environments the radius of which gradually expands until the entire nature is embraced. Conscious of law-governed system, human mind, is necessarily rational in essence. Man becomes conscious of the fact of this law-governed physical world and of the fact that every phenomenon is connected with some other phenomenon. This led to man's knowledge that nothing is uncaused. This experience leads him to think in causal terms and thus makes him rational. In order to explain human reason, he contends that reason is the simple, instinctive notion that every object of experience is connected with some other object or objects which may or may not have been already experienced. However, because of the belief in this connection, which holds the world of experience together, their existence is assumed. He considered reason as an echo of the harmony of the universe. In the instinctive level of the animal activity reason is expressed in rudimentary form. Thus, for him, human rationality is developed form of instinctive rationality present in the animals. The 'humanness', Roy held, was inherited from the mental and emotional equipment of the animals. Thus, reason is no longer a metaphysical category. Reason is the consciousness of the harmony of nature. Rationality becomes a biological function. Roy characterized reason in nature as physical determinism. Reason was considered a biological function because, with the help of his developed brain inherited from animals, man becomes conscious of the law-governed physical nature. But this contention has not been accepted by Deendayal Upadhyay. He conceives that spirit is the focal point of human existence. The man is not confined to rational level. He goes beyond that. Man is out and out self-conscious spiritual being. Roy observed in the fourth of his twenty second thesis that reason being a biological property is not antithesis of will, intelligence and emotion.

Historical determinism, therefore, does not exclude freedom of the will. Man's will and emotions are also determined or caused by physical factors. He rose out of the background of the physical universe. The latter is a cosmos a law-governed system. Therefore, man's being and becoming, his emotions, will, ideas are also determined. Man is essentially rational.

Integral humanism of Deendayal Upadhyay agrees that basic feature of human nature is the urge for freedom. As to the definition of freedom he thinks that freedom is progressive disappearance of all restrictions on the unfolding of the potentialities of individuals, as human beings, and not as cogs in the wheels of a mechanized social organism. The potentialities of the individual are not divine potentialities but inherent in man. He says that potentiality of man is divine and restricted to biological level. One dominant difference which I would like to streamline that humanism is considered by Dr. Radhakrishnan as a substitute of religion. Dr. Radhakrishnan, in his work 'The Idealist View of Life,' posits humanism as a viable alternative to traditional religious belief systems. Religion does both positive and negative functions. Dr. Radhakrishnan does not specifically label religion as either wholly positive or negative but recognizes its complex role in society. By proposing humanism, he aims to provide a framework that can unite people meaningfully without the divisive elements often associated with some religious practices. Humanism can be conceived as a substitute for religion, but this presents a different issue altogether. The contemporary Indian philosopher Dr. S. Radhakrishnan considers humanism as a potential substitute for religion.

Dharma can be possible with God or Without God. But religion is not possible without God. In religion, the presence of a divine entity and an institutional framework are deemed essential components of religious practice. However, Dharma stands out as a concept that can encompass both perspectives, with or without the presence of a deity. As we journey towards a nuanced understanding, it becomes imperative to engage in frank comparisons of diverse narratives. By exploring and critically analyzing the various dimensions of religious traditions, we can arrive at a more comprehensive and meaningful conclusion regarding the nature and essence of spirituality. Hinduism embraces pluralism, evidenced by its diverse array of scriptures rather than a single holy book.

Unlike many institutional religions, Hinduism allows for a wide range of beliefs and practices.

A Hindu can lead a devout life without visiting temples or believing in any specific deity. Similarly, Buddhism and Jainism, which do not worship a God, are still recognized as true religious paths. This pluralistic ethos reflects India's broader celebration of multiplicity in culture, geography, climate, and languages, making it a land rich in varied narratives and traditions.

In order to deliver a clear and impactful message that may resonate globally, it is essential to address the problem of clash of civilizations as stipulated by Harvard Professor Samual P. Huntington. This concept is fundamental to understanding contemporary conflicts and fostering a new narrative. The idea of integral humanism can provide a powerful message, as it contrasts sharply with the conflicts arising from dogmatic nationalism. Nationality may be understood in two ways: one is the dogmatic and the other is the enlightened one. Nationality is often perceived dogmatically, tied to rigid definitions based on borders and legalities. This emphasis on exclusivity can foster divisiveness. Conversely, an enlightened perspective on nationality acknowledges its fluidity, recognizing the diversity of identities within nations and appreciating the interconnectedness of humanity beyond borders. Embracing the enlightened view encourages inclusivity, empathy, and a deeper understanding of the complexities of identity in our increasingly globalized world. By emphasizing enlightened nationalism and integral humanism, we can offer a vision of global harmony and cooperation. Deendayal Upadhyay proposes the thesis of integral humanism that can lessen conflicts in the world. He asserts that national identity does not contradict global identity. One can be true to his nationality yet serve the entire humanity. In his book 'War and

Peace', Tolstoy highlighted that nationality is a cause of war. However, I do not subscribe to this view because I uphold that one can adhere to his nationality without undermining the others nationality. I contend that rigid nationalism often leads to conflicts. So, we must cherish to enlightened nationality and live without a sense hatred to others. I think that we cannot get rid of our nationality. To say that one should get rid of his nationality is to suggest that one should skip out of his own body. It is simply not feasible. Nationality is an intrinsic part of human existence.

Integral Humanism, whether conceived by Deendayal Upadhyay or Jacques Maritain, offers a holistic approach to social development. It emphasizes the integration of material and spiritual dimensions of human existence. Deendayal Upadhyay's vision focuses on the synthesis of traditional value system of India with modern needs. He advocates for a balanced growth that harmonizes individual and collective welfare. Similarly, Jacques Maritain's concept stresses the unity of human life, blending personal freedom with the common good, rooted in Christian philosophy and theology. M.N. Roy's philosophy champions the primacy of freedom and ethical values over determinism. He emphasizes the significance of individual agency and the ethical responsibility that comes with it, rejecting the notion of human actions being solely dictated by predetermined forces. For Roy, the pursuit of freedom and adherence to ethical principles are foundational to human existence. It enables individuals to shape their destinies and contribute meaningfully to society's progress. In his worldview, the cultivation of moral consciousness and the exercise of free will are essential for the realization of a just and harmonious world. These perspectives open new dimensions for the world by proposing frameworks that transcend mere economic or political considerations, urging societies to nurture the full potential of every individual within a cooperative and ethically grounded community. This comprehensive outlook promotes a sustainable and inclusive path forward, encouraging global systems that respect cultural diversity and uphold human dignity.

Integral Humanism, as a philosophy, offers a critical examination of antiquated value systems and advocates for the integration of new, dynamic moral principles in public life. This approach recognizes the limitations of old values in addressing contemporary issues and promotes a synthesis of traditional wisdom with modern insights. By doing so, Integral Humanism provides a framework that is both rooted in cultural heritage and adaptable to present-day challenges. It ensures that moral values remain relevant and effective in guiding public conduct. Furthermore, Integral Humanism stipulates a trend of moral values that emphasize holistic development and the interconnectedness of individual and social well-being. It calls for a balance between material progress and spiritual growth, advocating for values such as compassion, responsibility, and community welfare. This philosophy encourages individuals and leaders alike to prioritize ethical considerations in decision-making processes, thereby fostering a public life grounded in integrity and collective progress. In fact, Integral Humanism paves the way for a new value system that is both enduring and transformative, capable of nurturing a just and harmonious society.

Integral Humanism of both Deendayal Upadhyay and Jacques Maritain represents a paradigm shift in ethical frameworks, dismantling outdated values to pave the way for a revitalized system in public life. This philosophy not only deconstructs the old notions but also constructs a robust foundation for the infusion of novel moral values into the social fabric. By acknowledging the evolving dynamics of human existence, Integral Humanism advocates for a holistic approach that integrates individual well-being with societal progress. It fosters a renewed emphasis on empathy, compassion and social responsibility, guiding public discourse towards a more inclusive and ethical direction. Hence, Integral Humanism of Deendayal Upadhyay serves as a beacon for the cultivation of a new moral consciousness, one that resonates with the complexities of contemporary society and envisions a future rooted in integrity and solidarity.

Chapter Two

Universality, Traditionality and Historicity: A Metaphysical Approach to Integral Humanism

Claude Vishnu Spaak

The purpose of this paper is to open a philosophical discussion on Jacques Maritain and Deendayal Upadhyay regarding their respective conceptions of integral humanism. The aim is to show that the stakes of this philosophical discussion are the questions of universalism, tradition, and the meaning of human history. The thesis of this work is that if one puts aside the cultural differences between Maritain and Upadhyay regarding their respective notions of integral humanism (Maritain focuses on the relation of humanism to Christendom, whereas Upadhyay bases his approach on the Hindu dharmic tradition), one can see a strong shared commitment of both these thinkers to searching for a universal spiritual Absolute, in relation to which the integral human being would be standing. Yet the problem that we face regards the status of universalism itself: is it always already given in a set of eternal standards that govern the world order (dictating a more tradition-based approach to integral humanism)? Or is it intrinsically historical, in as much as it unfolds dialectically in history (in the latter case integral humanism is largely futural, the present humanity's purpose essentially being to prepare for its advent)? Of course, both perspectives can be compatible, and in this light Maritain and Upadhyay are two thinkers that seek, from two different cultural standpoints, to show how these two facets of universalism can be articulated to each other, yet with a major difference: Maritain, coming from the Western tradition, sees the road of history towards the universal integral man as a tragic one, paved with struggle; whereas Upadhyay, time and again, insists that the *Bharatiya* philosophical way of thinking categorically refuses the idea that conflict may have any philosophical fecundity, and that here lies a fundamental difference between the Indian and the Western traditions.

1. Humanism and Anthropocentrism in Maritain

One can start by examining the distinction, in Jacques Maritain, between, on the one hand, humanism in the true positive sense of integral humanism, and on the other hand, the so-called pseudo-humanism that developed during Modernity in Europe, which in Maritain's mind really should be renamed an anthropocentric conception of mankind. This anthropocentric paradigm culminates in the cartesian ontology of a scientific subjectivity that discovers within itself, through its own reflexive self-grounding powers, the methodological tools that it needs in order to know and dominate the material universe, through the lenses of the *mathesis universalis* ("universal mathematical knowledge"), human subjectivity becoming thereby the master and possessor of a disenchanted nature, ripped off of its sacred spiritual attributes and reduced to being a passive domain of corporeal being[1]. This is what

Descartes conceives in an explicit way in his *Discourse on the method*[2], in conformity with many other thinkers and scientists of the time, such as Bacon who professed that knowledge is power[3], or Galileo who asserted that the material universe is a book written in mathematical language, fully offered to the human mind to be deciphered[4]. As Maritain writes:

> "Much progress has (...) been made [since modernity], concerning above all the world of reflexivity and the *prise de conscience of self* (...). Science undertakes the conquest of created nature, the human soul makes unto itself a universe of its subjectivity, the profane world differentiates itself according to its own proper law, the creature knows itself"[5].

According to Maritain, this "anthropocentric spirit" has confronted modern man with "division" and "misfortune." As he writes:

> "[A]n experience of suffering and catastrophe has instructed us; it is onto the interior hell of man, a prey to himself, that incontestable enrichments of civilization have opened"[6].

This misfortune is due to the fact that the anthropocentric man of modernity has cut himself off from the transcendence of God:

> "Man, forgetting that in the order of being and of good it is God who has the first initiative and who vivifies our freedom, has sought to make his own proper movement as creature the absolutely first movement, to give to his freedom-of-creature the first initiative of his good"[7].

Such an experience, in Western modernity, of separation from the transcendence of God, leads to a process of immanentization of the spirit within the sphere of human subjectivity, as exemplified, for example, with the theory of transcendental subjectivity that one finds in Kant's *Critique of pure reason*, or in German Idealism (think here of Fichte), or later in Husserl's theory of absolute consciousness, in his transcendental phenomenology. What is forgotten here by modernity, according to Maritain, is the utter dependance of the human spirit towards "the movement of grace". Consequently, according to him:

> "[T]he age in question has been an age of dualism, of dissociation, of splitting in two, an age of humanism separated from the Incarnation, in which the effort of progress was to take on an inevitable character and itself contribute to the destruction of the human. In short, let us say that the radical vice of anthropocentric humanism has been its being anthropocentric, and not its being humanism"[8].

Thus, Maritain firmly maintains a theological conception of the transcendence of the Spirit that anthropocentric modernity has cut itself from, and this theological conception is specifically the Christian one, as one can see here from the Christological reference here to the Incarnation of Jesus Christ, by whom the transcendence of God is intimately linked in the Catholic faith to the movement of Grace, through the redemptive intervention of God in Creation. It is thus clear that Maritain's conception of integral humanism, as opposed to the false humanism of anthropocentric modernity, is grounded in the Christian faith:

> "We are thus led to distinguish two kinds of humanism: a theocentric or truly Christian humanism; and an anthropocentric humanism, for which the spirit of the Renaissance and that of the Reformation are primarily responsible"[9].

One can notice here that Maritain's extremely critical conception of the Reformation qualifies his theological humanism as essentially linked to the Roman Catholic and Apostolic Church (and it is worth noting in passing that Maritain was for a time the Ambassador of France to the Vatican). As Maritain continues:

> "The first kind of humanism recognizes that God is the center of man; it implies the Christian conception of man, sinner and redeemed, and the Christian conception of grace and freedom, of which we have noted the principles. The second kind of humanism believes that man himself is the center of man, and therefore of all things. It implies a naturalistic conception of man and of freedom. If this conception is false, one understands that anthropocentric humanism merits the name of inhuman humanism, and that its dialectic must be regarded as the *tragedy of humanism*"[10].

2. Upadhyay's Dharmic Conception of Integral Humanism

From here one can search for the areas of convergence and of divergence between Maritain and Upadhyay on integral humanism. Starting with the converging aspects, as is well known, Upadhyay concentrates his analysis of integral humanism with reference to the key concept of Hinduism, which is the four *Purusharthas*, or objectives of the ethical life: *Dharma* (fitting the harmonious order of the universe through our moral conduct, both at the individual level and at the level of groups, especially nations), *Artha* (the search for material wellbeing), *Kama* (the satisfaction of bodily needs) and *Moksha* (the search for spiritual liberation)[11]. Upadhyay, in the series of speeches that he gave on Integral Humanism for the philosophical and political doctrine of Jan

Sangh in 1965, repeatedly criticized the tendency of Western Modernity, especially in the development of capitalism and its individualistic paradigm (but also in the competing ideology that the West produced as a reaction to capitalism, namely socialism), to be exclusively focused on the domains of *Artha* and *Kama*. For Upadhyay, integral humanism can only stem from a spiritual quest that strives to conform, at the individual level but also at the level of the nation, or even of mankind in general, with the law of *Dharma*:

> "In Bharat, these [ethical] principles are termed *Dharma*—the laws of life. All those principles which bring about harmony, peace and progress in the life of mankind are included in this term *Dharma*. On the sound basis of *Dharma* then, we must proceed with the analysis of life as an integral whole"[12].

This clear dharmic conceptualization of integral humanism, with reference to the integral wholeness of life, is in alignment with Maritain's rejection of the anthropocentric Western conception of humanism, which, for Maritain no less than Upadhyay, focuses exclusively on the corrupted forms of *Artha* and *Kama*, on the economic exploitation of the world, and on the consumerist and sensualist attitude. Moreover, Upadhyay shares with Maritain the same analysis that Western modernity has created the conditions of division and struggle, both between the human being and nature, and also within the human social and cultural order. However, one could suspect, at first sight at least, that the convergence between Upadhyay and Maritain regards only their shared criticism of Western modernity, and not their respective positive views of the content of integral humanism, which as we have seen is highly dependent in Maritain on the Christian and even Catholic theology, whereas Upadhyay's central connection, throughout his 1965 Jan Sangh lectures series, between integral humanism and *Dharma*, would qualify his conception as grounded on the Hinduist religious tradition and culture.

Yet, such a differentiation between Maritain's Christian humanism and Upadhyay's alleged Hindu account of humanism would, in fact, be much too abrupt. Indeed, for Upadhyay, *Dharma* is by no means confined to the Hindu tradition or religion. On the contrary, *Dharma* regards the harmonious cosmic order of the entire universe:

> "A person is a member of his family as well as his community (...). Above all, he is a member of the Nation and Society. If we consider even the larger sphere, he is a member of the whole of mankind, and then the entire universe. (...). The most important is that, despite this multiple personality, he can and should behave in a way which does not bring different aspects of his life into mutual conflict, but which is mutually sustaining, complementary and unifying. This quality is inherent in man"[13].

Thus, the perspective of integral humanism can be seen as a universalist one, where the integral human being is the one able to fully integrate to the dharmic order of the universe, its non-conflictual oneness. In another passage, Upadhyay even says that *Dharma* is not reducible to a religious legislation. It can open to an integral trans-religious openness to the dharmic order of the universe:

> "*Dharma* is not confined to temples or mosques. Worship of God is only a part of *Dharma*. *Dharma* is much wider. In the past, temples had served as an effective medium to educate people in their *Dharma*. However, just as schools themselves do not constitute knowledge, so also temples do not constitute *Dharma*. A child may attend school regularly and yet may remain uneducated. So also, it is possible that a person may visit a temple or mosque

> without a break, and yet he may not know his *Dharma*. To attend a temple or mosque constitutes a part of a religion, sect, creed, but not necessarily *Dharma*"[14].

Thus, the reduction of *Dharma* to the religious-cultural worldview or world-experience of Hinduism would be a narrowing down of its universal dimension, a universal dimension which Hindu philosophy was able to conceive in Vedanta[15]. But if integral humanism, as dharmic wholeness, is universal, don't we have in the end a possible convergence with Maritain? This would entail, of course, that we expurgate Maritain's own conception of humanism from the narrow Christological aspects and find the universal aspects also at work in the Christian worldview. This for instance is the core of Hegel's works in his philosophy of Religion, where the Essence of Christianity should be understood as part of the dialectic development of the Universal Absolute Spirit[16]. One would then be in a position to show that Christianity and Hinduism designate two distinct cultural and religious worldviews, each contributing to shape different social and cultural identities, but which also serve as vectors towards understanding a universal spiritual order that the integral humanist experience strives to fit into.

3. Universality and Tradition

Yet, to do this, one needs to inquire more about the conditions for universality not to become an abstract dehumanized order. For Upadhyay it is essential to reconnect universality to traditionality. As Upadhyay stresses in his Jan Sangh lectures, the universality of *Dharma* is intimately linked to the traditional order of the universe:

> "Traditions are respected everywhere (...). We have a written constitution, but even this written constitution cannot go contrary to the traditions of this country. In

as much as it does go contrary to our traditions, it is not fulfilling *Dharma*."[17]

As he also writes:

"We have (...) thought over the integrated form of Humanism. On this basis, we shall be able to re-reconcile nationalism, democracy, socialism and world peace with the traditional values of *Bharatiya* culture, and think of all these ideals in an integrated form. (...) Thereby 'Man' can gain his lost status and attain the aims of his life."[18]

So, Upadhyay's emphasis on tradition is quite central for grasping the integral relation to *Dharma*. Integral humanism is deeply connected with tradition in the search for our spiritual identity at the individual level, the national level, the metaphysical level. Now, can this also be the case in the Western Christian worldview that Maritain belongs to? Is universalism not, in the Western experience, in a deep structural tension with tradition? Maritain here would doubtlessly say that such a conflict between universalism and tradition is what the anthropocentric worldview of modernity has secreted, and Maritain himself would plead for a unification of tradition and universality, precisely in the Christian religious experience since, as Maritain says: "for the Christian, true religion [...] transcends every civilization and every culture; it is strictly universal"[19].

4. The Historical Progressive Unfolding of Universalism

Here one must remark that Maritain, though attached to tradition, is not a traditionalist. Indeed, at the core of the Christian trinitarian concept of the Holy Spirit, which is archeologically linked to the Ancient Greek concept of *Logos*, lies the idea that the universal is not given once and for all in a traditional past that we need to reconnect with, but as a goal (a *telos*) that orients the movement of world history in a teleological way, i.e. in a linear and progressive way towards its full spiritual realization, which is yet to be achieved, and which is future-oriented. The deployment of history is part of the unfolding of the universal movement of Creation itself. From the Western point of view, we thus stand in a dharmic order that is still settling in, that is still incomplete in its constitution, a dharmic order in which God Himself has intervened at a certain point of History through the Incarnation of Christ. As Maritain writes, there is, after the first age of Christendom and the second age of modernity, a third age of the world yet to come:

> "This third age would witness first the general liquidation of post mediaeval humanism. (...) Man would remain in it that which he is, but he would be under a new temporal regime, a new historical sky, also destined to decline in the end for new dawns (...); and it is only under this regime that there would begin to flower the integral humanism, the humanism of the Incarnation"[20].

Have we reached here at a fundamental difference between the Western and Indian interpretations of the meaning of Integral Humanism, around two conflicting views regarding the status of universalism and its connection with tradition and historicity, one—Maritain's—that is future oriented, another—Upadhyay's—that is past oriented?

This would be a simplification. Even though Upadhyay relentlessly relates the integral man to the traditionality of *Dharma*, at the end of his 1965 lectures he also advocates for a very progressist vision of integral humanism, with the idea that humanity is on the linear road of history and has to embark on a journey towards the future, in order to fully actualize its potentialities:

> "We want neither capitalism nor socialism. We aim at the progress and happiness of 'Man', the Integral Man. (...) We have discussed here the philosophy. But the members of *Bharatiya Jana Sangh* are not mere philosophers or academicians. (...) We have taken due note of our ancient culture. But we are no archaeologists. We have no intention to become custodians of a vast archaeological museum. Our goal is not merely to protect the culture but to revitalize it so as to make it dynamic and in tune with the times. We must ensure that our Nation stands firm on this foundation and our society is enabled to live a healthy, progressive and purposeful life. We shall have to end a number of traditions and set in reforms which are helpful in the development of values and of national unity in our society"[21].

An example of this is of course what Upadhyay calls the evil of untouchability:

> "If today, society is gripped with evils like untouchability, which leads men to treat other human beings as lower than themselves, and thereby threaten the national unity, we shall have to end such evils"[22].

So, in the end, the soul of the nation, its *Chiti*, is by no means according to Upadhyay past-oriented, and tradition should never fall back on traditionalism, but serve as a driving force and shared identity on the nation's road towards progress. But what is then the conceptual positive content of such a progress? What is its full scope? Is it scientific? Can it be moral and political progress as well, like one finds for instance in Kant, who speaks of the rationalization of mankind under the moral law as a goal yet to be attained in a cosmopolitan world order still in the process of being implemented[23]? Here a tension probably emerges between, on the one hand, traditional knowledge and wisdom, and on the other hand, the linear historical movement of modernity as a spiritual movement of progress, of Enlightenment (*Aufklärung*). Is the metaphysical idea of history, seen as a process of universalization, one that Upadhyay would have accepted, or would he on the contrary have pointed out that such a conception leads inevitably to division, struggle, and only to an abstract humanism which, in the end, turns into an instrument of oppression against the human being, whether in the forms of capitalism or socialism? Put in another way, can *Sarvodaya*, which serves as the basis for Upadhyay's conception of progress, designate the progress of humanity towards understanding *Dharma* itself, leading to a new age of humanity yet to come? Or is it more exclusively a social and economic ideal, focusing on the dignity of labor, on an equitable distribution of wealth, communal self-sufficiency, and thus more centered on the sphere of *Artha* rather than that of *Dharma* itself?

Leaving these as open questions, what remains certain is that Upadhyay thought that human history should not be governed by conflict and struggle. He would thus have disagreed with the words of Kant who spoke of man's "unsociable sociability" as a positive driving force of history; or of Hegel, according to whom negativity is the engine of the progress of spirit. But again, for Hegel, conflict and negativity are not only proper to modernity, they go back to the dawn of Christianity, where redemption can only come through the tragic suffering of conversion and the saving intervention of Christ[24]. And further back, negativity is also for Hegel at the foundation of Greek thought itself, where the tragic, as Nietzsche puts in the *Birth of the Tragedy*, is seen as the most essential meaning of Being itself.

In Maritain himself, the theme of tragedy is central to his reflections on integral humanism, where he even speaks of the "tragedy of God", and the "naïve Christian civilization" that would "count on the native and naïve unity of man", meaning that the progress towards God implies the tragic movement of history as a struggle internal to man himself, precisely against anthropocentrism and atheistic materialism. Is this compatible with Upadhyay, who on the contrary puts forward the idea that struggle and negativity are always in a state of duality and ignorance about the oneness of the Harmonious Being? Maybe not, and it is here that we possibly reach a limit between not only Maritain and Upadhyay, but between the Western and Indian metaphysical worldviews that shape the respective visions of Maritain and Upadhyay on integral humanism

Conclusion

In his 1935 Vienna lecture on the crisis of the modern sciences, Husserl, the German philosopher and founder of phenomenology, showed that scientific progress had to overcome, through critical thinking, not only traditionality, but also the downfall of modernity plunged in the poison of naturalism. In this lecture, Husserl reflected on the identity of Europe, and he said that Europe is not merely a geographical concept; it is not simply a continent, but it is more profoundly a spiritual universal identity. Anyone, to Husserl's mind, can be a European if he or she steps into the scientific and philosophical community, sharing the universal task of serving scientific rationality, a rationality that knows no nationality, culture or religion. Now, in a controversial statement, Husserl noted in that text that "we Europeans will never be Indianized"[25], and what he meant there is that India was according to him the concept of a national cultural identity caught up in a tradition that is clouded by an overarching particularism. Such a Husserlian statement has, of course, been widely discussed and vividly criticized and condemned, often in a decolonial approach, and denounced for its ethnocentric bias (one can think here of Jacques Derrida's comments in "De l'esprit"[26]).

One of the great merits of Upadhyay's work is to remind us eloquently that India is not, and has never been imprisoned in any form of particularism, but that its relation to universality is the core of its spiritual spirituality.

Endnotes

1 On this, see J.-L. Marion, *Sur le prisme métaphysique de Descartes*, Paris, PUF, 1986, p. 130: "The structural homology between on the one hand the *cogitatio* [thinking], self-reflecting on an *ego*, and the *Mathesis universalis* (which implies a primal *Sapientia Universalis* [Universal knowledge]), answers to the same requirement: to ground the interpretation of *entia* (entities), seen as *cogitata* [thoughts], on an entity, an entity *par excellence*, itself conceived as a thinking entity *par excellence*, thus the self".

2 "But having no sooner acquired some general notions about physics, and begun to test them out on various particular problems, I noticed where they may lead and how much they differ from the principles that have been employed up to now, and I believed that I could not keep them hidden without sinning greatly against the law that obliges us to procure, as far as it is in our power, the general good of all mankind. For these notions have made me see that it is possible to attain knowledge which is very useful in life, and that unlike the speculative philosophy that is taught in the schools, it can be turned into a practice by which, knowing the power and action of fire, water, air, stars, the heavens, and all the other bodies that are around us as distinctly as we know the different trades of our craftsmen, we could put them to all the uses for which they are suited and thus make ourselves as it were the masters and possessors of nature" (R. Descartes, *A discourse on the method of correctly conducting one's reason and seeking truth in the sciences*, trans. by I. Maclean, Oxford, Oxford University Press, 2006, p. 51).

3 Cf. F. Bacon, *Novum Organum*, *The Works of Francis Bacon*, London, Basil Montagu ed., 1825, Vol. XIV, p. 31; F. Bacon, "Valerius Terminus: of the Interpretation of Nature", in *Miscellaneous Tracts upon Human Knowledge,* Works, Vol. I, p. 281.

4 "Philosophy is written in this grand book, the universe, which stands continually open to our gaze. But the book cannot be understood unless one first learns to comprehend the language and read the letters in which it is composed. It is written in the language of mathematics, and its characters are triangles, circles, and other geometric figures without which it is humanly impossible to understand a single word of it; without these, one wanders about in a dark labyrinth" (Galileo Galilei, The Assayer, trans. by S. Drake, pdf version put online by Stanford University, p. 4 (https://web.stanford.edu/~jsabol/certainty/readings/Galileo-Assayer.pdf).

5 J. Maritain, *Integral humanism. Temporal and spiritual problems of a new Christendom*, trans. by J. Evans, Notre Dame, University of Notre Dame Press, 1973 (from now on abbreviated as IH), p. 26.

6 IH, p. 27.

7 *Ibid*.

8 IH, p. 26-27.

9 IH, p. 27.

10 IH, p. 27-28.

11 "Here in Bharat, we have placed before ourselves the ideal of the four-fold responsibilities of catering to the needs of body, mind, intellect and soul, with a view to achieve the integrated progress of man. Dharma, Artha, Kama and Moksha are the four kinds of *Purusharthas* – human effort. *Purushartha* means effort which befit a man. The longings for *Dharma*, *Artha*, *Kama* and *Moksha* are inborn in man, and the satisfaction of these gives him joy. Of these four efforts too, we have thought in an integrated way" (D. Upadhyay, *Integral Humanism, Jan Sangh lectures*, pdf version in free internet access: https://deendayalupadhyay.org/images/book/Booklet%20on%20IntegralHumanism.pdf, p. 19 [now abbreviated as JS).

12 JS, p. 16.

13 JS, p. 28.

14 JS, p. 32.

15 Cf. Carl T Jackson, *Vedanta for the West: The Ramakrishna Movement in the United States (Religion in North America)*, Bloomington, Indiana University Press, 1994. In this book, C. T. Jackson notes that universalism is the main perceived quality of Vedanta to followers in the United States of America: "What precisely have been the attractions of the Ramakrishna movement's teaching for American followers? (...) Fortunately, there is some prospect of answering (...), thanks to a revealing series published in the 1950s in the journal *Vedanta and the West*. (...) Apparently, Vedanta's greatest attraction to Americans has been its perceived breadth and universalism. Series contributors repeated the universalist claim again and again" (p. 99-100).

16 As Hegel writes in the preface of his 1827 lectures on religion: "Absolute Religion. Here spirit, being in and for itself, no longer has singular forms or determinations of itself before it in its developed state, and knows itself no more as finite spirit, as spirit in some sort of determinateness or limitedness. Instead, it has overcome those limitations and is explicitly what it is implicitly. Spirit's knowing of itself as it is implicitly is the *being-in-and-for-self* of spirit, the consummate, absolute religion in which it is manifest what spirit is, what God is; and this religion is the Christian religion. That spirit must run its course in religion as in all else is necessary in spirit's concept. It is spirit only by virtue of the fact that it is for itself as the negation of all finite forms, as this absolute ideality. (...) This is the path and the goal by which spirit has attained its proper concept, the concept of itself, and has arrived at what it is in itself" (G. W. F. Hegel, *Lectures on the philosophy of religion*, volume 1: "Introduction and the concept of religion", trans. by R. F. Brown, P. C. Hodgson and J. M. Stewart, Berkeley, University of California Press, 1984, p. 183-184).

17 JS, p. 34.

18 JS, p. 54.

19 IH, p. 97.

20 IH, p. 244.

21 JS, p. 54.

22 JS, p. 55.

23 "To a high degree we are, through art and science, *cultured*. We are *civilized* (...) in all sorts of social grace and decorum. But to consider ourselves as having reached *morality* – for that, much is lacking. The ideal of morality belongs to culture; its use for some simulacrum of morality in the love of honor and outward decorum constitutes mere civilization. So long as states waste their forces in vain and violent self-expansion, and thereby constantly thwart the slow efforts to improve the minds of their citizens by even withdrawing all support from them, nothing in the way of a moral order is to be expected. For such an end, a long internal working of each political body toward the education of its citizens is required. Everything good that is not based on a morally good disposition, however, is nothing but pretense and glittering misery. In such a condition the human species will no doubt remain until, in the way I have described, it works its way out of the chaotic conditions of its international relations" (I. Kant, *Idea for a Universal History from a Cosmopolitan Point of View*, trans. by L. W. Beck, in I. Kant, *On History*, Indianapolis, Bobbs Merrill, 1963).

24 As Emilio Brito writes: "With a force undoubtedly unmatched, Hegel shows us that Christ is the speculative destiny of the Absolute: the manifestation of the infinite in the finite, the holocaust rendered to the spiritual community where he resurrects. Is this symbolism a poignant expression of the tragedy of the Absolute? And is this tragedy of the Spirit not resolved in the logical element of Absolute Knowledge? Hegel never denies that the Logos became flesh. However, it must be admitted that speculative sublation (*Aufhebung*) is predominant. In the shadow of the Hegelian cross, Easter only relays the absence of Jesus' body through the Gospel of the intimacy of the Spirit. Whatever the case, Hegel had the audacity to introduce the cross into God himself. (...) Entering 'into the strength of the adversary' is enriching humility, provided one knows how to resist the vertigo of dialectical sublimation" (E. Brito, "Valeur et limites du recours à Hegel en christologie" ["Value and limits of the recourse to Hegel in Christology"], in *Revue théologique de Louvain*, 1983, 14-4, p. 419 [our translation]).

25 "There is something unique here that is recognized in us [Europeans] by all other human groups, too, something that, quite apart from all considerations of utility, becomes a motive for them to Europeanize themselves even in their unbroken will to spiritual self-preservation; whereas we, if we understand ourselves properly, would never Indianize ourselves, for example. I mean that we feel (and in spite of all obscurity this feeling is probably legitimate) that an entelechy is inborn in our European civilization which holds sway throughout all the changing shapes of Europe and accords to them the sense of a development toward an ideal shape of life and being as an eternal pole" (E. Husserl, "The Vienna lecture. Philosophy and the crisis of European humanity", in *The crisis of European sciences and transcendental phenomenology*, trans. by D. Carr, Evanston, Northwestern University Press, 1970, p. 275).

26 Cf. J. Derrida, *Of spirit. Heidegger and the question*, trans. by G. Bennington and R. Bowlby, Chicago and London, University of Chicago Press, 1989, p. 120 sq.

Chapter Three

Humanism, Integrity and the Quest for an Inter-Religious Spirituality

Côme Carpentier de Gourdon

The Genesis of Humanism in the Humanities

The humanities are a field of knowledge encompassing the disciplines that are not concerned with the 'natural' and 'divine' sciences, according to a medieval classification that has its origins in Graeco-Roman antiquity. The Scholastic *Trivium* (grammar, rhetoric, and logic) provided the foundation for poetry, history, philosophy, and the other areas of study concerned with 'man', as described in Terence's famous adage "I am a man, I consider nothing that is human alien to me."

In the early 15th century, Francesco Petrarca, the famously erudite Italian bard, gave a new flavour to the literature of his time, and revived the study of the Classics of Antiquity, and he thus deserves to be called the first Humanist. He had many successors in the following two centuries, during which, partly thanks to the immigration of several Byzantine scholars to Western Europe, the intellectuals of Italy and other parts of Europe acquired more extensive and accurate knowledge about Graeco-Latin civilisation and its 'pagan' religion. As a result, many scholars and writers, later designated as Humanists, developed syncretic, universalistic views on cosmology and divinity, closely related to their scientific studies. The twin major influences of Pythagorean Neo-Platonism and Hermetic Esotericism reshaped Western European culture in the Renaissance by promoting an often-controversial synthesis between the polytheistic Mediterranean philosophies and arts and the Christian Revelation. The Council of Trent, held between 1545 and 1563, aimed at repressing the Reformation and defending the Catholic dogmas from 'heretical' challenges, but the resulting Baroque Era was pregnant with pre-Christian aesthetics and symbology, both in Roman Catholic and Protestant countries.

Humanism as Anthropocentric Rationality

The evolution of the subsequent Classical Age of Reason into the "Enlightenment,' with its corollary and skeptical theism, prepared and ushered in the Industrial Revolution of the late eighteenth century. In that progressivist, increasingly revolutionary context, religion and tradition that the Renaissance Humanists had not rejected but rather explored and enriched, were challenged and put on the backburner if not abandoned, at least by some. In the 19th century 'Age of Science', humanism was redefined as an alternative to the God-centric epistemology of the 'Ancien Regime' and manifested in the proclamation of the 'Rights of Man' and its codification by the French revolutionaries. Whereas the American founding fathers, who were mostly Deists, kept God as an overseeing presence in the Declaration of Independence and the Constitution of the United States, their French imitators were divided on the issue but, concerned to keep the hated royalist Church out of the picture, they firmly anchored the new dispensation in the elusive 'popular will' (that they promptly and repeatedly violated henceforth).

Humanism became an anthropocentric and anthropological paradigm (even before anthropology was invented) in which the human being is not only 'the measure of all things', as Protagoras had defined him, but also the only subject and object of investigation. Christianity describes man as the regent of Creation but also as a creature and servant of God, who is the sole master. Radical humanism, severed from theology, puts *genus homo* in the centre and top of the living universe. That comforting materialist *doxa* rests on the belief that all the virtues and positive qualities traditionally associated with the Divine (in the sense of a higher spiritual order) emanate from human intra-species solidarity, with no need for transcendence. To quote Wilde's ironic quip: 'it has no invisible means of support'.

Humanism in the literal sense is a philosophy related to Darwinism (whose negative effects on society it seeks to mitigate by emphasizing the cooperative impulse among members of most species) and invokes Locke and Rousseau's social contract. It was naturally adopted by Marx because it assumes that human beings have in them an innate tendency towards mutual help and solidarity, which amounts to morality. Humanism, in that sense, parts way with the original conservative ideology because it rejects the latter's scepticism about the primitive character of human beings that makes them fall prey to evil impulses. In Judaic and Christian societies, the belief in the Fall (of Eve and Adam) was the source of pessimism about human nature left to itself, while in China and India, the lower nature and ego (*ahamkara*) is seen as the origin of selfish and violent passions that may only be tamed by an inner awakening to the superior, universal soul. In contrast, optimism about man's ability to improve his lot and his species is a basic feature of the humanist worldview, which echoes Rousseau's theory that 'man is born good but society (that includes organised religion) makes him evil'.

Material progress, made possible by science and technology, was hailed by the French Encyclopaedists of the eighteenth century as the harbinger of a future in which justice, peace, and prosperity for all would be attained.

This ideology, which has extended its sway over the whole world for two centuries, has been severely challenged by the great wars and other anthropogenic tragedies that have occurred in that period, belying the theory that rising techno-scientific power would lead to general happiness and harmony in industrial societies by making people better educated and therefore wiser.

Towards the end of the eighteen hundreds, a reaction - partly inspired by the survival of Romanticism and partly by a religious revival- took place against materialistic utilitarianism, which had spawned various socialist theories.

Maritain's Calling

It is in that historical context that Jacques Maritain's spiritual journey and doctrine are to be situated. Born in a distinguished Protestant family with Liberal secular loyalties, he experienced as a young and brilliant student the spiritual emptiness and the 'death of meaning' that led him to contemplate suicide. Like some of his famous agnostic or anticlerical contemporaries, he was drawn by personal circumstances to Catholicism and embraced it with passion, together with his Russian-Jewish wife. Their conversion in 1906, shepherded by the controversial polemicist Léon Bloy, made Maritain a militant of the Church with a strong social commitment.

There is a tradition of anti-Capitalism in the Roman Church that invokes the Sermon of the Mount, the Gospels as a whole, and the Pauline epistles, to oppose capital accumulation, plutocracy, and the merchandisation of human labour. Social, often 'democratic,' and liberal Catholicism, illustrated by philosophers as activists such as Lacordaire, Ozanam, Albert de Mun, La Tour du Pin, and Frédéric Le Play in France fought Marxism and other forms of atheistic socialism, charting a middle course between the wild economic liberalism of the mid-19th century and the revolutionary Leftist ideology. They accepted the separation of Church and State and freedom of conscience, provided it included the freedom to believe in God and live a Christian life. Some were even comfortable living in a Republic, unlike their traditionally royalist fellow believers, but upheld the absolute authority of the Papacy in spiritual matters. Under the pontificate of Leo XIII from 1878 onwards, the Holy See became more concerned with the welfare of workers by supporting labour law reforms, promoted by the *Rerum Novarum* Encyclical in 1891.

As a renowned Aristotelian and Thomist scholar following in the footsteps of those modernist predecessors, Maritain soon became an authority on the Christian doctrine in its application to the society of his times. That he more than once defined himself as a man with leftist sympathies helped him to maintain a dialogue with socialist intellectuals, and the reformist Cardinal Montini, Archbishop of Milan, who would be crowned as Pope Paul VI in 1963, took his advice on various matters, particularly in the preparation of the Second Vatican Council, which ushered in a critical and controversial transformation of the Church's dogmas, teachings and rituals.

Maritain's Integral Humanism

Jacques Maritain was a prolific writer and many commentators have analysed his ideas more than the scope of this paper permits. The conjunction of the words 'integral' and 'humanism' says a lot about what he proposed and yet is so broad as to remain vague. Maritain was neither an economist nor a political scientist, and left relatively little material relevant to those two areas. He focused on the integration of spirituality with contemporary social institutions. 'Integration' is one of the modulations of the Latin word 'integra', also found in 'integrity' and 'integralism', now applied to conservative Catholics who reject the reforms of the Second Vatican Council, celebrate the Latin Mass according the rite of Saint Pius V and even deny the magisterial authority of the 'progressist' Popes who followed Pius XII, from 1958 onwards.

It is ironic that 'integral humanism' is at odds with 'integral Catholicism', perhaps because of Maritain's commitment to Christian ecumenical unity. His emphasis on humanism is suspect for traditional Christians, who regard it as a concession to atheistic progressivism and leftist innovations. Notably, Maritain's endorsement of the 'rights of man', later renamed 'human rights' (that he deemed rooted in natural law) is a departure from the Catholic dogma about God's absolute authority over His creation and the authority he delegates to His Church on Earth, whereas men have duties to Him and his representatives. Their rights, if any, flow out of the performance of their duties to God and society, quite like how Mahatma Gandhi saw it. Human dignity is recognized since man is in the Image and Likeness of God but only virtue, faith, and rectitude entitle him (or her) to receive the dues since neither God nor Nature owe anything to mankind. Indeed, rectitude (the Right) is at the origin of the legal concept of Right (as in 'the right path') which comes into being only in return for the accomplishment of Divine Law. No creature has any innate right in and as of itself in Nature. That right ensues from interrelations, out of reciprocal solidarity, and is satisfied by the duty of others to take care of their kith and kin and their fellow men.

Although he sees the concept of individual rights as a natural corollary of human dignity, Maritain, who upholds the Thomist distinction between the person (a qualitative category) and the individual (a quantitative label), acknowledged the supremacy of the common good (to which he dedicated one of his important books: *La Personne et le Bien Commun* (1947)) and denied the possibility of ethics solely derived from logical reasoning about material reality. His non-Kantian critical realism rests on an affirmation of the truth of human knowledge, sensorially acquired and reflectively confirmed, but it asserts an innate 'sense of the Absolute', manifesting as faith which can be the only basis for moral values. Therefore, in his view, secular (non-religious and agnostic) humanism, as professed by Kirkegaard for instance, is really counter-humanism. A sound moral philosophy can only be rooted in theology according to Maritain, and in Christianity it presupposes the recognition of the Original Sin and of an eschatological soteriology that lend meaning and purpose to human life.

How Maritain reconciled his doctrinal apologetism with his vision of democratic pluralism for world peace is not entirely clear. His support for ideas of global confederation and a world government implies that he accepted the validity of all civilisations, Christian and not, and his ecumenism attracted the opposition of some Conservative Catholic scholars; a few even accusing him of betraying the Faith for the sake of global conciliation, but that was not only the only ambiguity that he cultivated. His confession that he was at heart a 'leftist', critical of the hypocritical 'bourgeois pharisaism' (typical of many societies in his days as in the present), though he naturally rejected dialectical materialism, did not prevent him from playing leading roles in organisations dedicated to the fight against Communism.

In 1950, in Berlin, Maritain was the honorary Chairman of the CIA-funded Congress for Cultural Freedom, and his influence on Pope Paul VI (who through him became acquainted with the writing and social activism of Saul Alinsky) is regarded as a factor in the Vatican's shift to social democracy articulated by the aforesaid pope in his '*Populorum Progressio*' (1967), calling for a 'full-bodied humanism', in consonance with Maritain's concept. That was an initiative designed to move past the Church's implicit alignment with the Far-Right nationalist regimes of the earlier part of the century, acknowledged by Pius XI at that time in his famous statement that 'Catholicism too is totalitarian'.

An aspect of that course correction was the Roman Church's de facto reconciliation with the Jewish faith and people, a rather radical and one-sided about-turn that Maritain earnestly encouraged, possibly under the influence of his spouse, but also in response to the utterance in John's Gospel: 'Salvation comes from the Jews'.

In summary, it may be said that Jacques Maritain, just as his philosophical mentor Thomas Aquinas had done in his day, worked to update the Roman Catholic doctrine to restore its pre-eminence over science which he criticised, like Bergson, for being made into a new religion and usurping the traditional place and role of the humanities. He sought to revive the spirit of the Renaissance Humanists while borrowing intellectual contributions from the later secular Humanists who dominated the Western intellectual scene from the mid-nineteenth century. In essence, he reconciled the rationalistic agnosticism of his upbringing with the spiritual revelation that had led to his conversion. Was he not thereby emulating Thomas Aquinas, the 'Doctor Angelicus' who had fused Aristotle's Peripatetic philosophy with patristic theology and whom Leo XIII, the reformist Pope, had reinstated as the preeminent Church Father?

The Indic Interpretation of Integral Humanism (*Ekatma Manava Vad*)

In Indian civilisation, the words *manu, manava,* and *manushya* refer to the human being as a spiritual and physical entity, and the philosophical and legal texts associated with human beings and society are often prefixed with 'manava' (such as the *Manavadharmashastras*: the treatises on laws that pertain to the human species). It is from those sources, supported by a very profuse and ancient literature, that Deendayal Upadhyay's life work and doctrine drew their inspiration. He placed a strong emphasis on indigenous cultural nationalism and advocated for the Indianisation of the institutions and practices of modern India. He characterized the spirit of traditional Indic society as resting on the recognition of the organic unity between the material and the spiritual realms, between the secular and the sacred, and he saw in the Manu a microcosm, just as the Vedic scriptures define him. In consonance with Mahatma Gandhi's seminal *Hind Swaraj*, Upadhyay called for *Antyodaya*, the uplift of the most destitute and lowest in the social system, reminiscent of John Ruskin's evangelically inspired *Unto This Last*. To that end, Pandit Deendayal championed *Arthaneeti*: the politics of the common good, intended to make a state or polity (*Rajya*) Dharma-abiding and therefore duty-oriented, as opposed to the priority given to individual rights in modern secular societies. For him, every citizen or denizen of the Rajya is primarily, in accordance with the Vedic *Purushasukta hymn*, a member or limb (*rashtranga*) of the civilisational and spiritual entity (*Rashtra*) of which the Rajya is a political emanation, just as the individual (*vyakti* in Sanskrit) is a sovereign but interdependent expression of *Chitti*: the soul or essence of a Rashtra. The latter can be imperfectly described as the combination of the French historian and literary critic Hippolyte Taine's concepts of 'race' and 'milieu' that, combined with a third ingredient, the 'moment in time' structured human thought and cultural expressions[1].

In line with ancient Indian philosophical and sociological traditions, Upadhyay wanted the social order to be integrative and symbiotic, rather than polarised and competitive. He saw in Western-style democracy the risks posed by the sway of the *samskaras* (the passions and flaws of individuals) on individual and collective behaviour, and for that reason, he distrusted the reliance on liberty as the foundation of the social contract, since unlimited freedom is not only impossible in real life, but can be devastatingly harmful to its practitioners as well as to others and to the natural balance in general. The Scottish jurist and political philosopher Alexander Fraser Tytler explained why democracy left to itself as a system devoid of a higher superstructure, is doomed to decay[2].

The Integral Humanism of Upadhyay instead is grounded in *Samaj* (the family as an organic community) and regards the Rashtra and the Rajya as 'families of families' layered in concentric circles that expand beyond the national framework to embrace the whole world and the spiritual realms lying within and beyond it. Democracy left to itself, in his view, is a harbinger of chaos because it relies on the transient will or beliefs of a relative majority of people without higher guidance, and as a result of this metaphysical vacuum, can easily be subverted and overtaken by the manipulations of certain privileged groups, which is happening almost everywhere in modern nations as we witness daily.

Therefore, Deendayal's philosophy can be summarised as a set of principles and a praxis for socio-political and economic harmony through the practice of mutual service and duty which can alone, according to him, produce happiness (*sukha*) through a constant process of give-and-take between individuals and the community, the former contributing to the latter through their work and talent, while in turn the latter supports the former by supplying their needs and reasonable desires (*yogakshema*). In the economic domain, this system works for *Ekatma Arthaneeti*, the balanced use of resources that regulates production and consumption to avoid both waste and scarcity. By definition, in Integral Humanism, for Upadhyay, as for Maritain, man is not a mere economic producer and consumer of resources as an actor in a market, but is a holistic, multidimensional being: *sampurnamanava* (the integral man). While Jacques Maritain, raised in the European theological and philosophical cultural universe, emphasises that humans are physical creatures endowed with spirit and intellect, the Hindu Deendayal defines the Manu as a fragment of Brahman (the universal Divine Soul) that takes the shape of a body animated by a mind and an intellect.

The views of Maritain and Upadhyay about internationalism and global unity are generally convergent. However, while Maritain was an active promoter of a world government in the spirit of Catholic ecumenism (we have mentioned that he was involved in the movement for a world parliament, planetary federalism, and for inter-religious peace and cooperation), Deendayal's primary concern was to build or rebuild the Indian Rashtra by restoring her spiritual unity (*Ekatva*) as a supra-religious community ruled by the Chitti of the universal Dharma (*Vishwadharma*). For the Indian thought-leader, the many communities (*jati*s) and religious denominations of India could thereby find *ekatva*, also called Hindutva by some of his fellow RSS intellectuals. The new Bharat, that is India, could then play a founding role in the achievement of global peace and unity, going beyond the nation to embrace the surrounding universe.

We have shown how the combination of the two concepts, integral and humanism, was used by Jacques Maritain and Deendayal Upadhyay, among other social philosophers, to reconcile the seemingly opposite positions taken by spiritualists on the one hand and 'secular' materialists on the other. Their call for integrity affirmed their adhesion to the faith and traditions of their respective cultures, while their adoption of humanism implied their awareness of the need to take full account of the needs, desires, and conditions of human beings in all their universal and culturally specific dimensions. Jacques Maritain professed that the highest knowledge is supra-rational and can only be acquired through intuition (the Thomist connaturality); Deendayal Upadhyay taught that the Vedic tradition and the 'Dharmic' philosophies enshrine divine wisdom that reflects the natural order and is immanent in the human soul. Maritain's recognition of natural human rights may have been a political concession to the contemporary ideology, although he maintained that the natural corollaries of those rights were individual duties. Deendayal, based on the Indic social anthropology of the *Purusharthas*, knew that Dharma, together with the quest for *Moksha* (spiritual liberation and bliss) comprises both sides of the coin, and suffices to optimally regulate society. The yearning for Moksha, that denotes an innate subconscious awareness of it, is a distinctive factor of human beings also acknowledged in Christian moral philosophy as a quest for beatitude in communion with the Divine..

Both men rose above the not-so-old and clearly subjective divide between the Right and the Left of the political spectrum, Maritain by embracing some socialist ideas (including the affirmation of natural human rights that spiritual Conservatives have always been uncomfortable with) while remaining a defender of spirituality and religious tradition; and Upadhyay, by upholding the supra-ideological character of the Dharmic Law, anchored in a non-dualistic, holistic culture (which had no conception of a Left-Right dialectic) did not need to make the same concessions to be understood and accepted in the Indian civilisational context.

A Biological Vindication of Integral Humanism: Humanities as Natural Sciences.

Both the humanistic traditions, the Renascentist 'classical' and the secular 'rationalist', were strongly connected to the scientific knowledge and spirit of their respective periods. Jacques Maritain lost confidence in the prevalent mechanistic worldview of his time and eagerly accepted the 'vitalist' doctrine of Henri Bergson, born in an orthodox Jewish family but professing a form of scientific transcendentalism inspired by Spinoza and perhaps Kyeserling, who underlined the insufficiencies and fallacies of the sciences of the day, and brought spirituality back into the French intellectual Olympus of the time. Maritain remained a staunch Catholic, whereas Bergson's writings were banned by the Vatican on the grounds that he promoted a form of pantheism. After his conversion, Maritain and his wife Vera followed the biology lessons of Hans Driesch at the University of Heidelberg in Germany. Driesch also taught a vitalist interpretation of the life sciences, and was intellectually close to Bergson, who dedicated much of his lifework to the study of consciousness and its relation to nature and life. Driesch, a student of the illustrious Ernst Haeckel, also adopted some Thomist notions such as entelechy to define living beings and their organic development (*Theory of Organic Development* was the title of a book he published in 1894). He understood the 'life force' as a spiritual or 'psychoid' phenomenon, and was interested in psychic and parapsychic research, which made him somewhat suspect in the eyes of many of his colleagues. Maritain was impressed by Driesch's famous Theory of Order (1912) that anticipated more modern ecological discoveries and the Systems Theory, and he also saw himself as a scientific thinker. He insisted that philosophy and theology were the highest sciences, in keeping with the medieval epistemological hierarchy[3].

Deendayal Upadhyay had no academic training in the physical and natural sciences, as his background was in literature, philosophy, and sociology, but he always placed himself in an inter-religious, pan-spiritual dimension, rising above denominational and liturgical specificities. He saw in the Indic philosophical and ethical precepts the reflection of the universal laws of nature as was pointed out earlier. Therefore, a brief reference to some current discoveries and realisations in the 'sciences of life' is useful to determine the relevance of the conclusions separately reached by the French Catholic thinker and the Hindu social reformer.

In two of his books in French, entitled *La Vie des Plantes – Une Métaphysique du Mélange* and *Métamorphoses,* Emanuele Coccia, the exponent of 'radical botany,'[4] which is a play on the word radix (root), discusses in great detail the biological characteristics of vegetation, and concludes that no valid division is to be established between the humanities and the natural sciences, as both deal with living organisms, humans being one kind of animal and all animals depending on plants for their lives (breathing and nourishment). In the same synthetic vein, he argues that natural sciences are also spiritual, as they feed the reflections of ecology, philosophy, psychology, and even politics.

Coccia points out that in some ancient philosophical systems, the seed of a plant was seen as an allegory, analogue and physical kernel of Reason because it contains potentially the entire structure and architecture of the plant yet to be born. The seed enshrines the form that will evolve out of matter, thereby creating change and order at the same time. In the so-called 'Age of Enlightenment', according to Coccia, the concepts of spirit and reason were restricted to human beings. God was gradually downgraded and excluded, while the botanical and animal realms were regarded as machine-like lifeforms. Yet, modern genetics, by studying the DNA codes, acknowledges, at least tacitly, that chromosomes are organised, therefore 'rational', structures and that all naturally grown forms are alive at some level. This realisation powerfully supports the theories of immanent and transcendent natural law taught by both Maritain and Upadhyay, but the fact that plants are not 'individual' beings but are rather collective lifeforms, biological communities that grow while reproducing through their flowers and 'reincarnating' out of their seeds, exemplifies the universal interdependence of the global ecosystem.

The Franco-Italian writer analyses some other revealing properties of the botanical realm, such as their transmediumnity between the air and the earth, the celestial and chthonian domains. While their stems and leaves seek the Sunshine and the Carbon with which they manufacture organic matter and generate oxygen as waste, their roots dig into the soil to pump up minerals. All animals, including humans, fully depend on vegetal organisms to breathe and eat since flesh is transformed vegetal substance. Plants therefore link us to both the Sun in outer space and the subterranean foundations of our earthly home. Our modes of living and our laws must take into account and draw inspiration from plant life, as shown by agricultural/seasonal cycles, climates and our circadian rhythm that is a key factor in our instincts, thoughts and behaviour.

Coccia also provides us with a fascinating comparison between plant sexuality, manifested in the flower ('an attractor and a magnetic force' as he describes it) and ours (don't we offer flowers in many civilisations to those we wish to seduce?). The creation of beauty in a flower hints at the bio-psychic process that makes us admire beauty, imagine, and design or build beautiful things, whether it be songs, dances, paintings, sculptures or monuments. There is reproductive rationality in a flower as there is in the tail of a peacock, the mane of a lion, or the wings of a butterfly, and likewise, there is an elemental connection between human and anthropogenic aesthetics (the enjoyment of beauty leading to the creation of beautiful things) and the survival and reproductive imperative.

Can integral humanism, outside of particular cultural and political interpretations, be equated with the eco-metaphysical 'systems view of life' proposed by the late biologist and philosopher Francisco Varela? This essay has tried to answer this question in the conditional affirmative.

Endnotes

1 Hippolyte Taine (1828-1893) in his *Essais de Critique et d'Histoire* defined three basic factors that shape society and the individuals in it, particularly their literary and artistic creations. His influence on late 19th century Europe was extensive, and his philosophy, conservative but scientifically inspired, containing elements of positivism but rising above materialism has been 'irrationalist liberalism'.

2 Lord Alexander Fraser Tytler's (1747-1813) theory of democratic evolution https://www.al.com/opinion/2016/08/eight_stages_of_democracy.html

His main thesis has been summed thusly: Tytler identified "Eight Stages of a Democracy", from beginning to end. The eight stages go from bondage to spiritual faith; from spiritual faith to great courage; from courage to liberty; from liberty to abundance; from abundance to complacency; from complacency to apathy; from apathy to dependence, and finally from dependence back to bondage. Life and our universe move in cycles, and history is no different (quoted from above article).

3 The following essay proposes a scientific demonstration of the natural foundation of morality in the very fabric of the universe: https://medium.com/predict/the-foundation-of-morality-is-woven-into-the-fabric-of-the-universe-c42c5c27ff0c

4 Interview of E. Coccia by Olivier Zahm, *Purple Magazine, 28F/W2017, 28th Anniversary Issue.*

Chapter Four

The Human Person: Perspectives of Jaques Maritain

Felix Machado

Pandit Deendayal and Jaques Maritain offer valuable insights into the promotion of human dignity, ethical governance, and the integration of material and spiritual dimensions in the pursuit of a just society. From a Catholic Christian point of view, this paper underlines the Integral Humanism proposed by Jaques Maritain, which in many ways concurs with the profound thought of Pandit Deendayal Upadhyay. Obviously, an Indian would be proud to adhere their thinking to the philosophical, spiritual, and social tradition of their motherland. They would be delighted to discover that despite the cultural and religious diversity of their contexts, there is a universality of certain principles which emerges from both Pandit Upadhyay and Maritain. At the centre of Maritain's integral humanism[1] is a conception of the "human person" that is inherently and radically social and non-individualist. At the same time, though this philosophy is non-individualist, it is not anti-individualist, which is crucial to be appreciated.

1) The Human Person: For Maritain, following St.

Thomas Aquinas, the person is not a mere object — a thing that is merely acted upon. Rather, a person is a subject — a being that is an agent; a thinking and acting agent. A human person is able to act to achieve his own purposes — his own fulfilment and happiness. In that sense, Maritain's philosophy represents a kind of radical personalism, because it puts the person at the centre. But the person is not an isolated "individual" in the way conceived, for example, in the modern liberal social theories of Thomas Hobbes or John Locke. In the "state of nature" imagined by Hobbes and Locke, every individual is in a competition or struggle with every other individual. Because every individual is motivated by the pursuit of material self-interest and the pursuit of power, this competition or struggle has a zero-sum or win-lose quality. The reason is that the power and material advantages that individuals pursue — as conceived by Hobbes and Locke in their respective philosophies of individualism — are finite resources. One's gain is the other's loss; the other's gain is one's own loss.

Indeed, the "individual" as such according to the social and political philosophy of liberal individualism, is an essentially material and finite object, like a billiard ball that can only compete and collide with other billiard balls. Because individuals are inherently conflictual and competitive, there is no shared or "common good" for individuals to pursue in authentic partnership or civic friendship with each other. Instead, all that can be hoped for, at best, is that their constant conflict and competition can be managed in such a way that it does not become openly violent and destructive.

It is not that material individuality does not exist in Maritain's view. It is that the human person in his richness should not be reduced to this dimension of material individuality. Of great significance for our purposes is that

Maritain, in his attention to the multiple dimensions of the human person, goes out of his way to stress the similarity of his philosophical anthropology to that of Hinduism and indeed to the "intellectual heritage of humanity." As he says:

"The human being is held between two poles: a material pole, which in reality does not concern authentic personality, but rather the material condition and the shadow, as it were, of personality; and a spiritual pole, which concerns personality itself. It is this material pole, and the individual becoming the centre of all things, that the words of Blaise Pascal aim at. And it is on the contrary with the spiritual pole, and with the person, source of freedom and of goodness, that the words of St. Thomas are concerned. Herein we face the distinction, which I mentioned at the beginning, between individuality and personality.

The distinction between the 'ego' and the 'self' (*ahamkar* and *aham*) in Hindu philosophy is – with other metaphysical connotations – it's equivalent. This distinction is fundamental in the doctrine of St. Thomas Aquinas".

As he says later in the same work: "We are subject to the determinism of the physical world. But each man is also a person and, in so far as he is a person, he is not subject to the stars and atoms; for he subsists entirely with the very subsistence of his spiritual soul, and the latter is in him a principle of creative unity, of independence and of freedom" (Cf. *Scholasticism and Politics*).

2) The Human Person is not Absolute: In Jacques Maritain's social philosophy of "integral humanism," on the other hand, the "human person" is conceived of in higher and more multidimensional and thus more complete and "integral" terms than it is in the philosophy of Western liberalism. First, the human person possesses a transcendent dignity as a creature made in the image and likeness of God. Human persons come from God, as their First Efficient Cause and Creator. While human beings possess a bodily nature, they are also spiritual creatures, possessing a non-material soul, because they were created by God who is Pure Spirit. As Maritain writes: "The entire person is relative to the absolute, in which alone it can find its fulfilment. Its spiritual fatherland is the whole order of goods having an absolute value, and which serve as an introduction to the absolute Whole, which transcends the world. Finally, the human person not only bears to God the common resemblance born by other creatures; The human person not only resembles Him in a proper and peculiar fashion. It is the image of God. For God is spirit, and the person proceeds from Him, having as its principle of life a spiritual soul, a spirit capable of knowing and loving, and of being elevated by grace to participate in the very life of God, so as to finally love Him and know Him even as He knows and loves Himself".

Jacques Maritain, borrowing from St. Thomas Aquinas, views the human person not only as coming from God ("*exitus*") but also as returning to God ("*reditus*") as their Final Cause and Final End. God who is Spirit is our highest purpose and highest joy. Humans are therefore made not for isolation, but are made for communion. That is why they are given souls and spirits. They are given reason and will, so that they can freely enter a loving relationship with their Creator, a relationship in which they can understand and be conscious of God's nature and goodness and respond freely to his love — not as robots but as subjects. Their dignified independence as persons, their self-possession, is for the sake of enabling true self-giving and thus true communion.

"In order to be able to give oneself, one must first exist. And one must not only exist as other things, one must exist in an eminent way, by possessing oneself, by holding oneself in hand and by disposing of oneself; that is, one must exist through a spiritual existence, capable of enveloping itself by intelligence and freedom, and of super-existing in knowledge and free love. That is why the Western metaphysical tradition defines the person by independence: the person is a reality, which, subsisting spiritually, constitutes a universe by itself and an independent whole (relatively independent), in the great whole of the universe and facing the transcendent Whole, which is God. And that is why this philosophical tradition sees in God the sovereign personality, since God's existence consists itself in a pure and absolute super-existence of intellection and love. The notion of personality does not refer to matter, as does the notion of individuality applied to corporeal things. It refers to the highest and deepest dimensions of being; personality is rooted in the spirit, in so far as the latter stands by itself in existence and super-abounds in it. Metaphysically considered, personality, being in one's substance a signature or a seal enabling one freely to perfect and freely to give this substance, evidences in each of us that expansiveness of being which, in a corporeal-spiritual being, is linked to the spirit, and which constitutes, in the secret depths of our ontological structure, a source of dynamic unity and of inner unification" (Cf. Scholasticism and Politics).

That Maritain conceives of the human person as possessing by nature a capacity, orientation, and purpose that transcends the merely human is evident from his very definition of true "Humanism." And such a definition essentially tends to make man more truly human, and to manifest his original dignity by enabling him to participate in everything which can enrich him in nature and history (by 'concentrating the world in man', in Max Scheler's words, and by 'making man as large as the world'). "It demands that man develop his powers, his creative energies, and the life of reason, and at the same time labour to make the forces of the physical world instruments of his freedom. Certainly, the great pagan wisdom, which, according to the author of the Eudemian Ethics, aimed to link itself to 'that which is better than reason, being the source of reason', cannot be cut off from the humanistic tradition; and we are thus warned never to define humanism by excluding all reference to the superhuman and by foreswearing all transcendence..., Instead of an open human nature and an open reason, which are real nature and real reason, people pretend that there exists a nature and a reason isolated by themselves and shut up in themselves, excluding everything which is not themselves" (Cf. *Scholasticism and Politics*). In other words, true humanism or "integral humanism" cannot have a merely or reductively material understanding of the human person and his nature and purpose.

Indeed, it is precisely because of the fact that Maritain's "integral humanism" has a supernatural and ultimately Christian character — rooted in the Christian teaching of St. Thomas Aquinas — that it is a true humanism, that it is worthy of the lofty dignity of the human person. As Maritain observes: "Such a humanism which considers man in the wholeness of his natural and supernatural being, and which sets no *a priori* limit to the descent of the divine into man, we may call the humanism of the Incarnation is an 'integral' and 'progressive' Christian position which I believe conforms to principles representative of the genuine spirit of Thomism [— that is, to the theology and philosophy of St. Thomas Aquinas]" (*Scholasticism and Politics*).

3) The Social Nature of the "Human Person"

i. Maritain's "integral humanism" is inherently social, in that he views the human person as destined for communion not only with God but also with other human persons. And because human persons are not merely materialistic but spiritual creatures who also have spiritual ends or purposes and not merely material passions and interests, they can pursue shared goods and purposes — a truly "common good"[2] — with other human persons.

Maritain observes: "And why does the person demand for himself life in society? He demands this, first, by virtue of the very perfections which are inherent in him/her, and because of the fact of this being open to the communications of knowledge and of love and which require an entrance into relations with other persons. Taken in the aspect of its radical generosity, the human person tends to super-abound in social communications, according to the law of super-abundance which is inscribed in the very depths of being, of life, of intelligence, of love".

ii. It is because of his/her needs that the human person demands this life in society. Taken in the aspect of his indigence, he/she demands to be integrated to a body of social communications, without which it is impossible for him/her to attain to his full life and achievement. "Society thus appears as furnishing the person with the conditions of existence and development which he definitely needs". The human person cannot achieve his fullness alone, but only through receiving certain goods essential to him from society. "I do not mean only material needs, of bread, of clothes and lodging, for all of which man depends upon the aid of his fellows; but also, and first of all, the need of their aid in acting according to reason and virtue, which corresponds to the specific character of the human being".

iii. In order to attain to a certain degree of elevation in knowledge and perfection of moral life, man needs the education and the aid granted by his fellows. It is in this sense, in the words of Aristotle, that man is naturally a political animal. He is a political animal because he is a reasonable animal, because his reason seeks to develop with the help of education, through the teaching and the co-operation of other men/women, and because society is thus required to accomplish human dignity[3]. (Cf. *Scholasticism and Politics*).

iv. It is also important to see that Maritain's philosophy of integral humanism is nonetheless social in a way that prevents any human person from being conceived or used as a mere means or instrument of the political community. In Maritain's "integral humanism," because every human person is a being with an inherent spiritual dignity and an infinite spiritual end or purpose, he or she has a nature and a purpose that transcend any finite human community, including the political community — as great and noble and important as the political community may be. No human person can be reduced to being a mere cog in the wheel of a political or economic system.

As Maritain notes with great force in a characteristic passage: "[B]y reason of his destination to the absolute, and because he is called upon to fulfill a destiny superior to time, —in other words, according to the highest exigencies of personality as such, —the human person, as spiritual totality, referring to the transcendent Whole, surpasses all temporal societies and is superior to them. And from this point of view, —in other words, as regards the things that are not Caesar's, — "It is to the perfect achievement of the person and of its supra-temporal aspirations, that society itself and its common good are subordinated, as to the end of another order, which transcends them". He continues: "A single human soul is of more worth than the whole universe of bodies and material goods. There is nothing above the human soul, — except God. Regarding the eternal destiny of the soul, and its supra-temporal goods, society exists for each person and is subordinated to it" (Cf. *Scholasticism and Politics*). A bit later in *Scholasticism and Politics*, Maritain sharpens the point deploying the idea that certain "primordial rights" belong to the human person as such and must never be violated: "Man is constituted as person, made for God and for eternal life, before being constituted part of a human community; and he is constituted part of familial society before being constituted part of political society. Hence, there are primordial rights, which the latter must respect, and which it dares not wrong when it demands for itself the aid of its members because they are its parts" (Cf. *Scholasticism and Politics*).

v. Though Maritain's integral humanism has an important and in fact irreducible spiritual foundation and orientation, it is also animated by a strong respect for the irreducibly material and physical dimension of the human person and human society. True humanism for Maritain is not a Platonic or Cartesian dualism that separates the soul from the body, or mind from matter, in order to elevate the spiritual at the expense of the material. For Maritain's humanism is radically incarnational — as was seen above, where he calls the humanism, he advocates a "humanism of the Incarnation." It is incarnational in that it is founded on the central Christian claim that God Who is Spirit fully and completely assumed the nature of a flesh-and-blood human being in the Person of Jesus Christ. By assuming a fully human form, God elevated and ennobled the matter and the flesh of our human, material existence.

A striking illustration of this is that Maritain's most favourite and beloved song, which he loved to sing to the end of his life, was a simple spiritual ballad from the Picardy region of France, called "Jesus Christ s'habille en pauvre." Or literally in English, though the language is not as beautiful and poetic:

"Jesus Christ clothes himself as a beggar." In other words, by clothing himself as a beggar, essentially, and assuming the form of a materially impoverished person, God in Jesus Christ identifies with the materially poor and needy, investing them with an infinite dignity. And having done this Himself, He expects each of us to do the same — i.e. each of us is to love and honour the poor the way God does in Christ. Indeed, the little song Maritain loved so much, "Jesus Christ s'habille en pauvre," is ultimately about how a stingy husband who refuses to show any kindness to a poor beggar is condemned to hellfire; while his kind-hearted wife, who gives generously to the same beggar, is surrounded by heavenly light and is taken to Paradise.

vi. The fact that Maritain's integral humanism is a non-dualist or anti-dualist humanism that radically elevates — as well as integrates — both the spiritual and the material dimensions of human existence has direct and huge implications for politics. It means that no healthy politics can ignore or disrespect the spiritual dimension and the spiritual end or aspirations of the human person. It also means, however, that no healthy politics can ignore or disrespect the material dimension of the human person and of human society. Maritain writes with great power and clarity about the "social significance" of this kind of integrated and non-dualist humanism: "A characteristic of the humanism, which I call integral, would be that, far from being limited to the élite, it would care for the masses, for their right to work and to a spiritual life, and for the movement which brings them, we may say, to a historically full age. On the social significance of such a humanism, I will simply say that in my opinion it should assume the task of radically transforming the temporal order, a task which would tend to substitute for bourgeois civilization, and for an economic system based on the fecundity of money, not a collectivistic economy, but a 'personalistic' civilization and a 'personalistic' economy, through which would stream a temporal refraction of the truths of the Gospel." (Cf. *Scholasticism and Politics*).

Maritain continues: "This task is joined to a thorough awakening of the religious conscience, and I wish to insist for a moment on this point. One of the worst vices of the modern world is its dualism, the dissociation between the things of God and the things of the world. The latter, the things of the social, economic and political life, have been abandoned to their own carnal law, removed from the exigencies of the Gospel. The result is that they have become more and more unlivable; at the same time, Christian ethics, not really carried out in the social life of people, became in this connection, I do not say in itself or in the Church, I say in the world, in the general cultural behavior, a universe of formulas and words; and this universe of formulas and words was in effect vassalized, in practical cultural behavior, by the real energies of this same temporal world existentially detached from Christ. Such a disorder can be cured only by a renewal of the profoundest energies of the religious conscience, arising in temporal existence."

"On the other hand, modern civilization, which pays dearly to-day for the past, seems as if it were pushed, by the very contradictions and fatalities suffered by it, toward contrasting forms of misery and intensified materialism. To rise above these fatalities, we need an awakening of liberty and of its creative forces, we need the energies of spiritual and social resurrection of which man does not become capable by the grace of the State or any Party pedagogy, but by a love which fixes the centre of his life infinitely above the world and temporal history" (Cf. *Scholasticism and Politics*).

vii. According to Maritain, no dominant political philosophy or ideology of late modernity — whether Liberal Individualism, Communism, or Fascism — adequately respects the rights of the human person and the full requirements of an integral humanism as he has sketched this philosophy out in his work, *Scholasticism and Politics,* as well as many other writings. "I can only indicate briefly the criticisms to which we should submit the materialist philosophy of society, considered under its three chief forms: bourgeois individualism, communist anti-individualism; and the combined anti-individualism and anti-communism of the dictatorial or totalitarian type. These three doctrines equally ignore the human person and are reduced to considering instead the material individual alone".

viii. The only alternative is some kind of "personalist democracy" that is neither individualist, nor materialist, nor anti-individualist — a kind of "third way" democracy that eventually emerged in one form in Latin America and Europe as "Christian Democracy." Discussion of the details of political programmes is beyond the scope of this paper and was always largely beyond Jacques Maritain's own concerns and interests and beyond, he added, his competence and authority as a mere philosopher. Indeed, he deeply distrusted partisan politics, and even often dissociated himself from the partisanship of his own political and philosophical allies. It is sufficient to say, as Maritain said himself:

"Modern democracies suffer from a philosophy of life which undermines and annihilates their vital principle from within. If they must refine the sense of justice, and of risk, and of heroism, it is under condition of rejecting their materialist philosophy, and of viewing in full light a personalist conception of life and of society".

Conclusion

"To the inhuman humanism of the individual would thus succeed a new humanism—the integral humanism of the person, open to that which surpasses it and leads it to achievement, and open to the common service of justice and friendship".

This paper will be concluded by only saying very strongly that against inhuman humanism, and for the sake of realizing in India and elsewhere a truly integral humanism of the person, true Catholics and true Hindus have every reason to be the strongest of allies, and to work together, intellectually and socially, rather than against each other. And this volume represents a significant step in this constructive and collaborative direction.

Endnotes

1 (Jaques Maritain writes in his article, "Integral Humanism and the Crisis of Modern Times", which is published in *The Review of Politics*, January 1939, Vol 1, No. 1, University of Notre Dame, Indiana, U.S.A.): "To leave the discussion quite open, let us say that humanism (and such a definition may itself be developed along quite divergent lines) tends essentially to make man more truly human, and to manifest his original grandeur by enabling him to participate in everything which can enrich him in nature and history (by concentrating the world in man, almost in Max Scheler's words, and by making man as large as the world; it demands that man develop his powers, his creative energies and the life of reason, and at the same time labor to make forces of the physical world instruments of his freedom. Certainly, the wisdom of all religions, which according to the author of the Eudemian Ethics, aimed to link itself to 'that which is better than reason, being the source of treasure' cannot be cut off from the humanistic tradition; and we are also warned never to define humanism by excluding all reference to the superhuman and by foreswearing all transcendence". In this article Jaques Maritain spells out different kinds of humanism by different authors: e.g. there is "classical humanism" and its vices, within which these ideas operate and by the contingencies of history as well as by the acts of liberty produced in history, such as dialectic, but not in the sense of Hegelian nor Marxist. There is counter-humanism, rationalistic humanism (in fact, irrational), humanism of the Incarnation, etc. The New Humanism proposed by Maritain must: "re-assume in a purified climate all the work of the classical age; it must re-make

anthropology, find the rehabilitation and the "dignification" of the creature not in isolation, in a closed-inness of the creature on itself, but in its openness to the world of the divine and super-rational; and this implies in practice a work of sanctification of the profane and temporal; this means, in the spiritual order, the discovery of the *ways of childhood* whereby the "humanity of God our Savior" as St Paul Says, finds, with fewer human trappings, a readier way into man, and causes more souls to enter into this hidden task of suffering and vivifying; it implies, in the moral and social order, the discovery of a deeper and fuller sense of the dignity of the human person, so that man would re-find himself in God, and would direct social work toward an heroic ideal of brotherly love, itself conceived not as a spontaneous return of emotions to some illusory primitive condition, but as a difficult and painful conquest of the spirit, a work of grace and virtue".

2 What is common good? The sum total of those conditions of social life which allow people as groups and as individuals to reach their proper fulfillment. The common good involves the good of all, and of each individual because we are all really responsible for all. Respect for and promotion of the fundamental rights of the person, the development of the spiritual and temporal goods of persons and society, and the peace and security of all. So, one's authority is exercised legitimately when it acts for the common good and employs morally licit means to attain it. Therefore, political regimes must be determined by the free decision of their citizens. They should respect the principle of the 'rule of law' in which the law and not the arbitrary will of some, is sovereign. Unjust laws and measures contrary to the moral order are not binding in conscience.

When can one find the most complete realization of the common good? The most complete realization of the common good is found in those political communities which defend and promote the good of their citizens and of intermediate groups without forgetting the universal good of the entire human family. How do you participate in bringing about the common good? All according to the place and role that you occupy participate in bringing about the common good. The common good presupposes three essential elements: 1) You must respect the persons as such. Public authorities are bound to respect the fundamental and inalienable rights of the human person. Society should permit each of its members to fulfill his vocation. In particular, the common good resides in the conditions for the exercise of the natural freedoms' indispensable for the development of the human vocation, such as 'the right to act according to a sound norm of conscience and so safeguard... privacy, and rightful freedom also in matters of religion. 2) the common good requires the social well-being and development of the group itself. Development is the epitome of all social duties. Authority is to see and judge if there is conflict of interest, conflict between various particular interests; it should make accessible to each what is needed to lead a truly human life: food, clothing, health, work, education and culture, suitable information, the right to establish a family, and so on. 3) the common good requires peace, that is, stability and security of a just order. It presupposes that authority should ensure by morally acceptable means the security of society and its members. It is the basis of the right to legitimate personal and collective defense. Citizens also should take an active part in public life as far as possible.

3 The dignity of the human person: God created us and every other human being in his image and likeness. We are endowed with a spiritual and immortal soul, intelligence and free will. We are subordinate to God and called in soul and in body to eternal happiness. We attain this eternal happiness by the virtue of grace of Christ which makes us participate in the divine life. This grace of Christ is operative in every person who, following a correct conscience, seeks and loves the true and the good and avoids evil.

Happiness is not some vague and a sort of personally made idea but it is innate desire (we are created with this desire by God) and placed in our heart in order to draw us to God alone because, in the final analysis he alone can satisfy this innate desire.

Freedom is part of our God given dignity; freedom is our right and it must be respected, especially in moral and religious matters and must be protected by civil authority within the limits of the common good and a just public order. God has given us this power to act, to do this or that; we are responsible for our actions. The more does what is good; the freer one becomes. Freedom has a purpose, to attain perfection and this happens when we are directed towards God, our highest good. Freedom implies choosing between good and evil. The choice of evil is abuse of freedom and leads to slavery of sinful life. Freedom and responsibility are related. Freedom makes persons responsible for their actions; 'one does this or that because one wants this or that. There are aspects of ignorance, inadvertence, duress, fear, inordinate attachments or habits which diminish or cancel our freedom. Our freedom is weakened by original sin. This weakness is intensified with our successive sins. But Christ has set us free, 'so we should remain free (Gal 5:1). The Holy Spirit leads us to spiritual freedom to make us free co-workers with him in the Church and in the world.

The human person has communal dimension as an essential component of his nature and vocation. The goal of life for all is God. For us God is also Triune. Love of neighbor is inseparable from the love of God. How is the person related to community? The human person (not I, you, she, he) ought to be the principle, the subject and the end of all social institutions, national and international (family, society, the state, UN, etc.) with due respect for the principle of subsidiarity.

Chapter Five

Locating the Reflections of 'Self'

Lal Ji Pal and Sandeep E

The search for locating the original and dynamic nature of the self has always been a central concern of social thinkers. While mainstream thinkers have ascribed very little importance to this aspect, certain less celebrated thinkers, particularly from the peripheral world, including the eastern hemisphere, have given more significance to their thought. Indian political thinkers like Bankim Chandra Chatterjee, Swami Dayananda Saraswati, Swami Vivekananda, and Maharshi Aravindan stand at the forefront of this lineage. The particular socio-political landscape from which they tried to trace the roots and breadths of the self was unique from the Western landscape. The social life in the East was more family-centered and value-oriented. Here the relationship between the individual and society is more intrinsic.

Swami Vivekananda, denoting the organic relationship between both, describes the individual as "Vyasthi," whereas society is described as "Samasthi." The quest for a real 'self' had always been the crux of the social thoughts that emanated from these surroundings. However, following the early revivalist thinkers, the importance and charm of that quest had been beginning to dim. In the same way, Tilak and Gandhi also traced the value of society-centered life in the political spectrum of modern India. Later organizations, rooted in cultural nationalism, like the Rashtriya Swayamsevak Sangh, promoted the search for the self in the context of social and national reconstruction through man-making. The Baudhik Vibhags of the Sangh promoted such thoughts and discussions at the grass root level. It was in such a socio-intellectual context that Pandit Deendayal Upadhyay sorted out the basic tenets of the self as part of a wider horizon of integral humanism.

When it comes to the origin and prevalence of the concept of self in the mind of Jaques Maritain, we can contemplate a very distinct social trajectory. In the West, the prominence of society had faded due to the influences of the European Renaissance. Smith's economics, Lockean Liberalism, and Newtonian Physics have altogether elevated individuals to the zenith of socio-political order, surpassing the value-oriented social arguments of the orthodox Christian church. The Darwinian theory, which was borrowed by the socio-political realm too, in the form of social Darwinism, also furthered the relevance of acute individualism. However, positive readings on the self were also evolving parallelly. The religious reformation through the protestant revolution and Calvinism opened new avenues in Christianity to deliberate more philosophical aspects, including the Self. The revival of ancient and medieval literature, particularly in the regional languages of French, German, and Italian, also initiated discussions on the self. The Divine Comedy of Dante is a prime example. The English, French, and American revolutions ascribed some positive ramifications to Western individualism.

The trinities of liberty, equality, and fraternity enabled Western intellectuals to think about individuality more politely and humanely. Later, early socialist thinkers and communists, including Karl Marx, made some covert interpretations on the self. Karl Marx tried to locate the self in the materialistic world in his "Economic and Philosophic Manuscripts of 1844". His conception of Alienation, the sociological basis of Marxism, is an attempt to identify the complications faced by a worker's inner self due to the meddling of the intense materialistic interests of the capitalist class. According to him, the workers are alienated in four spheres- Alienation of the worker from their product; Alienation of the worker from the act of production; Alienation of the worker from other workers; and Alienation of the worker from their species-essence; with the fourth kind of Alienation being the most important one. It is directly related to the self, though Marx elaborated it differently. An individual's species-essence, or "Gattungswesen," contains a human being's full inborn capacities. Marx argues that an individual's identity and opportunity for self-development are taken away in a capitalist mode of production because he is considered nothing more than the seller of his own labor-power as a market commodity. It is in this way that the considerations of the self were evolving in the West at the time when Maritain invented his idea of the Self through his writing of Integral Humanism.

The above discussions shed light on the socio-political and ideological contexts in which Deendayal Upadhyay and Jaques Maritain evolved their thought on the Self. In pursuance of that, the following section outlines a brief overview of the integral humanism of Deendayal Upadhyay to unfold the description of the concept of Self.

Deendayal Upadhyay and Outline of Integral Humanism in the Indian Context

Deendayal Upadhyay was a versatile personality who heralded his presence across different dimensions of social and intellectual spheres. He was an ardent follower of the Rashtriya Swayamsevak Sangh. Benefiting from these ideological roots, he succeeded Shyama Prasad Mukherjee as a needed leader to lead the political party of the Bharatiya Jana Sangh in a new and dynamic way. He had a firm desire to do away with the conventional outlook of the Party. He thought to bring some new economic, philosophical, and political color to the policies and programmes of the Party. Integral humanism as a comprehensive philosophical document emerged out of this intention. Against this backdrop, he delivered four speeches in April 1965 in Bombay, the country's economic and business center. The talks presented a clear economic viewpoint in the context of the Congress government's almost ten years of Soviet-style economic planning. The Upadhyay alternative, on the other hand, was not free market capitalism, but rather a comprehensive ethical framework that outlined the proper role of an operating economy in realizing the potential of individuals and society as a whole[1].

His ideas on Dharma, Bharatiyata, Rama Rajya, and Antyodaya have always been important to establish Bharat as Vishwa Guru. Following in Deendayal Upadhyay's footsteps, the first BJP Prime Minister, Atal Bihari Vajpayee, worked toward good governance, which aims to provide everyone, especially those living in rural regions, with as many amenities as possible to enhance their quality of life. The new India that is "Vocal for Local" and striving for self-reliance under the leadership of Prime Minister Shri Narendra Modi also derives its energy from the conceptions of Deendayal Upadhyay[2]. The Deendayal Antyodaya Yojana, a comprehensive programme of the central government, aims to improve livelihood possibilities for the impoverished in both urban and rural areas through skill development as well as other ways[3]. All these are some of the legacies of Deendayal Upadhyay's Integral Humanism.

A close reading of his Integral Humanism proves that Deendayal Upadhyay· was very brilliantly furnishing an irrefutable and inalienable relationship between the three dimensions of Self- individual, societal, and national. These three notions of self are being amalgamated. However, a very visible upper hand has been given to the national self, which he describes as '*Chiti*'. Self is primarily affiliated with our identity. An individual as well as a society may have a special identity. However, it is also very important to consider our sense of national identity. Independence has no value without this identity, and it cannot be used as a tool for advancement and happiness. The primary reason behind Bharat's issues is the country's disregard for its national identity[4]. In an attempt to find out the prominent nature of the national self, he delves into the origin of the state. One dominant view is that society is a collection of people who created it by agreeing among themselves. "Social Contract Theory" is the name given to this perspective. This perspective places more emphasis on the individual[5].

Contradicting this, he says that it is believed that society is self-created. Similar to an individual, society develops naturally. Society is not created by people. It is not a registered cooperative society, a club, or a joint stock company. In actuality, society is an organic thing that has its own "Self," and an existence of its own. It is a sovereign creature, much like an individual. McDougal is credited with creating the field of "group mind" psychology. He acknowledges the group's unique mentality, psychology, and ways of thinking and doing. A collective has emotions as well[6].

The national self is the mainstay of national existence. Deendayal strives to correlate the vanishing of existing human civilizations to the decaying of the national self of those civilizations. Why Did Great Ancient Nations Succumb? He asks. Certain ancient nations are known to have vanished. The Greek country of antiquity came to an end. In the same vein, Egyptian civilization vanished. The fate of the Babylonian and Syrian civilizations is also similar. Cynthia passed away. Conversely, Israeli Jews coexisted with many ethnic groups for generations, dispersed throughout different regions, and managed to maintain their unique identity within their host communities[7]. Thus, it is evident that something other than settling on a specific plot of land is the root of national sentiment

A person is believed to have died when their relationship with their body is disengaged. The "Self" that resides in the body is the essence of the individual. In a similar vein, a nation's soul is this concept, ideal, or guiding principle[8]. A person can also be an avenue for attributing a life to the Nation's Chiti. Thus, a person represents his or her country in addition to themselves. Furthermore, he staffs the several organizations established to achieve the national objective thus also representing these. He also represents broader organizations than the Nation, including manhood. In summary, an individual is made up of many different qualities, but they do not conflict with one another; rather, they are cooperative, harmonious, and united[9]. Only a system that recognizes the fundamental harmony and mutual complementarity of the various human ideals, a system that creates laws to eliminate discord and increase cooperation and mutual usefulness, can bring about world peace and happiness and guarantee steady progress.

The theme of self has been addressed in this manner in the thought of Deendayal Upadhyay. Here it is very evident that the individual self and social self are ultimately supplementing the national self, that is Chiti. The mechanical view of society and state is negated. He establishes that just like the individual possesses a self, the nation also carries a similar one.

The Idea of Self in Maritain's Thought

The search for the self in Maritain's thought is rooted in his attachment to Christian theology. He was more resentful of the fact that materialistic rationalism, manifested in the form of dialectical materialism, Marxism, and finally, the more pessimistic Fascism, had severely hampered the purity and eternality of the individual self. Since the very early ages, Maritain had imbibed a notion that the believing soul, the spiritual life, had faced tremendous setbacks. The reading of certain novels written by pro-religious writers like Leon Bloy made this realization easier. Maritain embarked on a course that would guide him for the remainder of his career with his initial attempt to apply Thomist philosophy to modern-day social difficulties. Instilling humanism in thought was central to Maritain.[10] In books like Antimoderne, Théonas, and Three Reformers: Luther, Descartes, and Rousseau, Maritain remained mostly critical of modern philosophy, but he also found much to like in contemporary art, and saw the beginnings of a more compassionate politics in his time.

It is from this backdrop that he attempted to delineate the specifications of the new humanity, which he called Integral Humanism. It was a search for regaining the lost human self. Humanisme Intégral (Integral Humanism), written by Maritain in 1936, argued that modern humanism had lost sight of a spiritually affluent concept of the human being. He urged a New Christendom to be both aware of its place in a pluralistic society and true to its divine calling. When assessing the current state of affairs, Maritain was afraid that Catholics would just unite into a group inside one or more dominant political ideologies.[11] During the Spanish Civil War, the Republican and Nationalist groups forced violent conflict into every aspect of civil society, realizing this fear. Collaborating with his former pupil Yves R. Simon, Maritain organized aid for refugees seeking entry into France and sought to blunt the accusation made by both sides that the hundreds of thousands of casualties in the battle were only the fault of one party [12].

As seen before, the search for the self of Maritain was centered on Christian theology. However, he did not confine his thought process to any narrow view. His search for the self had surpassed religious or sectarian fissures. His approach towards the plight and cause of Jews at a point in time of growing antisemitism was very sympathetic and empathetic. Maritain committed himself to Jewish advocacy in the late 1930s, a time when European waves of violence and discrimination against Jews were growing. As a young, outspoken Dreyfussard, Maritain had long been aware of antisemitism both inside and outside of France.[13] Through writings like Les Juifs parmi les nations (English: Antisemitism), Maritain attempted to theologically consider Jewish-Christian ties and bring attention to the predicament of European Jews.

A piece of writing, 'Integral Humanism and the Crisis of Modern Times,' written by Maritain in 1939, sheds light on the idea of Integral Humanism and Self. Here, more focus is laid on the humanistic view of the self. He says that humanism, which could be defined in a variety of ways, tends to make man more fully human and to bring forth his inherent grandeur by allowing him to engage in everything that can enrich him in nature and history. It also requires that man cultivate his abilities, his creative energies, and the life of reason, while simultaneously working to make the forces of the physical world tools for his freedom.[14] It is clear from this that rationalism has endangered reason, and anthropocentric humanism has endangered humanism. But even here, this attitude yields to what one could term a counter-humanism, regardless of how intelligently the idea that intellect originates from the snake should be developed, or how generously they attempt to preserve human values.[15]

Maritain seeks to unfold his understanding of the fault lines of dialectical materialism in dealing with self and humanism. Because of its extreme atheism, it undermines the humanism that it claims to uphold in theory. Dialectical materialism's claim to be the heir of classical humanism is widely known. Man achieves his salvation by himself and by himself alone. Therefore, this salvation is solely and exclusively temporal; it cannot be achieved naturally without God, because man is truly alone and can only act truly alone in the absence of God, and even against God.[16]

Lastly, there is a stance that is both distinct from anti-humanist irrationalism and anthropocentric humanism. The Christian humanistic perspective holds that the failure of classical humanism was not humanism per se, but rather anthropocentric; it was not a hope in reason, but rather an isolation of reason and its eventual drying up; it was not a search for liberty, but rather an orientation toward the myth of the individual democracy rather than the historical ideal of the 'person democracy'.[17]

In summary, this perspective holds that the modern world has undermined the pursuit of real human values by pursuing good things through unethical means. Men must now preserve these values through an intellectual understanding of a deeper truth and a significant reinterpretation of national life, self, and identity. Resuming all of the work done by the classical era in a purified environment, the new humanism must reconstruct anthropology, and find the creature's "dignification" and rehabilitation not in isolation or its closed-offness to the divine and super-rational, but rather in its openness to the world of the divine and super-rational.[18] He says that we can refer to this kind of humanism as the humanism of the Incarnation, because it views man in the entirety of his natural and supernatural nature, and does not place restrictions on the divine's descent into man. It is a "progressive" and "integral" Christian stance that complies with the guiding ideals of the true Thomist philosophy.

Comparative Understanding of the Reflections on Self in Maritain and Deendayal Upadhyay

When we try to make a comparative understanding of the views on self of the two thinkers, the main divergence appears in the socio-moral context in which they cherished the idea of Integral Humanism. Both emphasized devising a new colour to the socio-political thinking of their own country. The challenges posed by materialism and capitalism had been rightly arrested by both of the thinkers. This led to their insistence on drafting a new plan centered on Integral humanism. When it comes to the mutual influence of these two thinkers, it is visible that Maritain is the pre-runner in the realm of Integral Humanism. Hence, an observation is that Deendayal Upadhyay was inspired by Maritain's thought. The Catholic social philosopher Jacques Maritain, whose book Integral Humanism described a Christian philosophy established in reaction to European social and political structures that presumed a priori materialism, appears to have been the inspiration behind the moniker Integral Humanism.[19] While Maritain is acknowledged as an intellectual interlocutor by Hindu nationalist sources, they are hesitant to attribute his impact to Upadhyay. With a revitalized Thomism that promoted a theologically specific view of human nature along with a legal and political structure that would allow for the possibility of human advancement based on this unique knowledge, Maritain's philosophical system sought to address the crisis of humanism[20]. Hence, a comparative study of the Self, inherent in both of the thinkers' writings, is also easy. Both try to discover the essence of the Self from the remains of the spiritual dominion of their respective societies. As Maritain's spiritual realm was the organized religion of Christianity, his thought on self is centered on the dominant Catholic stream of Christianity. On the other hand, as it is very difficult to find a similarly organized religious landscape on Indian soil, Deendayal Upadhyay tends to focus more on invoking the civilizational backdrop of Bharat.

It is evident that their thoughts have impacted subsequent generations in their respective countries. They established a way of thinking at a very turbulent time. The political thought of Deendayal was primarily aimed at the rejuvenation of a significant thought. The Hindu tradition of thought was sidelined with the emergence of other modes of thinking, including Nehruvian Secularism, Lohia's New Socialism, and the Social Justice ideas of B. R. Ambedkar. It is in this context that Deendayal attempted to revive the thought. In that mission, he attempted to pose an ideational challenge to both Capitalism and Socialism. It led to the identification of an alternative position that could make far-reaching changes in the ideological paradigm of India. There have been different actors to take over the legacy of Deendayal. Today, India is being led by a political party, the Bharatiya Janata Party, which is an organizational successor of the Bharatiya Jana Sangh. The BJP has openly owned the legacy of Deendayal Upadhyay in its policy formulation and implementation. Today there have been numerous policies and programmes in the social welfare sector of the government of India. Various state governments led by the BJP have initiated rural upliftment programmes in his name.

On the other hand, Maritain attempted to renovate Christianity by instilling more humanism into it. He upheld the idea of Integral Humanism in this mission. The blind pursuit of material welfare by priests and followers has been a major challenge to the religion for centuries. As a result, the true essence of the religion has been lost. It is in this context that he attempted to project the real intention of the religion through the idea of Integral Humanism. He succeeded in this mission.

Conclusion

The paper looks into the key features of the ideational understanding of the self in the thoughts of Deendayal Upadhyay and Jacques Maritain. Both were harbingers of Integral Humanism, which offered a third way in their respective socio-economic and political milieu. Both have introspected the scope of elevating the Self to a new level. Self is identity. This identity can be expanded into the social self and thereafter into the national self. Philosophical and ideological pathways such as dialectical materialism, Marxism, and Fascism have caused challenges to the very spirit of humanity. The humanism practiced in the present context is marred by numerous problems. A new approach to humanism needs to evolve. It can be termed as Integral Humanism. It will never oust anything from the purview of Human consideration. Rather, it is designed to encompass all the living and non-living organisms.

Endnotes

1 John Abraham. "In Search of Dharma: Integral Humanism and the Political Economy of Hindu Nationalism", *South Asia: Journal of South Asian Studies*, vol. 42, (February, 2019), p.16. https://doi.org/10.1080/00856401.2019.1557362

2 Bandaru Dattatraya. "Deendayal Upadhyay – A man of simple living, high thinking, and strong determination". Last modified 2021. Raj Bhavan Haryana https://haryanarajbhavan.gov.in/publication/pandit-deendayal-upadhyay-a-man-of-simple-living-high-thinking-strong-determination/

3 Ibid.

4 Upadhyay, Deendayal. *Integral Humanism*. 1965. http://www.chitrakoot.org/download/IntegralHumanism.pdf. p.7

5 Ibid., p.25

6 Ibid., p.26

7 Ibid., p.27

8 Ibid., p.28

9 Ibid., p.29-30

10 About Jacques Maritain." n.d. University of Notre Dame. https://maritain.nd.edu/about/about-jacques-maritain/.

11 Ibid.

12 Ibid.

13 Ibid.

14 Jacques Maritain. "Integral humanism and the crisis of Modern Times", *The Review of Politics*, vol.1, no.1, (1939), p. 1

15 Ibid., p.4

16 Ibid., p.6

17 Ibid., p.7

18 Ibid.p.7

19 John Abraham. op. cit p., 217.

20 Ibid.

Chapter Six

Integral Humanism and Radical Humanism: A Philosophical Inquiry

Krishna Mohan Upadhyay

Humanism stands as a reputed philosophical tradition that has profoundly influenced the development of human thought and society. It centres on the inherent dignity, rights, and capabilities of human beings, advocating for their welfare and flourishing within the framework of ethical principles and societal structures. Integral Humanism and Radical Humanism represent two distinctive philosophical paradigms within the broader spectrum of humanist thought, each offering unique perspectives on the nature of humanity and the organization of society.

In Western society, which is overly shaped by competing ideologies, the term "humanism" has multiple interpretations that are somewhat distinct from one another. An attempt has been made to bring nearly all of them together in a logical and convergent manner by introducing the term integral humanism. This approach relates to the profound unity of the three-part human situation, which is defined by the rational, imaginative, and spiritual behaviour of our minds. No one should be permitted to "supersede" the other two equally significant evident forms of the human mind, which are the rationality of "pure thought," the creative activity of imagination, and the spiritual interaction with "phenomena."[1]

Integral Humanism, with its roots in post-independence India, emerged as a response to the challenges of nation-building and cultural identity in a rapidly modernizing world. Deendayal Upadhyay, inspired by the rich tapestry of Indian civilization and its philosophical heritage, articulated Integral Humanism as a holistic approach that synthesizes the material and spiritual dimensions of human life.[2] It sought to reconcile traditional Indian values with the imperatives of modernity, aiming for a socio-political order that fosters both material progress and spiritual well-being. Integral Humanism, grounded in the concept of "Antyodaya" or the welfare of the last person in society, emphasizes the importance of social and economic policies that uplift the marginalized and disadvantaged. It advocates for a decentralized socio-political structure that respects the diversity of cultures and communities while promoting national unity and integrity. Integral Humanism also underscores the significance of self-reliance, cultural rootedness, and the synthesis of material progress with spiritual upliftment. Integral Humanism's emphasis on cultural rootedness and decentralized governance has had significant implications for Indian politics and policy-making. It has influenced debates on issues such as education, governance, and cultural preservation, often advocating for a balance between tradition and modernity. Integral Humanism has shaped the ideological landscape of nationalism in India, advocating policies and initiatives aimed at promoting cultural heritage and national identity.

Conversely, Radical Humanism arose in the early 20th century amidst global movements for social justice, secularism, and rationalism. Prominent thinkers like M. N. Roy, deeply influenced by Western Enlightenment ideals and Marxist principles, advocated for Radical Humanism as a progressive alternative to religious orthodoxy and authoritarianism.[3] Roy's philosophy emphasized individual freedom, scientific inquiry and social equality, advocating for a society free from dogma and superstition. It prioritizes secularism, rationalism, and individual freedom as its foundational principles. It calls for the separation of religion from the state, the primacy of reason and scientific inquiry in decision-making processes, and the protection of individual liberties against oppressive ideologies and structures. Radical Humanism champions social justice, equality, and human rights as essential components of a just and humane society. Radical Humanism's commitment to secularism, rationalism, and social justice has similarly left a mark on socio-political discourse, both in India and globally. It has inspired movements for social reform, gender equality, and freedom of expression, challenging entrenched power structures and orthodoxies.[4] Radical Humanism has contributed to the advancement of democratic values, human rights, and progressive social policies.

Integral Humanism and Radical Humanism have not been immune to criticisms and challenges from various counterparts. Integral Humanism has been accused of promoting a homogenizing and exclusionary vision of Indian culture, overlooking the diversity of traditions and identities within the country. Critics argue that its emphasis on cultural nationalism may marginalize minority communities and undermine secular principles.

Similarly, Radical Humanism has faced criticisms for its perceived neglect of cultural and spiritual dimensions of human existence. Its insistence on secularism and rationalism has been criticized as overlooking the significance of religion and tradition in people's lives, potentially leading to a superficial understanding of human nature and society.

In light of these considerations, this paper seeks to undertake a comprehensive comparative analysis of Integral Humanism and Radical Humanism, exploring their philosophical foundations, socio-political implications and relevance in contemporary discourse.

Integral Humanism

Integral Humanism emerges as a philosophical and socio-political doctrine within the context of post-independence India. It finds its roots in the ideological framework of the Rashtriya Swayamsevak Sangh (RSS) and the Bharatiya Jana Sangh (BJS), precursors to the Bharatiya Janata Party (BJP). The intellectual architect of Integral Humanism is often attributed to Deendayal Upadhyay, a prominent leader of the BJS and a revered figure within the Sangh Parivar.[5] Upadhyay wanted to provide a distinctive vision for India's sociopolitical development that drew inspiration from the country's ancient cultural heritage while addressing contemporary challenges. Integral Humanism is deeply rooted in the philosophy of Hindutva, a term often used to denote the cultural and civilizational identity of India. However, it goes beyond mere cultural nationalism by advocating for a synthesis of material progress with spiritual and cultural values. Upadhyay envisioned a society where economic development coexists harmoniously with ethical and moral principles derived from India's spiritual traditions, such as Dharma (duty/righteousness) and Seva (service/selflessness). This synthesis, according to Upadhyay, forms the essence of Integral Humanism.

Antyodaya (upliftment of the last person) is core to Integral Humanism, which emphasizes the welfare and empowerment of the utmost marginalized and disadvantaged sections of society. Upadhyay argued that the true test of a nation's progress lies in its ability to uplift the weakest and most vulnerable members of society. Integral Humanism advocates for a decentralized socio-political structure where power and decision-making authority are distributed at the grassroots level. This decentralization is seen as essential for fostering local initiatives, promoting cultural diversity, and ensuring effective governance. Additionally, Integral Humanism promotes the concept of Swadeshi or self-reliance, encouraging indigenous development and the utilization of local resources. Cultural rootedness and national unity are essential parts of Integral Humanism, as it emphasizes the importance of preserving and promoting India's cultural heritage as a source of unity and identity. While advocating for cultural rootedness, it also promotes a sense of national unity that transcends regional, linguistic and religious divides. Integral Humanism seeks to reconcile the diversity of India's cultural traditions with a shared commitment to the nation's progress and development.

The principles of Integral Humanism have had significant socio-political implications in India. They have influenced various aspects of governance, policymaking, and public discourse, particularly within the ideological spectrum of Hindu nationalism. Integral Humanism has shaped debates on issues such as education, healthcare, rural development, and cultural preservation. Policies and programmes inspired by Integral Humanism often prioritize the needs of the marginalized and promote indigenous development initiatives. Moreover, Integral Humanism's emphasis on cultural rootedness has led to efforts to revive traditional art forms, promote classical Indian languages and protect cultural monuments.

Integral Humanism has faced criticisms and challenges from various quarters. Critics argue that its emphasis on cultural nationalism may lead to the marginalization of minority communities and undermine secular principles enshrined in the Indian Constitution. Moreover, some critics contend that Integral Humanism's vision of society tends to be idealistic and impractical, overlooking the complexities of modern governance and socio-economic dynamics. Additionally, Integral Humanism has been accused of promoting a conservative and exclusionary worldview that limits individual freedoms and diversity of thought.

In brief, Integral Humanism represents a unique synthesis of traditional values and modern aspirations, advocating for a holistic approach to socio-political development. While it has garnered support from proponents of Hindu nationalism, it continues to be a subject of debate and critique within the broader discourse on Indian society and governance.

Radical Humanism

Radical Humanism emerges as a philosophical framework that advocates for secularism, rationalism, and individual freedom, challenging traditional religious and conservative ideologies. Rooted in the early 20th century socio-political context, particularly in response to colonialism, religious orthodoxy, and social inequalities, Radical Humanism offers a vision of society based on principles of reason, equality, and human dignity.[6] Radical Humanism finds its origins in the intellectual ferment of the early 20th century, marked by the rise of nationalist movements, socialist ideologies and anti-colonial struggles. Figures such as M. N. Roy, a polymathic Indian philosopher, political activist, and Marxist theorist, played a pivotal role in articulating the principles of Radical Humanism. Roy's engagement with Marxist thought, combined with his critique of religious dogma and authoritarianism, laid the groundwork for Radical Humanism as a distinct philosophical outlook.[7]

In the Indian context, Radical Humanism emerged as a response to the challenges posed by colonialism, caste discrimination, and religious conservatism. Roy and other proponents of Radical Humanism sought to emancipate Indian society from the shackles of tradition and superstition, advocating for a secular and rationalist ethos grounded in scientific inquiry and humanist values. At the heart of Radical Humanism lies a commitment to secularism, which advocates for the separation of religion from the state and the public sphere. Secularism, as conceived within the framework of Radical Humanism, ensures that individuals are free to practice their beliefs without state interference, while also safeguarding the rights of non-believers and promoting a pluralistic society.

Rationalism is another core principle of Radical Humanism, emphasizing the importance of reason, evidence and critical thinking in all aspects of human life. Rationalism entails a rejection of superstition, dogma, and blind faith, advocating for a scientific worldview grounded in empirical observation and logical reasoning. Individual freedom occupies a central place in the philosophy of Radical Humanism, emphasizing the autonomy and agency of individuals in shaping their lives and participating in society. This principle entails the protection of civil liberties, political rights, and personal autonomy against encroachments by state authority or societal norms.

Radical Humanism has profound socio-political implications, particularly in the domains of democracy, social justice, and human rights. By advocating for secularism, Radical Humanism promotes a democratic polity where all citizens, irrespective of their religious beliefs or affiliations, enjoy equal rights and opportunities. It seeks to mitigate religious conflicts and promote communal harmony by fostering a culture of tolerance and mutual respect. Furthermore, Radical Humanism's emphasis on rationalism fosters scientific temper and intellectual inquiry, which are essential for social progress and development. By prioritizing evidence-based decision-making and critical analysis, Radical Humanism seeks to address societal challenges such as poverty, illiteracy, and inequality through informed policy interventions and social reforms. In terms of human rights, Radical Humanism champions the dignity and equality of all individuals, irrespective of their caste, creed, gender, or socio-economic status. It advocates for the elimination of discriminatory practices and the promotion of inclusive policies that ensure the full realization of human potential and well-being.

Despite its principles and aspirations, Radical Humanism has faced criticisms and challenges from various quarters. Critics argue that its staunch secularism and rationalism may overlook the cultural and spiritual dimensions of human existence, leading to a narrow and reductionist view of society. They contend that Radical Humanism's emphasis on individual freedom may neglect the communal and collective aspects of human identity and solidarity. Moreover, Radical Humanism's association with Marxism and leftist politics has led to accusations of ideological bias and dogmatism. Critics argue that its commitment to class struggle and revolutionary change may undermine social stability and economic progress, perpetuating conflict and division within society.

In short, Radical Humanism offers a compelling vision of society based on secularism, rationalism, and individual freedom, challenging traditional orthodoxies and advocating for a more inclusive and egalitarian society. Despite its critics and challenges, Radical Humanism continues to inspire movements for social justice, human rights and democratic governance, reaffirming the enduring relevance of humanist ideals in the contemporary world.

Comparative Analysis of Integral Humanism and Radical Humanism

In this section, we delve into a comprehensive comparative analysis of Integral Humanism and Radical Humanism. By examining their shared values, points of divergence, potential synergies, and implications for contemporary society, we aim to elucidate the complex relationship between these two philosophical frameworks. Integral Humanism and Radical Humanism share certain core values and objectives. Both philosophies of Integral Humanism and Radical Humanism prioritize the inherent dignity and rights of every individual. They recognize the importance of respecting and safeguarding human autonomy, agency, and well-being.[8] Integral Humanism and Radical Humanism are equally concerned with addressing socio-economic disparities and promoting social justice. They advocate for policies and systems that ensure equitable distribution of resources and opportunities, albeit with differing approaches. Both frameworks emphasize the need for ethical governance and leadership. They advocate for transparency, accountability, and integrity in political and institutional processes, though with different emphases on cultural and secular values.

While Integral Humanism and Radical Humanism share certain commonalities, they also diverge on several ideas. Integral Humanism places a significant emphasis on the role of religion and spirituality in shaping individual and societal values. It advocates for a synthesis of material and spiritual aspects of life, often drawing from Hindu philosophical traditions. In contrast, Radical Humanism prioritizes secularism and rationalism, advocating for the separation of religion from the state and public sphere.[9] Integral Humanism advocates for a decentralized form of governance that respects the diversity of local cultures and communities. It emphasizes the importance of "Sarvodaya" or the welfare of all, through participatory decision-making processes. In contrast, Radical Humanism may lean towards more centralized governance structures, guided by principles of democracy and rational negotiation. Integral Humanism envisions a harmonious and integrated society that balances material progress with spiritual and cultural values. It emphasizes the idea of a 'Dharma Rajya' where ethical principles guide social and political life. Radical Humanism on the other hand, envisages a secular and rational society that prioritizes individual freedom, scientific inquiry, and social equality.

The comparative analysis of Integral Humanism and Radical Humanism has significant implications for contemporary society.

Interfaith Dialogue— The comparative analysis of Integral Humanism's emphasis on spirituality and Radical Humanism's commitment to secularism offers opportunities for constructive dialogue between religious and secular communities. By fostering mutual understanding and respect, such dialogue can contribute to social cohesion and harmony.

Social Movements— Social movements advocating for various causes, including environmental conservation, gender equality, and minority rights, can benefit from the philosophical perspectives offered by Integral Humanism and Radical Humanism. These frameworks can provide guiding principles and strategies for advancing social change while respecting diverse cultural and ethical values.

Policy Development— Policymakers can draw insights from both frameworks to develop holistic approaches to social and economic development. Integrating principles of social justice, cultural preservation, and individual freedom could lead to more inclusive and sustainable policies.

In short, the comparative analysis of Integral Humanism and Radical Humanism highlights their shared values, points of divergence, and potential synergies. By critically engaging with these frameworks, contemporary society can navigate complex socio-political challenges and aspire towards a more just, inclusive, and humane world.

The comparative analysis of Integral Humanism and Radical Humanism reveals nuanced insights into their philosophical underpinnings, socio-political implications, and potential contributions to contemporary discourse. While both frameworks offer distinct visions of human society and existence, their coexistence and interaction present opportunities for synthesis and dialogue.

Conclusion

In conclusion, the comparative analysis of Integral Humanism and Radical Humanism underscores the plurality of perspectives within humanist discourse and the importance of dialogue in navigating societal complexities. By critically engaging with these frameworks, scholars, policymakers, and activists can work towards fostering inclusive and equitable societies that uphold the dignity and rights of all individuals, regardless of cultural, religious, or ideological differences.

Through continued reflection, collaboration, and engagement with diverse viewpoints, it becomes possible to cultivate a more holistic understanding of humanism and its potential to shape a more just and humane world.

The comparative analysis presented in this paper serves as a starting point for further research and dialogue on the intersections between Integral Humanism and Radical Humanism. Future studies could delve deeper into specific areas of convergence and divergence between these frameworks, examining their implications for governance, ethics, and social justice. Additionally, interdisciplinary approaches that draw insights from philosophy, political science, sociology, and cultural studies can enrich our understanding of the complexities inherent in humanist thought.

Endnotes

1 Maritain, Jacques. "Integral humanism and the crisis of modern times." *The Review of Politics*, no. 1 (1939), pp. 1-17.

2 Upadhyay, Deendayal. *Integral humanism: An analysis of some basic elements* (New Delhi: Prabhat Prakashan, 2021), 12-13.

3 Talwar, S N. *Political Philosophy of M N Roy: Radical Humanism* (New Delhi: KK Publications, 2022), 56.

4 Saleem, Rakhshanda, Zenobia Morrill, and Justin M. Karter. "Introduction to the Special Issue on Radical Humanism, Critical Consciousness, and Social Change." *Journal of Humanistic Psychology* 61 (2019), 851-860.

5 Singh Sanjeet, Jagmeet Bawa, and Gagan Deep Sharma. "A Review Paper on Integral Humanism: Comparison of Deen Dayaal Upadhyay and His Counterparts." *International Journal of Multidisciplinary and Academic Research* (SSIJMAR), Vol. 5, no. 2 (2016), pp. 1-7.

6 Mahakul, Bibhuti K. "Radical Humanism of M N Roy." *The Indian Journal of Political Science* (2005), pp. 607-618.

7 Pal, Satarupa. "MN Roy: Journey from Marxism to Radical Humanism." *Pratidhwani the Echo*, vol. 6, no. 3 (2018), pp. 260-267.

8 Klassen, David. "Integral humanism or exclusive humanism? Reconsidering Maritain's political philosophy." *Philosophy, Culture and Traditions* vol. 7 (2011) pp. 87-101.

9 Durkin, K. "The Roots of Radical Humanism." In The Radical Humanism of Erich Fromm. *Critical Political Theory and Radical Practice* (New York: Palgrave Macmillan, (2014), pp. 41.

Social and Economic Dimensions of Integral Humanism

Chapter Seven

Integral Humanism and Integral Development

Alexis Rostand

India has long fascinated French and European thinkers. As an introduction to this chapter, it is important to acknowledge that, despite the deep historical connections between our cultures, the engagement of French intellectuals with India has not been as extensive as it could be. As a newcomer to India, I have explored the works of French-speaking scholars such as Mircea Eliade, Alain Daniélou, and Jean-Claude Carrière, which have guided my understanding of the cultural ties that bind our civilizations. This chapter represents an initial effort to build upon that foundation and explore the broader potential of India's influence on European thought.

As a Frenchman and European, I feel a sense of kinship with India, rooted in shared ancient histories that reach back beyond Alexander the Great. My perspective as an economist brings particular interest in India's unique approach to development—a vision that resonates with what Karl Polanyi described as an "embedded economy," where social relations shape and are shaped by economic structures. Polanyi's assertion that "social relations are embedded in the economic system" offers a valuable model for contemporary global challenges. As a Christian, I am moved by India's spiritual heritage and seek to explore the philosophical bridges between our worlds, a dialogue exemplified by the exchanges between Jacques Maritain and Deendayal Upadhyay.

Maritain, the Third Way, and the Neo-Thomist Revival

This chapter examines the fundamental concept of Integral Development and its application within the social and economic spheres, rooted in the philosophical and metaphysical framework of Integral Humanism as articulated by Jacques Maritain and integrated into the Social Doctrine of the Church. Emerging from the particular context of the neo-Thomist revival in Europe, in which Maritain played a pivotal role, this concept became a core element of the Church's doctrinal teachings. This chapter offers a brief introduction to this living tradition, which has continued to evolve and develop in recent years.

Jacques Maritain did not focus extensively on economic matters in his writings; however, as a philosopher of integrality, he naturally incorporated economic phenomena into his broader philosophical framework. His lifelong dedication to the pursuit of the common good led him to recognize the economic sphere as an essential aspect of human life.

During the 1930s and 1940s—a critical period for Europe when many of his key works were published—Jacques Maritain can be meaningfully compared to a group of thinkers associated with the concept of *la troisième voie*, or the "third way." This group included notable figures such as Bertrand de Jouvenel, Denis de Rougemont, and Emmanuel Mounier. Although not all of these thinkers were Catholic, they shared a common pursuit of integrality through their intellectual and spiritual journeys. They sought to chart a new, virtuous path that avoided the extremes and totalitarian ideologies of their time, offering an alternative during a period of intense geopolitical tension. This approach aligns with Aristotle's notion of the "mean" or *le juste milieu*, captured in the phrase *in medio stat virtus*, meaning that "virtue lies in between extremes."

Each of these thinkers proposed a unique path that offered an alternative to the prevailing ideologies of their time, such as individualism and collectivism; liberalism and socialism; nationalism and internationalism. Their approaches included personalism, advocated by Mounier; corporatism, championed by Jouvenel; and federalism, promoted by Rougemont.

Maritain's role in the neo-Thomist renewal was particularly significant, especially following the publication of Pope Leo XIII's encyclical *Aeterni Patris*, which called for a return to the teachings of Saint Thomas Aquinas. Alongside other intellectuals like Étienne Gilson, Marie-Dominique Chenu, and Réginald Garrigou-Lagrange, he played a crucial role in reintroducing Aquinas—often referred to as the "angelic doctor"—whose theology remains a cornerstone of European intellectual tradition.

Saint Thomas Aquinas produced indeed the most comprehensive synthesis of Christian theology and Aristotelian philosophy that influenced Roman Catholic doctrine for centuries. It was officially adopted as the Church's philosophical framework in 1917 by Canon Law.

This historical context is essential to understanding how the Social Doctrine of the Church began to take shape through a renewed engagement with Thomistic thought. It is within this framework that the concepts of Integral Humanism and Integral Development arose as distinct yet interrelated ideas in the late 19th and early 20th centuries. This background also explains why the influence of Maritain, and others of his time, remains present in contemporary Catholic doctrine and beyond.

As a leading Catholic intellectual, Maritain exerted considerable influence over his peers. Even when his landmark work *Humanisme Intégral* was published in 1936, it played a pivotal role in shaping the development of the Church's Social Doctrine. Maritain's contributions, both direct and indirect, continue to resonate within the Church's teachings, providing a foundation for the enduring relevance of Integral Humanism in the modern era.

Introduction to Social Doctrine of the Catholic Church

The Social Doctrine of the Catholic Church is a collection of principles rooted in the teachings of the Church's Magisterium. As stated in the opening paragraphs of the *Compendium of the Social Doctrine of the Church*, it offers Christians "principles for reflection, criteria for judgment, and directives for action" that serve as a foundation for fostering an integral and solidarity-based humanism"[1].

While the social teaching of the Church traces its origins to sacred scriptures, the Gospels, the Apostles, the Fathers of the Church, and great thinkers throughout history, the formal effort to articulate a Christian doctrine addressing economic and social issues under papal authority emerged more clearly in the late 19th century. This effort took shape with the publication of Pope Leo XIII's encyclical *Rerum Novarum* in 1891, which focuses on the relationship between capital and labor. The Latin title, *Rerum Novarum*, translates to "Of New Things."

The term "Social Doctrine" was first introduced by Pope Pius XI in his 1929 encyclical *Quadragesimo Anno*. Over time, it was enriched by a series of encyclicals and other writings, culminating in the *Compendium of the Social Doctrine of the Church*, published in 2004 under the guidance of Pope John Paul II. This document, which distills the wealth of Christian wisdom into 13 chapters, begins with the phrase "An integral and Solidary Humanism."

In this context, Integral Humanism finds its expression in the economic realm as Integral Development. This paper will present a brief genealogy of Integral Development, demonstrating the enduring influence of Jacques Maritain on the economic world up to the present day.

The Genealogy of Integral Development

According to the *Compendium of the Social Doctrine of the Church*, the pursuit of integral development requires us to view economic actions—particularly investment—holistically, situating them within a perspective of salvation that is inherently "universal and integral [and] concerns the human person in each of its dimensions: personal and social, spiritual and corporeal, historical and transcendent." [2].

The concept of "integral development" was first introduced in Pope Paul VI's 1967 encyclical *Populorum Progressio*. It appears as early as the fifth paragraph and serves as the title of the first section, which concludes with reflections on "full humanism."

> "42. *The ultimate goal is a full-bodied humanism (44). And does this not mean the fulfillment of the whole man and of every man? A narrow humanism, closed in on itself and not open to the values of the spirit and to God who is their source, could achieve apparent success, for man can set about organizing terrestrial realities without God. But "closed off from God, they will end up being directed against man. A humanism closed off from other realities becomes inhuman." (45)*[3]
>
> *True humanism points the way toward God and acknowledges the task to which we are called, the task*

> *which offers us the real meaning of human life. Man is not the ultimate measure of man. Man becomes truly man only by passing beyond himself. In the words of Pascal: "Man infinitely surpasses man." (46)*[4]

The reference to the great Blaise Pascal here is deeply significant, as his profound influence on Maritain cannot be overlooked. Pascal, who passed away 400 years ago, embodied the spirit of integrality through his remarkable and diverse genius. A mathematician, physicist, moralist, philosopher, polemicist, and entrepreneur, this "terrifying genius," as Chateaubriand famously described him, stands as a towering figure in the history of ideas—not only in France but far beyond. He lived at a time when the emerging tension between science and religion was just beginning, offering a glimpse of the more intense conflicts that would follow. While this may not be the moment to delve into Pascal's legacy, it would undoubtedly be worthwhile to explore his influence beyond the boundaries of Christianity.

Returning to the *Compendium*, it is important to note that in footnote 44, which follows the mention of "full-bodied humanism," the text explicitly references Jacques Maritain. It cites Maritain's work *Les conditions spirituelles du progrès et de la paix*, published in an anthology titled *Rencontre des cultures à l'UNESCO sous le signe du Concile Oecuménique Vatican II*. Maritain directly and explicitly influenced the first reference to "Integral" or "fully-bodied Humanism" in *Populorum Progressio*, marking its initial introduction.

Earlier in the document, in footnote 15, the text also references Father Louis-Joseph Lebret, a Dominican priest and a profound thinker in the field of human economy. In 1961, he published the remarkable work *Concrete Dynamics of Development*, in which he eloquently wrote: "*We do not accept separating the economic from the human, the development of the civilizations in which it is inscribed. What matters to us is man, every man, every group of men, up to all humanity.*"[5]

Twenty years later, in his 1987 encyclical *Sollicitudo Rei Socialis*, Saint John Paul II dedicates a significant passage to the concept of "authentic human development." He contrasts the idea of progress as a linear process, rooted in the principles of Enlightenment philosophy, with a view of development reduced to the mere accumulation of goods and services. Without moral purpose, such development ultimately turns against humanity, enslaving it. Saint John Paul II emphasizes the primacy of being over having and highlights the "transcendent reality of the human being."

Discussing the various dimensions of development, Saint John Paul II asserts that "development, which is not merely economic, is measured and oriented according to this reality and vocation of man considered in his entirety, that is to say, according to an inner parameter which is proper to him."[6] This inner parameter refers to humanity's divine vocation and the salvation of the soul.

Twenty years later, in 2009, Pope Benedict XVI, in his encyclical *Caritas in Veritate*, expanded on his predecessor's teachings. Reflecting on the true meaning of growth—what it means "to be more"—he emphasized that "the truth of development lies in its entirety: if it is not for all of man and all men, development is not true development."[7]

Highlighting how development factors have evolved in an increasingly interconnected world with greater labor mobility, Pope Benedict XVI observes that the issue of development has become more complex. He points out that the denial of religious freedom—often manifesting in many countries, particularly developed ones, through the "programmed promotion of religious indifference or practical atheism"—ultimately deprives citizens of the moral and spiritual strength needed to pursue integral human development."[8] In doing so, he echoes Pope Paul VI, who cautioned against the dangers of "moral underdevelopment," which arises from "the exclusive pursuit of wealth that stifles the growth of being and opposes true greatness."

The emphasis on integrality is crucial because it lies at the heart of the salvific path to which every Christian is called. Thus, speaking of integral economic development through investment involves re-examining how we perceive the act of investing. It must serve as a means to "advance on the path toward the true and integral well-being of man."

This brief overview of fifty years of social teaching highlights the profound influence of Maritain's work and the central role the concept of integral development has assumed in Church doctrine. Over time, it has been enriched by the teachings of successive Popes, notably Saint John Paul II and Benedict XVI, culminating in the most recent document, *Oeconomicae et Pecuniariae Quaestiones*, published in 2018—a text worth pausing to reflect upon.

The Contemporary Legacy of Jacques Maritain with reference to *Oeconomicae et Pecuniariae Quaestiones*

In *Oeconomicae et Pecuniariae Quaestiones*, we find an even more detailed exploration of how the issue of Christian salvation is applied to the financial sphere. The text situates itself firmly within the perspective of integral development, critically examining economic strategies in light of the fundamental principles of the Church's Magisterium.

In the opening paragraph, it encapsulates this principle of integrality by emphasizing that the necessary alliance between technical expertise and human wisdom is essential for advancing toward the true and integral well-being of humanity. Without this harmony, all human actions risk becoming "distorted" or "perverted."

It is a common and pervasive flaw to consider—and analyze—economic phenomena solely through their economic dimension. This issue arises from the compartmentalization of knowledge, driven in part by the growing complexity of the systems we inhabit. At its core, it stems from an excessively fragmented understanding of social functions and human existence, leading to significant confusion.

Specifically, this flaw manifests in the tendency to confine the economy—and, by extension, the finance of investing—within a narrow domain of knowledge. This reductionist approach treats it as a purely technical field, isolated within its own paradigm and disconnected from other forms of understanding, resulting in many of its failures.

Finally, the temptation to view finance as an exact science, reducible to mathematical equations, has been a key contributor to some of the most significant financial and human disasters of recent history. One might argue that the separation of economics from philosophy, of which it was once a branch, represents a "divorce" whose harmful consequences have been gravely underestimated.

In this text, Pope Francis, remaining faithful to the teachings of his predecessors, underscores the tendency to interpret the world through a "homogeneous and one-dimensional paradigm." This echoes Pope Benedict XVI's warning that "technological development can lead one to think that technique is self-sufficient when man, by questioning only the how, neglects to consider the whys that drive him to act."

Drawn to the allure of pure technique and the "illusion of its omnipotence," economic science has suffered from the "fragmentation of knowledge." To address this, it must engage in meaningful dialogue with other fields of knowledge, particularly philosophy, from which the social sciences have distanced themselves—a separation lamented by Benedict XVI. This shift has neglected the fundamentally interdisciplinary nature of the Church's social doctrine.

True Well-Being

The document *Oeconomicae et Pecuniariae Quaestiones* opens with a powerful reminder: only an "alliance between technical knowledge and human wisdom" can address the pressing need for an ethical foundation, a need increasingly voiced, especially by those in the economic and financial sectors. This call carries a sense of urgency and gravity, underscored by the warning in the same sentence that without this alliance, there looms the risk of "all human action being perverted."

The proposed union is described as essential to progress on the path toward "a true and integral well-being of man," a phrase that encapsulates the essence of the document's message. From its introduction, the text invites readers to reflect on the concept of well-being itself, emphasizing its depth and significance. The use of the term "true" as a qualifier for well-being is particularly noteworthy. Unlike previous Church documents, such as the *Compendium* or *Caritas in Veritate*, where the term "well-being" appears in various contexts—whether referring to future generations, individuals, peoples, or a country's economic condition—it is rarely central. Instead, it is closely tied to the broader notion of integral development.

Typically, well-being is understood as an emotional or psychological state. Pope Benedict XVI highlighted this in *Caritas in Veritate*, critiquing modern technocratic thought for its tendency to reduce issues of inner life to psychological terms alone. He observed that the challenge of development is deeply intertwined with our understanding of the human soul[9].

In presenting "true and integral well-being" as its cornerstone, *Oeconomicae et Pecuniariae Quaestiones* urges a more profound engagement with this idea, advocating for an approach that transcends superficial or materialistic interpretations and aligns with the holistic vision of flourishing humanity.

At the heart of the Christian perspective on human development lies the challenge of contributing to the salvation of the soul in all its dimensions. By emphasizing that well-being must be "true," the text of *Oeconomicae et Pecuniariae Quaestiones* draws attention back to the original meaning of the term—something often overlooked in its common usage.

Well-being, as the term itself suggests, denotes a human existence that is inherently good. It is synonymous with the "good life" or the "blessed life," encompassing the full dimensions of human existence. Thus, for "well-being to be authentic, it must always be integral—addressing the entirety of the human person and the collective well-being of all humanity."[10]

The emphasis on integral aspect is crucial because it lies at the heart of the salvation process to which every Christian is called. In this document, inspired by the message of *Oeconomicae et Pecuniariae Quaestiones*, we aim to reevaluate how we approach the act of investing, which should serve as a means to "progress on the path towards a true and integral well-being of man." A commitment to integral development calls us to consider economic actions—especially investment—in their full complexity, ensuring they are aligned with a vision of salvation that is both universal and holistic. This perspective encompasses every dimension of the human person: *"personal and social, spiritual and bodily, historical and transcendent"*[11].

The text further emphasizes that, to be truly authentic and integral, economic strategies must prioritize "the overall quality of life and well-being," even before the pursuit of indiscriminate profit growth. This well-being, it insists, must always be comprehensive—encompassing the whole person and all people. Moreover, if profit is regarded as the primary measure and goal of investment, the text issues a strong reminder: "No profit is legitimate if it lacks a vision of the integral promotion of the human person, the universal destination of goods, and the preferential option for the poor."

Conclusion

This chapter has briefly explored the economic dimensions of Integral Humanism, the economic philosophy of Jacques Maritain, and the rich tradition of the Church's Social Doctrine, from which the concept of Integral Humanism originates. The purpose of this concise overview is to introduce the foundational principles, offering a framework from which individuals of goodwill can develop tools for judgment, enabling them to discern and act for the common good in various areas of economic life.

If these reflections have illuminated even a fraction of how Maritain and his contemporaries have influenced modern thought, then this chapter has served a meaningful purpose. It is intended as a starting point for fostering deeper dialogue between the political, economic, and spiritual realms, encouraging us to explore the treasures each tradition holds.

In the West, there is a frequent tendency to overlook or even deliberately dismiss the richness of our cultural, intellectual, and philosophical heritage—the wisdom found in sacred scriptures, classical literature, and foundational thinkers. Many prefer to pursue new and untested ideas, succumbing to the allure of reinventing the wheel. This inclination is regrettable, particularly when a vast reservoir of timeless knowledge is readily available. Our responsibility is to engage with the works of those who came before us, to rediscover the truths they unveiled, and to apply these insights to address the pressing challenges of our time, including those in the economic sphere.

Endnotes

1 *Compendium of the Social Doctrine of the Church*, 2005, n°7

2 Idem, n°38

3 Saint Paul VI, *Populorum progressio*, 1967, n° 14.

4 Idem, n° 42

5 L. J. Lebret, O.P., *Dynamique concrète du développement Paris: Economie et Humanisme, Les editions ouvrières (1961), 28.*

6 Saint Jean Paul II, *Sollicitudo Rei Socialis, 1967, n°29*

7 Pape Benoît XVI, *Lettre encyclique Caritas in veritate, 2009, n. 18.*

8 *Idem.*

9 Pape Benoît XVI, *Ecyclical Letter Caritas in veritate, 2009, n° 76.*

10 *Idem, n°18*

11 *Compendium of the Social Doctrine of Church, 2005, n. 38*

Chapter Eight

Economic Implications of Integral Humanism

Sanjay K. Jha

Integral Humanism, as expounded by Pandit Deendayal Upadhyay, offers a profound economic philosophy that seeks to harmonise individual well-being with collective advancement by embedding human values into economic planning.[1] Drawing extensively from traditional Indian thought, Integral Humanism addresses the shortcomings of capitalist and socialist paradigms, which fail to encompass the full spectrum of human needs and potential.[2] By challenging contemporary economic models' reductionist tendencies, Upadhyay advocates for a balanced approach that fosters overall well-being.[3] Integral Humanism diverges from Western capitalist and socialist paradigms by advocating a value-driven approach that integrates economic growth with spiritual and ethical development, thereby presenting a holistic perspective on human progress.[4] It proposes that economic systems should elevate human life in its entirety rather than solely focusing on wealth accumulation.[5] In Bharat's evolving socio-economic landscape, there is an increasing acknowledgment of the need to align policy-making with Integral Humanism. This framework provides a compelling alternative to capitalist and socialist models by embedding ethical and cultural values into economic systems, thereby ensuring that progress respects and preserves cultural integrity.[6] Integral Humanism advocates for a balance between material and spiritual growth, challenging the materialistic orientation of contemporary economic models and suggesting a shift towards ethical living and holistic growth.[7]

1. Context

Bharat's ambition to attain developed nation status by 2047 highlights the relevance of integrating Integral Humanism into economic policy formation. The nation's economic and social transformations are influenced by both global trends and national aspirations, necessitating a synthesis of traditional values with contemporary economic strategies.[8] The emphasis on decentralisation, self-reliance, and value-driven development within Integral Humanism resonates with Bharat's strategic objectives as it approaches its centenary of independence.[9] Integral Humanism provides a framework for evaluating economic and social policies. It advocates for a development model that respects human dignity and cultural heritage while pursuing modern economic objectives, offering insights into reconciling rapid industrialisation with cultural preservation and social equity.[10]

2. Conceptual Foundations of Integral Humanism

Integral Humanism presents a philosophical framework that transcends conventional economic systems by integrating ethical, spiritual, and material dimensions. It advocates for a decentralised and morally grounded approach to economic organisation, sharply contrasting with capitalist models that centralise power and prioritise profit and socialist doctrines that impose restrictive controls.[11] His philosophy critiques the narrow focus on material and class struggles found in Western capitalist and socialist theories, proposing an alternative that harmonises economic progress with cultural and spiritual values.[12] Formulated by Deendayal Upadhyay, Integral Humanism proposes a synthesis that aligns with Bharat's cultural ethos and fosters economic progress in harmony with spiritual and ethical dimensions.[13] Upadhyay envisioned this philosophy as a means to harmonise individual aspirations with societal well-being, integrating ethical principles into economic activities to ensure that human development encompasses both material prosperity and spiritual growth.[14]

2.1 Core Principles

Integral Humanism emphasises a human-centric approach to development. The core principles of Integral Humanism highlight holistic development, a value-centric approach, and decentralisation. Upadhyay asserts that economic systems should align with Dharma (ethical living), Artha (material wealth), and Kama (pleasures), with Dharma guiding both the means of earning wealth and its utilisation. This integration of ethical values into economic pursuits contrasts with profit-driven or state-controlled models.[15] Integral Humanism's principles advocate for local self-governance and economic independence, empowering communities and reducing reliance on external aid.[16] This philosophy encompasses respect for human dignity, holistic development, and the integration of traditional wisdom with modern advancements.

2.2 Critique of Existing Economic Models

Integral Humanism proposes a radical rethinking of economic systems. It critiques both Western capitalism and socialist ideologies for their limitations in addressing human needs holistically.[17] Upadhyay argues that existing models fail to address the full spectrum of human needs and aspirations, advocating for a framework that balances material prosperity with spiritual growth.[18] He contends that capitalist models often result in inequality and environmental degradation, while socialist models can lead to loss of individual freedoms and inefficient central planning.[19] Upadhyay's critique underscores the deficiencies of both Western and Socialist economic models, positioning Integral Humanism as a comprehensive alternative that addresses holistic human development.[20] This philosophy advocates for an economic system that balances material progress with ethical and spiritual development, respecting human dignity, and promoting societal well-being.[21]

3. Economic Critiques and Alternatives

Integral Humanism offers a profound critique of contemporary economic systems, often failing to foster holistic human development. Capitalism's relentless pursuit of profit and centralisation of power typically results in monopolistic practices and socio-economic disparities, undermining equitable resource distribution and human welfare.[22] In contrast, socialism's rigid state control and focus on class struggle can suppress individual freedoms and economic innovation, revealing its limitations in achieving balanced social equity.[23] Western economic theories, by prioritising material wealth, frequently overlook the integration of ethical and spiritual values into economic planning. Integral Humanism advocates for a more inclusive and sustainable approach to development.[2425]

3.1 Capitalism and Integral Humanism

Capitalism's focus on profit maximisation and centralisation of power often leads to monopolistic practices, diminishing consumer choice and holistic human development.[26] Integral Humanism criticises capitalism for exacerbating socio-economic disparities and concentrating power, and detracting from equitable resource distribution and opportunities.[27] By prioritising profit, capitalism overshadows holistic human development, conflicting with Integral Humanism's principles of equitable resource allocation and moral alignment.[28] Integral Humanism advocates for integrating ethical principles with material pursuits, promoting decentralisation and fairness to address systemic inequalities perpetuated by capitalism.[29] This philosophy seeks to mitigate the adverse effects of centralised economic power by supporting local empowerment and equitable resource distribution, aligning with societal welfare and ethical considerations.[30] Deendayal Upadhyay highlighted the need for an economic model prioritising sustainable development and equitable resource distribution— as central tenets of Integral Humanism.[31]

3.2 Socialism and Integral Humanism

Integral Humanism critiques socialism's state control and focus on class struggle, arguing that such approaches can suppress individual freedoms and hinder economic innovation.[32] It challenges the deterministic approach of Marxist theory, suggesting that socialism's emphasis on class conflict and state ownership can lead to totalitarian outcomes, conflicting with values of individual autonomy and moral development.[33] Upadhyay's critique of socialism highlights its reductionist view, potentially undermining personal initiative and economic dynamism. Integral Humanism offers an alternative that respects personal freedoms while promoting collective well-being, advocating for a balance between individual rights and social equity.[34] The focus on eliminating private property within socialism is seen as counterproductive to personal motivation and societal progress, addressed by Integral Humanism through its value-centric economic framework.[35]

4. Economic System for Bharat

Integral Humanism envisions an economic system for Bharat that aligns material progress with ethical and cultural values, prioritising minimum living standards, employment generation, and national defence, while advocating for decentralisation and self-reliance. This system critiques excessive reliance on foreign aid and supports a model that fosters local industries and utilises indigenous resources, integrating traditional wisdom with modern technological advancements to ensure that economic growth respects and enhances cultural integrity.[36] Integral Humanism sets clear economic development objectives: to ensure basic living standards, create employment opportunities, and reinforce national defence.[37] This model aims to balance material progress with cultural and ethical values, asserting that economic policies should address immediate needs while supporting long-term societal well-being and aligning with ethical and cultural principles.[38] As Upadhyay emphasises, economic systems must reflect these values to benefit all societal segments while preserving national integrity and security.[39]

The framework envisions an economy where basic necessities are accessible to all, with policies promoting both material and ethical considerations. It advocates for a balanced approach that includes ensuring minimum living standards, fostering employment, and sustaining national defence, aiming for a model that is inclusive and respects fundamental values of Dharma.[40] Integral Humanism's approach thus seeks to enhance societal progress while respecting cultural values.[41] Upadhyay asserts that "economic policies should focus on ensuring that every citizen has access to basic necessities and opportunities for employment",[42] reflecting a balanced approach that harmonises economic growth with the protection of human values and cultural integrity.[43]

Integral Humanism also stresses the importance of self-reliance and sustainability, aiming to reduce dependency on external resources and promote sustainable practices. This approach seeks to build a resilient economy capable of withstanding external shocks while supporting national autonomy. Sustainability ensures that economic activities do not deplete resources or harm the environment, aligning development with long-term ecological health.[44] Furthermore, it integrates cultural and spiritual values into the economic framework, fostering a development model that respects and enhances societal identity while pursuing progress.[45]

4.1 Decentralisation and Swadeshi

Integral Humanism underscores decentralisation and self-reliance (Swadeshi) as fundamental to its economic philosophy, critiquing over-reliance on foreign aid and advocating for nurturing local industries and resources. Decentralisation is viewed as essential for reducing external dependencies and strengthening local economic resilience.[46] The Swadeshi concept promotes using locally produced goods and services, strengthening regional economies and national resilience against external shocks, aligning with Bharat's cultural values.[47] This philosophy offers a model that builds a more resilient economy while honouring cultural values.[48] Upadhyay highlights the importance of self-reliance, asserting that decentralising the economy promotes local autonomy and reduces vulnerabilities associated with dependence on foreign aid. By advancing local industries and utilising indigenous resources, the Swadeshi approach aims to construct a more self-sufficient and resilient economic structure.[49] Upadhyay asserts, "A decentralised economy that relies on local resources and self-reliance is crucial for sustainable development".[50] This model contrasts with centralised systems that may undermine local stability and self-sufficiency.

Integral Humanism advocates for an economic system centred on local decision-making and self-reliance. Upadhyay emphasises that reducing dependence on foreign resources is crucial for maintaining national sovereignty and achieving sustainable development, stating, "The promotion of a Swadeshi approach is essential for maintaining economic sovereignty".[51] This viewpoint underlines the need for economic policies that empower local communities and leverage local resources for resilience.

4.2 Human-Centric Development

Integral Humanism underscores human-centric development by advocating for a fusion of traditional wisdom with modern technology while preserving cultural and ethical values. It promotes a balanced approach to progress, ensuring that economic development complements rather than compromises societal values and environmental sustainability.[52] Upadhyay highlights the need for development that integrates ethical and cultural dimensions, arguing that economic progress should not come at the expense of human values and environmental health.[53] By emphasising the importance of aligning economic activities with moral and spiritual values, Integral Humanism offers a critique of purely materialistic development models, advocating for an approach that fosters holistic well-being and respects cultural heritage.[54] Human-centric development entails a focus on human dignity and environmental stewardship, ensuring that economic policies and practices support overall societal well-being.[55] Integral Humanism proposes an economic model where technological advancements are harmonised with ethical considerations, promoting a development framework that integrates material progress with spiritual and cultural values.[56] This approach aims to create an economy that values both human and environmental integrity, addressing the limitations of conventional economic systems.[57]

Integral Humanism's economic vision for Bharat is centred on a harmonious blend of material and ethical values, promoting self-reliance, decentralisation, and human-centric development. By critiquing both capitalism and socialism, this model offers an alternative that balances economic growth with cultural and moral principles, aiming for a more inclusive and sustainable development paradigm.[58]

5. Approaches and Policies of Current Government

The contemporary economic policies of Bharat reveal an intricate fusion between modern economic strategies and traditional values. Efforts to weave the principles of Integral Humanism into policy frameworks are evident, though their depth and consistency vary. Initiatives like 'Make in India' and 'Digital India' demonstrate a commitment to self-reliance and technological progress, aligning with Deendayal Upadhyay's vision of economic independence and cultural resurgence.[59] Despite these efforts, critical scrutiny reveals gaps in fully embodying Integral Humanism, particularly concerning social equity and environmental sustainability. Inadequate decentralisation, inconsistent cultural integration, and uneven ethical considerations underscore the need for a more holistic approach that harmonises economic growth with the values espoused by Integral Humanism.

5.1 Current Policies

The examination of Bharat's economic policies uncovers varying degrees of alignment with Integral Humanism. While some efforts to integrate ethical and cultural values into these frameworks are apparent, their extent requires closer inspection.[60] The policy landscape reflects a blend of liberalisation and global integration, alongside initiatives that promote local industries and self-reliance. This blend suggests an attempt to merge modern strategies with traditional values. However, an analytical assessment suggests that while some policies align with Integral Humanism, others fall short of its holistic approach. Upadhyay's framework underscores the necessity of aligning economic policies with these principles to balance growth with ethical considerations.[61] Although policies often incorporate elements of Integral Humanism, such as decentralisation and self-reliance, alignment remains inconsistent. Upadhyay's emphasis on Dharma in policy-making serves as a benchmark for evaluating these policies, highlighting the need for ongoing assessment to ensure they genuinely reflect Integral Humanism's ideals.[62] While some policies effectively integrate decentralisation and cultural preservation, others prioritise immediate economic benefits over long-term sustainability and ethical values. Evaluating these policies through the lens of Integral Humanism helps identify areas for improvement and offers a basis for enhancing coherence with these principles.[63] Recent initiatives such as 'Make in India' and 'Digital India' illustrate a significant move towards embodying Integral Humanism. These policies reflect an earnest attempt to bolster self-reliance and technological advancement, resonating with Upadhyay's vision.[64] However, a detailed examination reveals that while these initiatives reflect aspects of Integral Humanism, substantial gaps remain, particularly in social equity and environmental sustainability. Despite efforts to promote rural development and local industries, significant shortcomings in policy implementation persist, suggesting a need for stronger alignment with Integral Humanism's ethical and social dimensions.

The alignment of Bharat's economic policies with Integral Humanism is scrutinised through decentralisation and ethical considerations. Policies like 'Make in India' aim to enhance domestic manufacturing and reduce foreign dependency, yet their effectiveness in promoting community-level development and equitable resource distribution remains uneven.[65] This partial alignment underscores the challenge of integrating holistic principles into practical policy frameworks, where economic progress often overshadows cultural and ethical considerations. The review of policies indicates both progress and gaps. While significant efforts have been made towards self-reliance and technological innovation, addressing the discrepancies between policy objectives and Integral Humanism's holistic principles remains crucial.[66]

5.2 Policy Critiques

Evaluating contemporary policies against Integral Humanism reveals notable gaps, particularly concerning decentralisation and cultural values. Current policies often fall short of fully embracing Integral Humanism, with issues such as inadequate decentralisation and insufficient cultural integration being prominent.[67] Upadhyay's framework suggests that policies must align with Dharma for effective development, asserting, "Policies should align with the principles of Dharma for effective development".[68] Despite efforts to promote growth, policies often fail to align with Integral Humanism, leading to overreliance on foreign aid and neglect of cultural values, potentially compromising self-reliance and ethical development objectives. Recommendations for improvement include enhancing policy frameworks to reflect Integral Humanism principles more thoroughly.[69]

An examination reveals a lack of focus on decentralisation and holistic development as critical aspects of Integral Humanism. Upadhyay advocates for improved coherence with Integral Humanism principles, stating, "Effective policies must integrate the core principles of Integral Humanism to address contemporary challenges".[70] Implementation gaps persist, with bureaucratic inefficiencies and a lack of focus on ethical considerations. Recommendations include bolstering ethical enforcement and supporting local initiatives, noting, "Policy gaps exist in implementation and alignment with Integral Humanism, necessitating improvements in ethical enforcement and local support".[71] The review indicates both alignment and discrepancies with Integral Humanism. While some policies reflect its principles, others fail to achieve comprehensive integration of human-centric and culturally rooted development goals. Recommendations propose a greater emphasis on balancing economic growth with social equity and environmental sustainability in order to align more closely with Integral Humanism.[72] A major critique involves insufficient focus on decentralised governance. Integral Humanism advocates for decentralisation to empower local communities and foster participatory governance. Yet, current policies often favour centralised planning, undermining local innovation and self-reliance.[73] This centralisation disconnects national policies from local needs, missing opportunities to leverage Bharat's diverse cultural strengths. Shortcomings in the healthcare and education sectors also reflect a lack of alignment with Integral Humanism's emphasis on social equity and universal access to basic services. This misalignment suggests a need for policies that more effectively address income inequality and infrastructure deficits in healthcare and education.[74]

Recommendations for aligning policies with Integral Humanism include a stronger focus on decentralisation and local governance, enabling better-tailored strategies and ensuring equitable distribution of growth benefits across regions.[75] Integrating traditional knowledge and cultural values into policy frameworks is also crucial for supporting a development model that respects Bharat's cultural heritage while promoting sustainable practices. The critique extends to the lack of cultural considerations in economic planning. Integral Humanism asserts that economic systems should nurture material prosperity alongside spiritual and cultural well-being. The current focus on economic efficiency often neglects these broader dimensions, suggesting the need to embed cultural values into the policy-making process for a truly holistic development model.[76]

6. Basic Needs and Employment Guarantee

Integral Humanism, as articulated by Deendayal Upadhyay, envisions an economic system where fulfilling basic needs and ensuring employment are central to human progress. This philosophy contends that addressing fundamental necessities such as food, education, and healthcare is vital for maintaining human dignity and fostering equitable growth.[77] It critiques demand-driven economic models for their failure to offer a holistic development strategy, advocating instead for a balanced structure that integrates both material and spiritual well-being.[78] The goal of Integral Humanism is to establish a just, sustainable, and inclusive economic system by focusing on basic needs and full employment, supporting both individual and collective advancement.

6.1 Basic Necessities

Integral Humanism places significant importance on securing fundamental rights—food, education, and healthcare—as central to human development.[79] It advocates for an economic system that guarantees these necessities for all, promoting human dignity and holistic development. Upadhyay argues that addressing these basic needs is not merely an economic issue but a fundamental aspect of human progress.[80] Ensuring access to food, education, and healthcare is crucial for achieving holistic development and societal well-being, highlighting that these provisions are foundational for broader human advancement and social equity.[81] Upadhyay's principle that "ensuring basic necessities is fundamental to achieving holistic human development"[82] aligns with Integral Humanism's vision of integrating spiritual and material well-being, thereby fostering individual potential and collective progress.[83] Historical examples of societies that provided education and medical care as collective duties underscore the enduring relevance of this principle.[84] Upadhyay's assertion that "meeting basic needs is a pre-requisite for meaningful economic development and social stability"[85] underscores the critical role these necessities play in ensuring a just and stable society.

Integral Humanism posits that the state must play a crucial role in securing these basic needs, especially in rural and underdeveloped areas where access to quality education and healthcare is often limited. Economic development should enhance life quality rather than serve as an end in itself, calling for economic policies aligned with social goals to ensure inclusive growth benefiting marginalised communities.[86] Food security is a primary concern; access to sufficient and nutritious food is seen as a fundamental right essential for other forms of human development. State policies must secure food supply chains, support sustainable agricultural practices, and provide adequate nutrition, particularly to vulnerable populations.[87] This focus aligns with the broader aim of achieving a self-reliant and resilient economy capable of withstanding external shocks and internal disparities.

Education, a cornerstone of Integral Humanism, is viewed not just as a tool for economic advancement but as crucial for fostering a just and equitable society. The philosophy advocates for an education system that is accessible, equitable, and designed to develop individuals' full potential, including basic literacy and numeracy as well as values promoting social cohesion and moral development.[88] The state's responsibility includes ensuring educational opportunities for all and bridging gaps between different social strata.

Healthcare, within Integral Humanism, is considered a universal right that should be accessible to all. The philosophy calls for a comprehensive healthcare system that is both preventive and curative, enabling citizens to lead healthy, productive lives. This involves robust public health infrastructure, adequate funding for medical facilities, and policies prioritising preventive care and health education.[89] This emphasis reflects a holistic view of human well-being, integrating physical, psychological, and social dimensions.

Integral Humanism links the provision of basic necessities to the broader goal of holistic human development, advocating for a development model that values both spiritual and material prosperity. Addressing basic needs is seen as foundational for creating a society that values material and spiritual well-being, fostering a balanced social order.[90] True development must be multidimensional, incorporating ethical and cultural dimensions alongside economic and social advancements.

Integral Humanism underscores the necessity of full employment to ensure economic security and social stability. It advocates for capital formation within a decentralised economy, promoting small and medium enterprises, and encouraging worker participation in economic decision-making. This model aims to create a more equitable and inclusive economic system, addressing unemployment and underemployment while ensuring that economic growth benefits all societal segments.[91] By promoting decentralised planning and labour-intensive production methods, Integral Humanism seeks to harness the potential of all citizens, reduce economic disparities, and foster a stable economy.[92] Worker participation is essential for economic efficiency, ensuring that the benefits of development are shared equitably and that economic policies are both growth-oriented and human-centric, focusing on the comprehensive development of all individuals.[93]

6.2 Economic Structure

Integral Humanism critiques demand-driven economies for their failure to support holistic human development adequately.[94] Such economies often emphasise immediate market responses, neglecting the broader human and ethical dimensions necessary for comprehensive growth.[95] Demand-driven models inadequately support holistic development, and an economic structure aligned with ethical principles is essential for balancing material requirements with spiritual and cultural considerations.[96] Integral Humanism proposes an economic framework that transcends short-term gains to foster overall well-being and development. It critiques demand-driven models for prioritising immediate economic output over sustainable progress.[97] To address these shortcomings, Integral Humanism proposes a decentralised economic structure. Upadhyay argues that "An economic system that supports comprehensive human development requires a shift away from mere demand-driven approaches towards those that foster genuine human growth and well-being".[98] This model aims to create an economic framework that supports human and environmental well-being, addressing the limitations of demand-driven models and promoting sustainable development.[99] Integral Humanism contrasts sharply with prevalent demand-driven economies, which focus primarily on material wealth accumulation at the expense of holistic development. It envisions an economic system that prioritises comprehensive human development, incorporating not just economic growth but also moral and spiritual dimensions.[100] This philosophy challenges the conventional reliance on GDP and other economic indicators, advocating instead for a model that balances economic efficiency with ethical responsibility, community well-being, and cultural integrity.[101]

A central feature of this economic structure is its emphasis on decentralisation and local self-sufficiency. Integral Humanism contends that centralised economies tend to concentrate wealth and power, marginalising communities and individuals. By promoting decentralisation, it aims to empower local economies, reduce disparities, and ensure a more equitable distribution of economic benefits.[102] This approach supports the growth of small and medium enterprises, which are vital for employment and sustaining local cultures and traditions.

Moreover, Integral Humanism calls for integrating social, cultural, and ethical considerations into economic policies. This integration is crucial for creating an economic environment that respects human dignity and promotes holistic well-being. The philosophy advocates for policies that encourage ethical business practices, environmental stewardship, and community engagement, challenging the notion that economic growth alone leads to societal well-being.[103] It proposes a model that values human and cultural development alongside economic progress.

In practical terms, this economic structure involves a shift towards sustainable and equitable practices, encouraging technologies and methods that reduces environmental impact and conserve resources. Integral Humanism highlights the importance of prioritising education and healthcare in economic planning, reflecting a commitment to human capital development. A healthy and well-educated populace is essential for long-term economic stability and growth.[104]

Integral Humanism presents a vision of an economic system that harmonises material prosperity with ethical and cultural growth. It challenges dominant economic paradigms, proposing a more inclusive and holistic approach that integrates economic activities with broader human development goals. This perspective underscores the importance of aligning economic policies with social justice, environmental sustainability, and cultural preservation.[105]

7. Paradoxes and Future Trajectories

Navigating Bharat's economic future requires addressing complex domestic and global paradoxes while integrating the principles of Integral Humanism. The juxtaposition of rapid economic growth with persistent inequality underscores the need for policies that harmonise progress with social equity and cultural integrity.[106] Bharat's role in a multipolar world demands balancing traditional values with modern economic imperatives.[107] This balancing act is further complicated by the rapid pace of globalisation, which often prioritises economic efficiency over holistic well-being.[108] Intellectuals and academics play a crucial role in shaping policies that integrate ethical considerations and cultural values to ensure Bharat's economic trajectory reflecting its heritage and contemporary realities.[109] Reconciling traditional values with modern economic practices, supported by a robust intellectual framework, is essential.[110]

7.1 Domestic and Global Paradoxes

The interplay between Bharat's domestic diversity and the global shift towards multipolarity reveals paradoxes influencing

Integral Humanism's implementation. Bharat's vast cultural, ethnic, and socio-economic diversity presents challenges in aligning national policies with global economic trends. This paradox emerges in reconciling these varied domestic elements with the need for a coherent economic strategy on the global stage.[111] The convergence of Bharat's domestic diversity with the global trend towards multipolarity highlights the difficulty of integrating traditional values with modern economic policies. Upadhyay's Integral Humanism offers a method to address these paradoxes by embedding ethical and cultural values within economic strategies. This approach seeks to harmonise local needs with global ambitions, ensuring development policies are both culturally grounded and internationally competitive.[112] Integral Humanism provides a framework that integrates ethical and cultural dimensions into economic planning, addressing the paradoxes of Bharat's domestic diversity and global multipolarity. By incorporating traditional values into contemporary economic frameworks, this approach aims to create a balanced development strategy that respects local traditions while engaging effectively with global trends.[113] Further examination of Bharat's economic trajectory reveals that its diverse cultural landscape and position within a multipolar world create challenges for conventional economic models. Integral Humanism proposes a development model that respects cultural diversity and adapts to shifting global dynamics, supporting inclusive policies that address both domestic and international economic shifts.[114] Upadhyay's Integral Humanism advocates a nuanced approach to these paradoxes, promoting a development strategy that harmonises traditional values with contemporary global realities. This model encourages unity among various social and economic institutions while adapting to a multipolar world. As Upadhyay's vision suggests, "Integral Humanism provides a framework for reconciling domestic diversity with global multipolarity, supporting a development model that respects cultural and global considerations".[115] Integral Humanism offers a framework to reconcile Bharat's domestic diversity with global multipolarity. It offers a framework to address these paradoxes by promoting a balanced approach that integrates economic efficiency with social justice and cultural integrity.[116]

A central domestic paradox is the coexistence of economic progress with significant inequality. Despite substantial GDP growth, wealth remains unevenly distributed, with pockets of prosperity amidst widespread poverty. Integral Humanism critiques this uneven development, advocating for an economic system that prioritises holistic human well-being over mere material wealth accumulation. This philosophy stresses aligning economic policies with social goals to ensure growth benefits to all societal segments, particularly the marginalised.[117] It calls for a development model that is economically sustainable, socially inclusive, and culturally respectful.

Globally, Bharat's position in a multipolar world presents challenges in balancing strategic interests with cultural and ethical values. Integral Humanism provides guidance for this balance, emphasising ethical governance and cultural integrity. It suggests Bharat should pursue a path that reflects its unique cultural and philosophical heritage rather than merely adopting Western economic models. This includes advocating for a more equitable global economic order where diverse cultures and nations are respected and integrated into global governance structures.[118] The concept of cultural integrity is crucial amidst globalisation, which often leads to cultural homogenisation and erosion of local traditions. Integral Humanism advocates for a model of global engagement that preserves cultural diversity, enriches the global cultural landscape, and strengthens Bharat's identity. This approach resists cultural assimilation and maintains national and cultural pride.[119]

Addressing these paradoxes requires a nuanced approach integrating diverse perspectives into economic and social planning. Integral Humanism proposes fostering dialogue and collaboration among different cultural, economic, and social groups. This inclusive approach ensures that all voices are heard and policies reflect the diverse needs and aspirations of the population, while maintaining ethical governance that considers social and cultural impacts.[120]

Bharat's domestic and global paradoxes present significant challenges but also opportunities for redefining its development trajectory. Integral Humanism offers a comprehensive framework for navigating these complexities, advocating for a development model that is inclusive, culturally sensitive, and ethically grounded. This philosophy encourages Bharat to forge a unique path that honours its rich cultural heritage while engaging constructively with the global community, ensuring a balanced and harmonious future.[121]

7.2 Economic Trajectory

Examining Bharat's current economic trajectory through the lens of Integral Humanism involves analysing how contemporary economic policies align with traditional values and holistic principles as outlined by Upadhyay.[122] This assessment seeks to gauge the extent to which Bharat's development strategies incorporate ethical and cultural values while addressing modern economic challenges.[123] A detailed examination reveals both opportunities and challenges in aligning Bharat's economic trajectory with Integral Humanism. Upadhyay's framework offers insights into how economic policies can reflect ethical and cultural values, aiming for sustainable development that respects traditional values while meeting contemporary needs.[124] Current economic policies show a mixed alignment with Integral Humanism. This analysis evaluates how well these policies embody Upadhyay's principles and address Bharat's traditional aspirations. Upadhyay asserted that "economic policies should reflect the principles of Dharma to achieve meaningful progress".[125] Integrating Integral Humanism into Bharat's economic policies is crucial for achieving modernisation while preserving traditional values. This alignment is essential for addressing contemporary economic challenges and maintaining cultural integrity. As stated, "evaluating Bharat's economic trajectory in relation to Integral Humanism involves assessing alignment with holistic development and traditional values."[126] This alignment is fundamental for achieving sustainable development and supporting Bharat's aspirations for 2047.[127] It's economic trajectory, characterised by significant growth, presents challenges when examined through Integral Humanism. This philosophy, advocating for a development model that integrates ethical governance, cultural values, and human welfare, contrasts with conventional focuses on economic metrics like GDP growth and industrialisation. The divergence between traditional values and modern economic policies suggests a need for realignment to achieve truly sustainable and inclusive development.[128]

The rapid pace of globalisation and technological advancement has shaped Bharat's economic policies, often prioritising efficiency over holistic well-being. While this focus has led to impressive economic gains, these benefits have not been evenly distributed. Integral Humanism critiques this disparity, advocating for a model that values human dignity and community welfare alongside economic efficiency. It calls for policies that are not solely market-driven but also grounded in Bharat's social and cultural contexts.[129] Reassessing Bharat's economic trajectory involves integrating traditional values with modern economic practices. This is not about rejecting modernity but about finding a balanced approach that respects the nation's rich cultural heritage. For instance, incorporating ethical considerations into business practices and economic strategies ensures that growth is not only measurable but also meaningful and equitable.[130]

8. Final Analysis

Integral Humanism, as articulated by Pandit Deendayal Upadhyay, offers a profound framework for addressing Bharat's economic challenges. It advocates for a development model that integrates ethical values, cultural integrity, and human welfare into economic planning. The alignment of Bharat's economic policies with these principles is crucial for achieving a balanced and sustainable future.[131] This approach ensures that economic policies not only drive growth but also promote social justice and cultural respect. As Bharat advances towards 2047, integrating these principles into its economic strategy is essential for achieving holistic development and preserving its cultural heritage.[132] By integrating Integral Humanism into economic planning, Bharat can pursue a development model that respects its unique cultural and ethical dimensions while addressing contemporary economic challenges. This alignment is key to achieving a balanced and sustainable future, reflecting the principles of ethical governance and human welfare.[133]

Endnotes

1 Upadhyay, Deendayal. 2002. Integral Humanism: Our Direction. Deendayal Research Institute. https://deendayalupadhyay.org/images/book/Booklet%20on%20IntegralHumanism.pdf.

2 Bhatt, Kartikey, R Sharma, Pinky Desai, Tekpalsingh Anand, Gautambhai Vaghela, and Sanjay Kamaliya. 2016. "Economic Thoughts." In Economics, 121–34. Gujarat State Board of School Textbooks. https://drive.google.com/file/d/1-Rp7YNJlGNZC7Tem-5DaHtB3M7oNq8_C/view.

3 Upadhyay, Manjula. 2018. "Economic Thought of Deen Dayal Upadhyay." International Journal of Innovative Social Science & Humanities Research 5 (1): 172–77. https://www.researchgate.net/publication/332684114_ECONOMIC_THOUGHT_OF_DEEN_DAYAL_UPADHYAY.

4 Upadhyay, Deendayal. 2002. Integral Humanism: Western Versus Bharatiya View. Deendayal Research Institute. https://deendayalupadhyay.org/images/book/Booklet%20on%20IntegralHumanism.pdf.

5 Upadhyay, Deendayal. 2002. Integral Humanism: Economic Structure Suited to National Genius. Deendayal Research Institute. https://deendayalupadhyay.org/images/book/Booklet%20on%20IntegralHumanism.pdf.

6 Upadhyay, Deendayal. 2002. Integral Humanism: Western Versus Bharatiya View. Deendayal Research Institute. https://deendayalupadhyay.org/images/book/Booklet%20on%20IntegralHumanism.pdf.

7 Verma, Rajesh, and Vijay Srivastava. 2021. "Relevance of Economic Vision of Deen Dayal Upadhaya: An Analysis In Gandhian Framework." Indian Journal of Public Administration New Series Vol. XVIII (2): 129–38. https://www.researchgate.net/publication/359451872_RELEVANCE_OF_ECONOMIC_VISION_OF_DEEN_DAYAL_UPADHAYA_AN_ANALYSIS_IN_GANDHIAN_FRAMEWORK.

Also see Sharma, Sanjeev Kumar, and Ansuiya Nain. 2018. "Integral Humanism of Deen Dayal Upadhyay and its Contemporary Relevance." The Indian Journal of Political Science Vol. LXXIX (1): 13–20. https://www.researchgate.net/publication/342305382_Integral_Humanism_of_Deen_Dayal_Upadhyay_and_its_Contemporary_Relevance.

8 Upadhyay, Deendayal. 2002. Integral Humanism: Our Direction. Deendayal Research Institute. https://deendayalupadhyay.org/images/book/Booklet%20on%20IntegralHumanism.pdf.

9 Upadhyay, Deendayal. 2002. Integral Humanism: Harmony Between the Individual and The Collectivity. Deendayal Research Institute. https://deendayalupadhyay.org/images/book/Booklet%20on%20IntegralHumanism.pdf.

10 Bhatt, Kartikey, R Sharma, Pinky Desai, Tekpalsingh Anand, Gautambhai Vaghela, and Sanjay Kamaliya. 2016. "Economic Thoughts." In Economics, 121–34. Gujarat State Board of School Textbooks. https://drive.google.com/file/d/1-Rp7YNJlGNZC7Tem-5DaHtB3M7oNq8_C/view.

11 Upadhyay, Deendayal. 2002. Integral Humanism: Our Direction. Deendayal Research Institute. https://deendayalupadhyay.org/images/book/Booklet%20on%20IntegralHumanism.pdf.

12 Ibid.

13 Upadhyay, Deendayal. 2002. Integral Humanism: Western Versus Bharatiya View. Deendayal Research Institute. https://deendayalupadhyay.org/images/book/Booklet%20on%20IntegralHumanism.pdf.

14 Upadhyay, Deendayal. 2002. Integral Humanism: Harmony Between The Individual And The Collectivity. Deendayal Research Institute. https://deendayalupadhyay.org/images/book/Booklet%20on%20IntegralHumanism.pdf.

15 Upadhyay, Deendayal. 2002. Integral Humanism: Western Versus Bharatiya View. Deendayal Research Institute. https://deendayalupadhyay.org/images/book/Booklet%20on%20IntegralHumanism.pdf.

16 Upadhyay, Deendayal. 2002. Integral Humanism: Harmony Between The Individual And The Collectivity. Deendayal Research Institute. https://deendayalupadhyay.org/images/book/Booklet%20on%20IntegralHumanism.pdf.

17 Upadhyay, Deendayal. 2002. Integral Humanism: Our Direction. Deendayal Research Institute. https://deendayalupadhyay.org/images/book/Booklet%20on%20IntegralHumanism.pdf.

18 Ibid.

19 Upadhyay, Deendayal. 2002. Integral Humanism: Western Versus Bharatiya View. Deendayal Research Institute. https://deendayalupadhyay.org/images/book/Booklet%20on%20IntegralHumanism.pdf.

20 Upadhyay, Deendayal. 2002. Integral Humanism: Economic Structure Suited To National Genius. Deendayal Research Institute. https://deendayalupadhyay.org/images/book/Booklet%20on%20IntegralHumanism.pdf.

21 Ibid.

22 Upadhyay, Manjula. 2018. "Economic Thought of Deen Dayal Upadhyay." International Journal of Innovative Social Science & Humanities Research 5 (1): 172–77. https://www.researchgate.net/publication/332684114_ECONOMIC_THOUGHT_OF_DEEN_DAYAL_UPADHYAY.

23 Bhatt, Kartikey, R Sharma, Pinky Desai, Tekpalsingh Anand, Gautambhai Vaghela, and Sanjay Kamaliya. 2016. "Economic Thoughts." In Economics, 121–34. Gujarat State Board of School Textbooks. https://drive.google.com/file/d/1-Rp7YNJlGNZC7Tem-5DaHtB3M7oNq8_C/view.

24 Sharma, Sanjeev Kumar, and Ansuiya Nain. 2018. "Integral Humanism of Deen Dayal Upadhyay and its Contemporary Relevance." The Indian Journal of Political Science Vol. LXXIX (1): 13–20. https://www.researchgate.net/publication/342305382_Integral_Humanism_of_Deen_Dayal_Upadhyay_and_its_Contemporary_Relevance.

25 Verma, Rajesh, and Vijay Srivastava. 2021. "Relevance of Economic Vision of Deen Dayal Upadhaya: an Analysis in Gandhian Framework." Indian Journal of Public Administration New Series Vol. XVIII (2): 129–38. https://www.researchgate.net/publication/359451872_RELEVANCE_OF_ECONOMIC_VISION_OF_DEEN_DAYAL_UPADHAYA_AN_ANALYSIS_IN_GANDHIAN_FRAMEWORK.

26 Upadhyay, Deendayal. 2002. Integral Humanism: Our Direction. Deendayal Research Institute. https://deendayalupadhyay.org/images/book/Booklet%20on%20IntegralHumanism.pdf.

27 Upadhyay, Deendayal. 2002. Integral Humanism: Western Versus Bharatiya View. Deendayal Research Institute. https://deendayalupadhyay.org/images/book/Booklet%20on%20IntegralHumanism.pdf.

28 Ibid.

29 Upadhyay, Deendayal. 2002. Integral Humanism: Harmony Between the Individual and the Collectivity. Deendayal Research Institute. https://deendayalupadhyay.org/images/book/Booklet%20on%20IntegralHumanism.pdf.

30 Ibid.

31 Upadhyay, Deendayal. 2002. Integral Humanism: Economic Structure Suited to National Genius. Deendayal Research Institute. https://deendayalupadhyay.org/images/book/Booklet%20on%20IntegralHumanism.pdf.

32 Upadhyay, Deendayal. 2002. Integral Humanism: Our Direction. Deendayal Research Institute. https://deendayalupadhyay.org/images/book/Booklet%20on%20IntegralHumanism.pdf.

33 Ibid.

34 Upadhyay, Deendayal. 2002. Integral Humanism: Western Versus Bharatiya View. Deendayal Research Institute. https://deendayalupadhyay.org/images/book/Booklet%20on%20IntegralHumanism.pdf.

35 Upadhyay, Deendayal. 2002. Integral Humanism: Harmony Between the Individual and The Collectivity. Deendayal Research Institute. https://deendayalupadhyay.org/images/book/Booklet%20on%20IntegralHumanism.pdf.

36 Upadhyay, Deendayal. 2002. Integral Humanism: Our Direction. Deendayal Research Institute. https://deendayalupadhyay.org/images/book/Booklet%20on%20IntegralHumanism.pdf.

37 Ibid.

38 Upadhyay, Deendayal. 2002. Integral Humanism: Western Versus Bharatiya View. Deendayal Research Institute. https://deendayalupadhyay.org/images/book/Booklet%20on%20IntegralHumanism.pdf.

39 Ibid.

40 Upadhyay, Deendayal. 2002. Integral Humanism: Harmony Between the Individual and The Collectivity. Deendayal Research

Institute. https://deendayalupadhyay.org/images/book/Booklet%20on%20IntegralHumanism.pdf.

41 Ibid.

42 Ibid.

43 Ibid.

44 Upadhyay, Manjula. 2018. "Economic Thought of Deen Dayal Upadhyay." International Journal of Innovative Social Science & Humanities Research 5 (1): 172–77. https://www.researchgate.net/publication/332684114_ECONOMIC_THOUGHT_OF_DEEN_DAYAL_UPADHYAY.

45 Verma, Rajesh, and Vijay Srivastava. 2021. "Relevance of Economic Vision of Deen Dayal Upadhaya: An Analysis in Gandhian Framework." Indian Journal of Public Administration New Series Vol. XVIII (2): 129–38. https://www.researchgate.net/publication/359451872_RELEVANCE_OF_ECONOMIC_VISION_OF_DEEN_DAYAL_UPADHAYA_AN_ANALYSIS_IN_GANDHIAN_FRAMEWORK.

46 Upadhyay, Deendayal. 2002. Integral Humanism: Our Direction. Deendayal Research Institute. https://deendayalupadhyay.org/images/book/Booklet%20on%20IntegralHumanism.pdf.

47 Bhatt, Kartikey, R Sharma, Pinky Desai, Tekpalsingh Anand, Gautambhai Vaghela, and Sanjay Kamaliya. 2016. "Economic Thoughts." In Economics, 121–34. Gujarat State Board of School Textbooks. https://drive.google.com/file/d/1-Rp7YNJlGNZC7Tem-5DaHtB3M7oNq8_C/view.

48 Upadhyay, Manjula. 2018. "Economic Thought of Deen Dayal Upadhyay." International Journal of Innovative Social Science & Humanities Research 5 (1): 172–77. https://www.researchgate.net/publication/332684114_ECONOMIC_THOUGHT_OF_DEEN_DAYAL_UPADHYAY.

49 Upadhyay, Deendayal. 2002. Integral Humanism: Western Versus Bharatiya View. Deendayal Research Institute. https://deendayalupadhyay.org/images/book/Booklet%20on%20IntegralHumanism.pdf.

50 Upadhyay, Deendayal. 2002. Integral Humanism: Economic Structure Suited to National Genius. Deendayal Research Institute. https://deendayalupadhyay.org/images/book/Booklet%20on%20IntegralHumanism.pdf.

51 Upadhyay, Deendayal. 2002. Integral Humanism: Harmony Between the Individual and The Collectivity. Deendayal Research Institute. https://deendayalupadhyay.org/images/book/Booklet%20on%20IntegralHumanism.pdf.

52 Upadhyay, Deendayal. 2002. Integral Humanism: Our Direction. Deendayal Research Institute. https://deendayalupadhyay.org/images/book/Booklet%20on%20IntegralHumanism.pdf.

53 Upadhyay, Deendayal. 2002. Integral Humanism: Western Versus Bharatiya View. Deendayal Research Institute. https://deendayalupadhyay.org/images/book/Booklet%20on%20IntegralHumanism.pdf.

54 Upadhyay, Deendayal. 2002. Integral Humanism: Harmony Between the Individual and The Collectivity. Deendayal Research Institute. https://deendayalupadhyay.org/images/book/Booklet%20on%20IntegralHumanism.pdf.

55 Upadhyay, Deendayal. 2002. Integral Humanism: Economic Structure Suited to National Genius. Deendayal Research Institute. https://deendayalupadhyay.org/images/book/Booklet%20on%20IntegralHumanism.pdf.

56 Ibid.

57 Upadhyay, Manjula. 2018. "Economic Thought of Deen Dayal Upadhyay." International Journal of Innovative Social Science & Humanities Research 5 (1): 172–77. https://www.researchgate.net/publication/332684114_ECONOMIC_THOUGHT_OF_DEEN_DAYAL_UPADHYAY.

58 Verma, Rajesh, and Vijay Srivastava. 2021. "Relevance of Economic Vision of Deen Dayal Upadhyay: An Analysis in Gandhian Framework." Indian Journal of Public Administration New Series Vol. XVIII (2): 129–38. https://www.researchgate.net/publication/359451872_RELEVANCE_OF_ECONOMIC_VISION_OF_DEEN_DAYAL_UPADHAYA_AN_ANALYSIS_IN_GANDHIAN_FRAMEWORK.

59 Upadhyay, Deendayal. 2002. Integral Humanism: Our Direction. Deendayal Research Institute. https://deendayalupadhyay.org/images/book/Booklet%20on%20IntegralHumanism.pdf.

60 Upadhyay, Deendayal. 2002. Integral Humanism: Western Versus Bharatiya View. Deendayal Research Institute. https://deendayalupadhyay.org/images/book/Booklet%20on%20IntegralHumanism.pdf.

61 Upadhyay, Deendayal. 2002. Integral Humanism: Harmony Between the Individual and The Collectivity. Deendayal Research Institute. https://deendayalupadhyay.org/images/book/Booklet%20on%20IntegralHumanism.pdf.

62 Ibid.

63 Upadhyay, Deendayal. 2002. Integral Humanism: Economic Structure Suited to National Genius. Deendayal Research Institute. https://deendayalupadhyay.org/images/book/Booklet%20on%20IntegralHumanism.pdf.

64 Bhatt, Kartikey, R Sharma, Pinky Desai, Tekpalsingh Anand, Gautambhai Vaghela, and Sanjay Kamaliya. 2016. "Economic Thoughts." In Economics, 121–34. Gujarat State Board of School Textbooks. https://drive.google.com/file/d/1-Rp7YNJlGNZC7Tem-5DaHtB3M7oNq8_C/view.

65 Upadhyay, Manjula. 2018. "Economic Thought of Deen Dayal Upadhyay." International Journal of Innovative Social Science & Humanities Research 5 (1): 172–77. https://www.researchgate.net/publication/332684114_ECONOMIC_THOUGHT_OF_DEEN_DAYAL_UPADHYAY.

66 Sharma, Sanjeev Kumar, and Ansuiya Nain. 2018. "Integral Humanism of Deen Dayal Upadhyay and Its Contemporary Relevance." The Indian Journal of Political Science Vol. LXXIX (1): 13–20. https://www.researchgate.net/publication/342305382_Integral_Humanism_of_Deen_Dayal_Upadhyay_and_its_Contemporary_Relevance.

67 Upadhyay, Deendayal. 2002. Integral Humanism: Our Direction. Deendayal Research Institute. https://deendayalupadhyay.org/images/book/Booklet%20on%20IntegralHumanism.pdf.

68 Upadhyay, Deendayal. 2002. Integral Humanism: Western Versus Bharatiya View. Deendayal Research Institute. https://deendayalupadhyay.org/images/book/Booklet%20on%20IntegralHumanism.pdf.

69 Ibid.

70 Upadhyay, Deendayal. 2002. Integral Humanism: Harmony Between the Individual and The Collectivity. Deendayal Research Institute. https://deendayalupadhyay.org/images/book/Booklet%20on%20IntegralHumanism.pdf.

71 Upadhyay, Deendayal. 2002. Integral Humanism: Economic Structure Suited to National Genius. Deendayal Research Institute. https://deendayalupadhyay.org/images/book/Booklet%20on%20IntegralHumanism.pdf.

72 Ibid.

73 Bhatt, Kartikey, R Sharma, Pinky Desai, Tekpalsingh Anand, Gautambhai Vaghela, and Sanjay Kamaliya. 2016. "Economic Thoughts." In Economics, 121–34. Gujarat State Board of School Textbooks. https://drive.google.com/file/d/1-Rp7YNJlGNZC7Tem-5DaHtB3M7oNq8_C/view.

74 Ibid.

75 Verma, Rajesh, and Vijay Srivastava. 2021. "Relevance Of Economic Vision of Deen Dayal Upadhaya: An Analysis In Gandhian Framework." Indian Journal of Public Administration New Series Vol. XVIII (2): 129–38. https://www.researchgate.net/publication/359451872_RELEVANCE_OF_ECONOMIC_VISION_OF_DEEN_DAYAL_UPADHAYA_AN_ANALYSIS_IN_GANDHIAN_FRAMEWORK.

76 Sharma, Sanjeev Kumar, and Ansuiya Nain. 2018. "Integral Humanism of Deen Dayal Upadhyay and its Contemporary Relevance." The Indian Journal of Political Science Vol. LXXIX (1): 13–20. https://www.researchgate.net/publication/342305382_Integral_Humanism_of_Deen_Dayal_Upadhyay_and_its_Contemporary_Relevance.

77 Upadhyay, Deendayal. 2002. Integral Humanism: Our Direction. Deendayal Research Institute. https://deendayalupadhyay.org/images/book/Booklet%20on%20IntegralHumanism.pdf.

78 Upadhyay, Deendayal. 2002. Integral Humanism: Western Versus Bharatiya View. Deendayal Research Institute. https://deendayalupadhyay.org/images/book/Booklet%20on%20IntegralHumanism.pdf.

79 Upadhyay, Deendayal. 2002. Integral Humanism: Our Direction. Deendayal Research Institute. https://deendayalupadhyay.org/images/book/Booklet%20on%20IntegralHumanism.pdf.

80 Upadhyay, Deendayal. 2002. Integral Humanism: Western Versus Bharatiya View. Deendayal Research Institute. https://deendayalupadhyay.org/images/book/Booklet%20on%20IntegralHumanism.pdf.

81 Ibid.

82 Ibid.

83 Ibid.

84 Upadhyay, Deendayal. 2002. Integral Humanism: Economic Structure Suited to National Genius. Deendayal Research Institute. https://deendayalupadhyay.org/images/book/Booklet%20on%20IntegralHumanism.pdf.

85 Ibid.

86 Bhatt, Kartikey, R Sharma, Pinky Desai, Tekpalsingh Anand, Gautambhai Vaghela, and Sanjay Kamaliya. 2016. "Economic Thoughts." In Economics, 121–34. Gujarat State Board of School Textbooks. https://drive.google.com/file/d/1-Rp7YNJlGNZC7Tem-5DaHtB3M7oNq8_C/view.

87 Ibid.

88 Upadhyay, Manjula. 2018. "Economic Thought of Deen Dayal Upadhyay." International Journal of Innovative Social Science & Humanities Research 5 (1): 172–77. https://www.researchgate.net/publication/332684114_ECONOMIC_THOUGHT_OF_DEEN_DAYAL_UPADHYAY.

89 Verma, Rajesh, and Vijay Srivastava. 2021. "Relevance of Economic Vision of Deen Dayal Upadhyay: An Analysis in Gandhian Framework." Indian Journal of Public Administration New Series Vol. XVIII (2): 129–38. https://www.researchgate.

net/publication/359451872_RELEVANCE_OF_ECONOMIC_VISION_OF_DEEN_DAYAL_UPADHAYA_AN_ANALYSIS_IN_GANDHIAN_FRAMEWORK.

90 Sharma, Sanjeev Kumar, and Ansuiya Nain. 2018. "Integral Humanism of Deen Dayal Upadhyay and its Contemporary Relevance." The Indian Journal of Political Science Vol. LXXIX (1): 13–20. https://www.researchgate.net/publication/342305382_Integral_Humanism_of_Deen_Dayal_Upadhyay_and_its_Contemporary_Relevance.

91 Bhatt, Kartikey, R Sharma, Pinky Desai, Tekpalsingh Anand, Gautambhai Vaghela, and Sanjay Kamaliya. 2016. "Economic Thoughts." In Economics, 121–34. Gujarat State Board of School Textbooks. https://drive.google.com/file/d/1-Rp7YNJlGNZC7Tem-5DaHtB3M7oNq8_C/view.

92 Verma, Rajesh, and Vijay Srivastava. 2021. "Relevance of Economic Vision of Deen Dayal Upadhyay: An Analysis in Gandhian Framework." Indian Journal of Public Administration New Series Vol. XVIII (2): 129–38. https://www.researchgate.net/publication/359451872_RELEVANCE_OF_ECONOMIC_VISION_OF_DEEN_DAYAL_UPADHAYA_AN_ANALYSIS_IN_GANDHIAN_FRAMEWORK.

93 Sharma, Sanjeev Kumar, and Ansuiya Nain. 2018. "Integral Humanism of Deen Dayal Upadhyay and its Contemporary Relevance." The Indian Journal of Political Science Vol. LXXIX (1): 13–20. https://www.researchgate.net/publication/342305382_Integral_Humanism_of_Deen_Dayal_Upadhyay_and_its_Contemporary_Relevance.

94 Upadhyay, Deendayal. 2002. Integral Humanism: Our Direction. Deendayal Research Institute. https://deendayalupadhyay.org/images/book/Booklet%20on%20IntegralHumanism.pdf.

95 Ibid.

96 Upadhyay, Deendayal. 2002. Integral Humanism: Western Versus Bharatiya View. Deendayal Research Institute. https://deendayalupadhyay.org/images/book/Booklet%20on%20IntegralHumanism.pdf.

97 Upadhyay, Deendayal. 2002. Integral Humanism: Harmony Between the Individual and The Collectivity. Deendayal Research Institute. https://deendayalupadhyay.org/images/book/Booklet%20on%20IntegralHumanism.pdf.

98 Upadhyay, Deendayal. 2002. Integral Humanism: Economic Structure Suited to National Genius. Deendayal Research Institute. https://deendayalupadhyay.org/images/book/Booklet%20on%20IntegralHumanism.pdf.

99 Ibid.

100 Bhatt, Kartikey, R Sharma, Pinky Desai, Tekpalsingh Anand, Gautambhai Vaghela, and Sanjay Kamaliya. 2016. "Economic Thoughts." In Economics, 121–34. Gujarat State Board of School Textbooks. https://drive.google.com/file/d/1-Rp7YNJlGNZC7Tem-5DaHtB3M7oNq8_C/view.

101 Ibid.

102 Upadhyay, Manjula. 2018. "Economic Thought of Deen Dayal Upadhyay." International Journal of Innovative Social Science & Humanities Research 5 (1): 172–77. https://www.researchgate.net/publication/332684114_ECONOMIC_THOUGHT_OF_DEEN_DAYAL_UPADHYAY.

103 Verma, Rajesh, and Vijay Srivastava. 2021. "Relevance of Economic Vision of Deen Dayal Upadhyay: An Analysis in Gandhian Framework." Indian Journal of Public Administration New Series Vol. XVIII (2): 129–38. https://www.researchgate.net/publication/359451872_RELEVANCE_OF_ECONOMIC_VISION_OF_DEEN_DAYAL_UPADHAYA_AN_ANALYSIS_IN_GANDHIAN_FRAMEWORK.

104 Sharma, Sanjeev Kumar, and Ansuiya Nain. 2018. "Integral Humanism of Deen Dayal Upadhyay and its Contemporary Relevance." The Indian Journal of Political Science Vol. LXXIX (1): 13–20. https://www.researchgate.net/publication/342305382_Integral_Humanism_of_Deen_Dayal_Upadhyay_and_its_Contemporary_Relevance.

105 Bhatt, Kartikey, R Sharma, Pinky Desai, Tekpalsingh Anand, Gautambhai Vaghela, and Sanjay Kamaliya. 2016. "Economic

Thoughts." In Economics, 121–34. Gujarat State Board of School Textbooks. https://drive.google.com/file/d/1-Rp7YNJlGNZC7Tem-5DaHtB3M7oNq8_C/view.

106 Upadhyay, Deendayal. 2002. Integral Humanism: Our Direction. Deendayal Research Institute. https://deendayalupadhyay.org/images/book/Booklet%20on%20IntegralHumanism.pdf.

107 Ibid.

108 Bhatt, Kartikey, R Sharma, Pinky Desai, Tekpalsingh Anand, Gautambhai Vaghela, and Sanjay Kamaliya. 2016. "Economic Thoughts." In Economics, 121–34. Gujarat State Board of School Textbooks. https://drive.google.com/file/d/1-Rp7YNJlGNZC7Tem-5DaHtB3M7oNq8_C/view.

109 Upadhyay, Deendayal. 2002. Integral Humanism: Harmony Between the Individual and The Collectivity. Deendayal Research Institute. https://deendayalupadhyay.org/images/book/Booklet%20on%20IntegralHumanism.pdf.

110 Upadhyay, Deendayal. 2002. Integral Humanism: Economic Structure Suited to National Genius. Deendayal Research Institute. https://deendayalupadhyay.org/images/book/Booklet%20on%20IntegralHumanism.pdf.

111 Upadhyay, Deendayal. 2002. Integral Humanism: Our Direction. Deendayal Research Institute. https://deendayalupadhyay.org/images/book/Booklet%20on%20IntegralHumanism.pdf.

112 Upadhyay, Deendayal. 2002. Integral Humanism: Western Versus Bharatiya View. Deendayal Research Institute. https://deendayalupadhyay.org/images/book/Booklet%20on%20IntegralHumanism.pdf.

113 Ibid.

114 Upadhyay, Deendayal. 2002. Integral Humanism: Harmony Between the Individual and The Collectivity. Deendayal Research Institute. https://deendayalupadhyay.org/images/book/Booklet%20on%20IntegralHumanism.pdf.

115 Upadhyay, Deendayal. 2002. Integral Humanism: Economic Structure Suited to National Genius. Deendayal Research

Institute. https://deendayalupadhyay.org/images/book/Booklet%20on%20IntegralHumanism.pdf.

116 Bhatt, Kartikey, R Sharma, Pinky Desai, Tekpalsingh Anand, Gautambhai Vaghela, and Sanjay Kamaliya. 2016. "Economic Thoughts." In Economics, 121–34. Gujarat State Board of School Textbooks. https://drive.google.com/file/d/1-Rp7YNJlGNZC7Tem-5DaHtB3M7oNq8_C/view.

117 Ibid.

118 Upadhyay, Manjula. 2018. "Economic Thought of Deen Dayal Upadhyay." International Journal of Innovative Social Science & Humanities Research 5 (1): 172–77. https://www.researchgate.net/publication/332684114_ECONOMIC_THOUGHT_OF_DEEN_DAYAL_UPADHYAY.

119 Verma, Rajesh, and Vijay Srivastava. 2021. "Relevance of Economic Vision of Deen Dayal Upadhyay: An Analysis in Gandhian Framework." Indian Journal of Public Administration New Series Vol. XVIII (2): 129–38. https://www.researchgate.net/publication/359451872_RELEVANCE_OF_ECONOMIC_VISION_OF_DEEN_DAYAL_UPADHAYA_AN_ANALYSIS_IN_GANDHIAN_FRAMEWORK.

120 Sharma, Sanjeev Kumar, and Ansuiya Nain. 2018. "Integral Humanism of Deen Dayal Upadhyay and its Contemporary Relevance." The Indian Journal of Political Science Vol. LXXIX (1): 13–20. https://www.researchgate.net/publication/342305382_Integral_Humanism_of_Deen_Dayal_Upadhyay_and_its_Contemporary_Relevance.

121 Bhatt, Kartikey, R Sharma, Pinky Desai, Tekpalsingh Anand, Gautambhai Vaghela, and Sanjay Kamaliya. 2016. "Economic Thoughts." In Economics, 121–34. Gujarat State Board of School Textbooks. https://drive.google.com/file/d/1-Rp7YNJlGNZC7Tem-5DaHtB3M7oNq8_C/view.

122 Upadhyay, Deendayal. 2002. Integral Humanism: Our Direction. Deendayal Research Institute. https://deendayalupadhyay.org/images/book/Booklet%20on%20IntegralHumanism.pdf.

123 Ibid.

124 Upadhyay, Deendayal. 2002. Integral Humanism: Western Versus Bharatiya View. Deendayal Research Institute. https://deendayalupadhyay.org/images/book/Booklet%20on%20IntegralHumanism.pdf.

125 Upadhyay, Deendayal. 2002. Integral Humanism: Harmony Between the Individual and The Collectivity. Deendayal Research Institute. https://deendayalupadhyay.org/images/book/Booklet%20on%20IntegralHumanism.pdf.

126 Upadhyay, Deendayal. 2002. Integral Humanism: Economic Structure Suited to National Genius. Deendayal Research Institute. https://deendayalupadhyay.org/images/book/Booklet%20on%20IntegralHumanism.pdf.

127 Ibid.

128 Bhatt, Kartikey, R Sharma, Pinky Desai, Tekpalsingh Anand, Gautambhai Vaghela, and Sanjay Kamaliya. 2016. "Economic Thoughts." In Economics, 121–34. Gujarat State Board of School Textbooks. https://drive.google.com/file/d/1-Rp7YNJlGNZC7Tem-5DaHtB3M7oNq8_C/view.

129 Ibid.

130 Bhatt, Kartikey, R Sharma, Pinky Desai, Tekpalsingh Anand, Gautambhai Vaghela, and Sanjay Kamaliya. 2016. "Economic Thoughts." In Economics, 121–34. Gujarat State Board of School Textbooks. https://drive.google.com/file/d/1-Rp7YNJlGNZC7Tem-5DaHtB3M7oNq8_C/view.

131 Upadhyay, Deendayal. 2002. Integral Humanism: Our Direction. Deendayal Research Institute. https://deendayalupadhyay.org/images/book/Booklet%20on%20IntegralHumanism.pdf.

132 Upadhyay, Deendayal. 2002. Integral Humanism: Western Versus Bharatiya View. Deendayal Research Institute. https://deendayalupadhyay.org/images/book/Booklet%20on%20IntegralHumanism.pdf.

133 Ibid.

Chapter Nine

Crisis of Modern Times and Integral Humanism

Sonu Trivedi

The perceived decline of the fundamental value systems due to cultural dissociation, social inequality and unsustainable economic practices has raised critical challenges that threaten the global ecosystem and sustainability of our modern times. Deendayal Upadhyay's philosophy of 'Integral Humanism' offers a framework that addresses these crises by advocating a balanced development model that integrates the spiritual and material aspects of human existence. Integral Humanism presents a specific philosophical and socio-political perspective that addresses such crises from a nationalist perspective. It seeks to harmonise individual's material and spiritual needs with the collective welfare of society, rejecting both extreme individualism and collectivism.

Deendayal Upadhyay was a prominent Indian philosopher and political thinker who offered a holistic approach to human development, emphasising the integration of spiritual, material, individual, and collective aspects of human life. Structured upon the concept of 'Integral Humanism' as propounded by Upadhyay, this paper argues on how Integral Humanism's emphasis on the balance between material and spiritual growth can offer an alternative towards more sustainable and equitable development amidst the prevailing uncertainties and disruptions in modern times. Further, by analysing Deendayal Upadhyay's ideals of cultural rootedness and his socio-economic model based on the principles of decentralisation, self-reliance, and the promotion of a moral and ethical foundation in governance and society, this paper addresses the critical concerns in society reinforcing moral and ethical values through the lens of Integral Humanism.

Civilisational Heritage and Cultural Rootedness

Deendayal Upadhyay's views on civilisational heritage and cultural rootedness form a crucial part of his philosophy of Integral Humanism. He stressed the importance of understanding and preserving a society's civilisational heritage while fostering cultural rootedness to ensure holistic development. He views life as integrated not only in the case of collective or social life but also in the individual life. "Body, mind, intelligence and the soul — these four make up an individual. But these are integrated. We cannot think of each part separately"[1]. In Bharat, Deendayal Upadhyay believes, "we have placed before ourselves the ideal of the four-fold responsibilities, of catering for the needs of body, mind, intellect and soul with a view to achieve the integrated progress of man." Furthermore, "Dharma, Artha, Kama and Moksha are the four kinds of Purushartha which befit a man. The longings for Dharma, Artha Kama and Moksha, are inborn in man, and satisfaction of these four efforts too, we have thought in an integrated way"[2].

Deendayal Upadhyay emphasised the importance of historical continuity, arguing that a society must understand and appreciate its past to build a prosperous future. He believed that historical consciousness provides a sense of identity and direction. According to him, every civilisation has unique values and principles that contribute to its distinct identity. He says, "It is essential that we think about our national identity. Without this identity there is no meaning of independence, nor can independence become the instrument of progress and happiness."[3] He says. "The basic cause of the problems facing Bharat is the neglect of its national identity."[4] While finding solutions to problems of our country, he says, "Every country has its own peculiar historical, social and economic situations and its leaders decide the remedies to the ills that beset the country from time to time taking into consideration its background. It is illogical to believe that remedies which the leaders of one country decided to try for their problems are likely to be applicable as such to all other peoples. Therefore, it is neither possible nor wise to adopt foreign 'Isms' in our country in the original form in toto. It will not be helpful in achieving happiness and prosperity."[5] From a nationalist perspective, he talks about the importance of Bhartiya culture and how it could point direction to the world.

Integral Humanism also stresses the importance of cultural and civilisational heritage. Deendayal Upadhyay believed that a society's development should be rooted in its cultural values and traditions, ensuring that modernisation does not lead to cultural erosion. He characterises Bhartiya culture as viewing life as an integrated whole. From an integral view point according to him, "To think of parts may be proper for a specialist but it is not useful from the practical standpoint. The confusion in the West arises primarily from its tendency to think of life in sections and then to attempt to put them together by patch work."[6] He accepts the diversity and plurality in life but endeavours to discover the unity behind them. According to him, "Unity in diversity and the expression of unity in various forms has remained the central thought of Bhartiya culture."[7]

Discussing about his idea of 'Akhand Bharat,' Deendayal Upadhyay not only calls it as a symbol of the geographical unity of the country but it also reflects the Indian outlook which sees unity in diversity.[8] According to him, "Akhand Bharat is not a political slogan which we have accepted because it is popular in a particular situation, but it is the foundation of our entire philosophy. The description of India in our Puranas is not only based on land but also based on people and culture. We did not separate land, people and culture from each other but it was in their integration that we realized the nation." The term Akhand Bharat includes all those basic values of a national and integral culture. It also encompasses, the feeling that "entire land from Attock to Cuttack, from Kutch to Kamrup and from Kashmir to Kanyakumari as not only virtuous and sacred but as intimate to us. The people who have been born on this holy land since time immemorial and are there today, no matter how superficial the differences may be in terms of place and time, every devotee of 'Akhand Bharat' sees the basic unity in their entire life."[9]

The erosion of cultural values and identities in the face of modern culture is a significant concern. Integral Humanism's focus on cultural rootedness can help societies preserve their unique identities while engaging with global modernity, fostering a more pluralistic and harmonious global order. He regarded western science and the western way of life as two different things. "Whereas western science is universal and must be absorbed by us if we wish to go forward, the same is not true about the western way of life and values. In fact, thoughtless imitation of the West must be scrupulously discarded."[10] Deendayal Upadhyay emphasised the need for individuals and societies to remain rooted in their cultural identity. He believed that cultural rootedness provides a sense of belonging, pride, and stability and resist the forces of cultural imperialism.

To quote Vajpayee on this, "Every moment of his life, as every atom of his body, was an offering at the feet of the nation, which was his God."[11] He further says, "Panditji derived inspiration from India's glorious past because he wanted to build a glorious future. Though his ideas received their vital nourishment from the age-old and inexhaustible springs of our national culture, he was far from being a traditionalist. He wanted to lay the foundation of a glorious future by making India a prosperous, modern nation. He was a great thinker and taught us to be proud of the past but at the same time ready to accept the challenges of the future."[12]

Walter Anderson, in his tribute to Deendayal Upadhyay says, "Contemporary politics in India, according to Upadhyay was based on partial, if not incorrect, understanding of man and his role in society. The political leadership of post-independence India, he asserted, had attempted to apply western notion of the good society to Indian conditions and the result was unsatisfactory. Economic growth was sluggish, unemployment and exploitation had increased, national integration was undermined, and cultural progress was slow."[13]

Referring to the 'divine form of our culture', Deendayal says, "With the support of Universal knowledge and our heritage, we shall create a Bharat which will excel all its past glories, and will enable every citizen in its fold to steadily progress in the development of his manifold latent possibilities and to achieve through a sense of unity with the entire creation, a state even higher than that of a complete human being; to become Narayan from Nar."[14]

Socio-economic Model of Decentralisation and Self-reliance

Deendayal Upadhyay's philosophy deeply rooted in Indian cultural and spiritual traditions, provides a comprehensive framework for addressing the socio-economic challenges of contemporary society. The core of Upadhyay's socio-economic model is the concept of holistic development. He believed that economic policies should not only aim at increasing wealth but also at promoting overall well-being and happiness. This involves creating a balance between material and spiritual needs, ensuring that economic progress does not lead to moral and ethical decline. He advocates for self-reliance and decentralised governance. He argued that local self-governance and self-sufficiency are crucial for sustainable development and the empowerment of individuals and communities as it seeks to balance material progress with spiritual well-being, rejecting the extremes of both capitalism and socialism.

A key principle of Upadhyay's socio-economic model is self-reliance or Swadeshi. He encouraged the use of indigenous resources and technologies to reduce dependence on foreign goods and services. This principle aims to build a robust and resilient economy that can withstand global economic fluctuations. Giving general directions for developing our economy, he says, "Swadeshi and Decentralisation are the two words which can briefly summarise the economic policy suitable for the present circumstances."[15] Standing high against the extremes of both Capitalism and Socialism, Upadhyay says, "In the capitalist system the industrialist creates capital with the help of surplus value. In a socialist system, the state undertakes this task. In both the systems, the entire production is not distributed among the workers. If production is carried on through centralised large-scale industries, the sacrifice on the part of the worker in creating the capital is not given due recognition. The advantage in decentralisation is in the fact that the workers have a sense of direct participation in the management of this surplus value or capital."[16] This approach not only fosters self-reliance but also ensures that economic benefits are distributed more equitably.

Leaders like Gandhi, Lohia and Deendayal have also envisaged the establishment of an enduring social order based on justice, equality and freedom that would be economically, politically and technologically decentralised. Comparing these great personalities of Indian social and political life, Keshava Prasad Singh acquaints us with what these leaders shared in common.[17] "The decentralised economic set-up envisaged by them has close affinity. They have identical views on the vital constituents and issues of their decentralised economic order. Gandhi's Sarvodaya, Lohia's 'decentralised socialism' and Panditji's 'Integral Humanism' meet and also merge indissolubly on the splendid confluence of decentralised economic order."[18]

However, D. B. Thengdi asserts that, "Deendayal Upadhyay differed from the Gandhian school of thought in as much as he laid greater stress on mechanisation."[19] According to Thengdi, "he also differed from the Nehruvian approach. Wholesale transplantation of technology and industrial structure from the west would not suit Indian conditions, he said. No doubt Charkha is to be replaced by machines. But this replacement should not necessarily be by automatic machines aggravating the problems of unemployment, idle capacity, complete decapitalisation of the existing means of production, dearth of foreign exchange and domestic capital, and colossal waste of available raw material. The factors, such as, wind, water, steam, oil, gas, electricity and atomic power that can supply the motive power must also be taken into consideration. The available managerial skills must be fully utilised. The production should be suited to the needs of the society. For this purpose, we should design suitable machines, introduce reasonably adaptable changes in the traditional techniques of production, and develop a 'Bhartiya' Technology."[20]

Thengdi, further compares Marx and Deendayal as both believed that "Statelessness as an ideal condition of any society.

Both were against exploitation and the system that gives rise to it."[21] According to him, "The ideology of Deendayal ji as well as of Marx is essentially humanistic. The maxim 'from each according to his ability; to each according to his needs' is quite consistent with the spirit of Integral Humanism. Both thought-systems consider freedom from want and production or action for the sake of self-fulfilment, as an ideal condition. The final stage of communism consisting of 'socialised humanity' that is "a classless, stateless, and generally a structureless collectivity of complete individuals who live in harmony with themselves and with each other" is broadly compatible with the ultimate goal of Integral Humanism."[22] However, they differ on the point that "Marx advocated bloody revolution for destroying not only the superstructure but also the foundations of the existing social order; Panditji stood for mass awakening, mass education and mass mobilisation through appropriate sanskaras with a view to alter the superstructure, leaving intact the eternal foundation of Dharma."[23] He further says, "Both these thinkers visualised full development of all the faculties of every individual. But while Deendayal ji considered man in an integrated way, Marx, under the influence of the then prevailing objective conditions, treated man as an economic being."[24]

With a focus on social reformation, D. B. Thengdi makes an interesting similarity in the thoughts of Jaya Prakash Narayan, M. N. Roy and Deendayal Upadhyay. "Both the concepts, 'total revolution' put forth by J. P. and 'Integral Humanism' propounded by Pt. Deendayal Upadhyay ultimately conceives of a party less democracy."[25] According to him, M. N. Roy also clearly said, "So long as parties exist, culture in the true sense cannot evolve. While a representative form of government can come up through the party system, a truly democratic government envisages a government run by people themselves."[26] Fully consistent with Indian tradition, Thengdi puts all the three thinkers at the same level.

Deendayal Upadhyay was critical of the Western models of development which could result in the loss of indigenous cultural practices and wisdom that are vital for a balanced and sustainable way of life. Focussing on self-reliance and criticising the third five-year plan in 1961, he argues, "There is too much dependence on foreign sources for the implementation of the industrial programme. Too much dependence on foreign sources has forced for plan to orientate all its production programmes to augment export earnings. Requirements of this programme go counter to the needs of developing internal markets, establishing prices, dispersal of industries and labour-intensive methods of production. They impose added burdens on the people. Thus, we find ourselves in the grip of a vicious circle."[27] To add further, he says, "Westernism apart, the planners are also obsessed with the idea of ushering in a socialist era. There would hardly be any difference with the ultimate objectives of socialism that is imbuing every citizen and his activities with a social purpose as against private profit, reduction of economic inequalities and granting of social justice to all. But the means adopted by socialist countries to achieve these objectives are hardly suitable to the purpose. The State comes forward to own all factors of production and the citizens, big and small, lose their identity."[28] Thus, he was opposed to the adoption of Western values and lifestyles, which he saw as leading to cultural erosion and alienation.

Deendayal Upadhyay calls socialism as a system which reduces people to the status of labourers as there is no independent ownership and bloody revolution is invoked for its establishment. As this system is based on the conflict between individual and society through class struggle, according to Upadhyay, "this system does not go well with the Indian culture and tradition."[29] He believed that this approach fosters division and antagonism within society, undermining social harmony and cohesion. Upadhyay argued for a more inclusive and integrative approach to social issues. He says, "we are not socialists of this type, nor are we individualists in Western sense. The Indian system calls for blend of the two. Our effort is to merge the individual in the social, because the individual can die but society never."[30] Upadhyay's critique of socialism is particularly significant, as it highlights the limitations of this ideology from the perspective of Indian cultural and social contexts.

Nationalism, democracy and socialism, according to Deendayal Upadhyay, "are incomplete and mutually opposing ideals."[31] "Each had a certain merit but taken alone each provided only a partial solution to the human quest for the good life. Nationalism posed a threat to world peace. Democracy when linked with capitalism, gave free reign to exploitation. Socialism, the reaction to the linked concept of democracy-capitalism, robbed the individual of dignity and freedom. Each of these concepts exacerbated material acquisitiveness and thus stimulated greed, class antagonism, exploitation and social anarchy."[32]

He advocated for a balanced development where each authority – public and private, "should be allowed to contribute its best to the development of the nation." According to him, the history of development strategies in the decade of 1950s "shows that the private sector has shown greater virility and capacity to invest and produce, why should its services be not utilized? If we can tolerate a Birla and a Tata, what is the harm if a few more spring up?"[33] He believed that the needs of "social justice can be secured through fiscal measures."

Deendayal Upadhyay calls 'Right to Food' as a 'birthright.' According to him, "slogan should be that the one who earns will feed and every person will have enough to eat. In a society even those who do not earn must have food. The children and the old, the diseased and the invalids, all must be eared for by the society. Any economic system must provide for the minimum basic necessities of human life to everyone. Food, clothing and shelter constitute, broadly speaking these basic necessities.[34] Similarly, he also talks about, "The guarantee of work to be given to every able-bodied member of the society."[35] This should be the aim of our economic system. "IF a vote for everyone is the touch-stone of political democracy, work for everyone is a measure of economic democracy. This right to work does not mean slave labour as in communist countries. Work should not only give a means of livelihood to a person but it should be of the choice of that person. If for doing that work the worker does not get a proper share in the national income, he would, be considered unemployed. From this point of view a minimum wage, a just system of distribution and some sort of social security are necessary."[36]

Within the framework of Integral Humanism, Upadhyay favours for the economic system, "which helps in the developments of our humane qualities, or civilization and enables us to attain a still higher level of all round perfection. We should have a system which does not overwhelm our humane quality; which does not make us slaves of its own grinding wheels."[37] Deendayal Upadhyay's socio-economic model based on the philosophy of Integral Humanism offers a holistic framework for addressing the complex challenges of modern society. By integrating material, social, and spiritual dimensions of development, Upadhyay's model offers valuable insights for sustainable and inclusive growth.

Moral and Ethical Foundations

Integral Humanism places a strong emphasis on Dharma. It suggests that societal progress should be guided by ethical considerations and a sense of duty towards others. According to Deendayal Upadhyay, Dharma and religion need not be equated. "Religion means a creed or a sect; it does not mean

Dharma. Dharma is very wide concept. It is concerned with all aspects of life. It sustains the society. Even further, it sustains the whole world. That which sustains is "Dharma."[38] He further says that, "Dharma is not confined to temples or mosques. Worship of God is only a part of Dharma. Dharma is much wider." According to him, "the English word 'religion' is not the correct word for 'Dharma'. The nearest equivalent English term for Dharma can be 'Innate law.' Since 'Dharma' is supreme, our ideal of the state has been "Dharma Rajya". The king is supposed to protect Dharma." Dharma Rajya, however, does not mean a 'theocratic state' to Deendayal Upadhyay. Dharma includes principles which bring about harmony, peace and progress in the life of mankind. "Dharma Rajya accepts the importance of religion in the peace, happiness and progress of an individual. Therefore, the state has the responsibility to maintain an atmosphere in which every individual can follow the religion of his choice and live in peace."[39]

Deendayal Upadhyay views society as an organic entity and is self-born having its own life. It comes into existence in an organic way. It has its body, mind, intellect and soul.[40] Fundamental principle of a nation, according to Deendayal Upadhyay, is its soul, which he calls as 'Chiti.' "Chiti is fundamental and is central to the nation from its very beginning. Chiti determines the direction in which the nation is to advance culturally. Whatever is in accordance with Chiti, is included in culture. On the strength of this 'Chiti', a nation arises, strong and virile. It is this 'Chiti' that is demonstrated in the actions of every great man of a nation."[41] He says, "if the soul of the society weakens, then all the different limbs of the society will grow feeble and ineffective. The laws that help manifest and maintain Chiti of a Nation are termed Dharma of that nation. Hence it is this 'Dharma' that is supreme. Dharma is the repository of the nation's soul. If Dharma is destroyed. the Nation perishes. Anyone who abandons Dharma betrays the nation."[42] According to Upadhyay, "In a Dharma Rajya, the state is not absolutely powerful. It is subject to Dharma. We have always vested sovereignty in Dharma."[43]

Vajpayee while talking about Deendayal Upadhyay says, "Politics for Deendayal Upadhyay was a means, not the end, a way, not the goal. He wanted to spiritualize politics."[44] In an article titled 'Your Vote', Deendayal Upadhyay addresses ethical questions related to the entire election process in India which goes beyond the specific time frame. He touches upon the present set of voters, candidates and political parties as well.

For voters Deendayal says, "Vote is a matter of conscience. Do not sell it. Do not destroy it. The voter should not complain; he should command. He should not desire; he must demand. He should not grumble and grudge; but should assess and assert. The voter should see that he votes for a principle and not for a party, that he votes for a party and not for a personality, that he votes for a person and not for the purse. Let him consider the cause and not the caste; go with the worthy rather than with the winner. Choose the right man and see that the man you choose wins; that will be your victory."[45]

For candidates, he says, "A suitable candidate to a man of commonsense should be one who can represent the party's views in the legislature, who has been nursing his constituency and can claim to air the feelings of its people. As an individual he should be devoted to the people and as a member of the party he seeks to represent, he should be disciplined and dedicated to its cause. If he has any other qualifications they may add to his stature, but they cannot be substituted for these basic ingredients of suitability."[46]

Answering to what is a good party he says, "Evidently the one that is not simply a collection of individuals but is a body corporate with a distinctive purposeful existence different from its desire to capture power. Political power should be a means rather than an end to the members of such a party. There should be devotion to a cause in the rank and file of the party. Devotion leads to dedication and discipline. Discipline does not mean simply outward conformity to certain dos and don'ts. The more you impose discipline from above the less is the internal strength of a party. Discipline is to a party what Dharma is to a society. If there is a devotion and discipline, there will not be any groups and factions in the party. When party interests are subordinated to self-interest, factionalism begins. It is a social manifestation of an egoistic and perverse mind. A faction-ridden party becomes ineffective and loses all capacity for doing good."[47]

Speaking against the recommendation of Ford Foundation on 'cow slaughter,' Deendayal says, often foreign institutions are involved in advising and giving guidance on subjects that they do not even know. The recommendations he says, "ignore the socio-economic importance of cow in India. Without understanding the economic aspects of Hindu sociology, these recommendations become unrealistic."[48] "The concept of 'Swaraj' presupposes the resuscitation of 'our' values of life and points of honour. And the cow, by far, constitutes the centre of all our points of honour. Those who want to establish foreign values of life in Bharat, who want to base the future of Bharat on a new foundation borrowed from abroad, having wiped out our ancient way of life entirely, they raise their eyebrows and twist their nose on the problem of cow protection. The nation, in fact, is the inspiring mind–force behind the physical human conglomeration. It derives its existence from the spiritual traditions and faiths which alone pour life and vivacity into its limbs. And the cow forms not only the centre of national mind but she permeates through our entire existence like 'Brahma.' The slogan of cow–protection will not only help us realize the fulfilment of our long-cherished aspirations but will send through the entire national life a new wave of self–consciousness.

This will bring about a thorough metamorphosis in the present setup of our government."[49]

Based on moral and ethical considerations, Deendayal Upadhyay calls education as a social responsibility. "To educate a child is in the interest of the Society itself. By birth a child is an animal. He becomes a responsible member of the society only by education and culture."[50] He advocates for free and compulsory education of children and uses the metaphor of a tree for explaining the same. "We do not charge fee from trees for sowing the seed and caring for it. On the contrary we invest our money and efforts. We know that when the tree grows, we shall reap fruits. Education is a similar investment. An educated individual will indeed serve the society."[51]

According to Deendayal Upadhyay, "The modern world recognises unity only in the drab mechanical aspect. Uniformity has been assumed to be the essential characteristic of unity. In a living organism, the inner unity seldom manifests itself in uniform ways. A machine can repeat the same action any number of times and in any place. But a human being is not capable of acting in this mechanical manner."[52] The blind imitation to western world and running towards centralisation has "rung the death knell of all our decentralised institutions in the political, economic and social spheres. If we cannot escape the impact of the modern world and cannot find our new ways on our own, better suited to modern conditions, we go down with the rest of the world."[53] He further says, "We can still hold to our own and pave the ways for others to follow. But this calls for a total reorientation of our outlook towards life. Towards policies and towards planning."[54]

Conclusion

To conclude, while challenges due to the crisis of modern world poses serious threat to the mankind today, Deendayal

Upadhyay's Integral Humanism offers a philosophical framework that addresses these crises by advocating for an economic system aligned with natural laws and ethical values.

Deendayal Upadhyay's Integral Humanism offers a perspective that critiques modernity's excesses while advocating for a return to traditional Indian values and a more balanced approach to development. It views the crisis as stemming from a disconnect between material progress and spiritual well-being, advocating for a reintegration of these dimensions to ensure sustainable and harmonious societal development. By advocating for a balanced development model that respects cultural values, promotes ethical governance, and fosters sustainable practices, Integral Humanism offers a pathway towards a more harmonious and resilient global society. Integrating these principles into contemporary policy and societal norms can help mitigate the multifaceted crises facing modern world.

Integral Humanism underscores the need for a balanced relationship between humans and nature and promotes a society where economic progress benefits all individuals. Amidst the crisis of modern times, the cultural roots of Integral Humanism inspire the mankind to adopt more ethical and responsible behaviours, leading to more just and effective governance.

Endnotes

1 Deendayal Upadhyay, "Integral Humanism," Lecture -2, April 23 1965. URL: https://deendayalupadhyay.org/images/book/Booklet%20on%20IntegralHumanism.pdf?ref=quillette.com

2 Ibid.

3 Deendayal Upadhyay, "Integral Humanism," Lecture -1, April 22 1965.

4 Ibid.

5 Deendayal Upadhyay, "Integral Humanism," Lecture -2, April 23 1965.

6 Ibid.

7 Ibid.

8 Deendayal Upadhyay, "Akhand Bharat," *Rashtriya Chintan*. URL: http://library.bjp.org/jspui/handle/123456789/439

9 Ibid.

10 Deendayal Upadhyay, "Integral Humanism," Lecture -1, April 22 1965.

11 Vajpayee, Atal Bihari, "From Funeral Oration," Feb 18, 1968. URL: https://deendayalupadhyay.org/accept.html

12 Ibid.

13 Andersen Walter K., "The Political Philosophy of Deendayal Upadhyay," in *Destination: Nation's Tribute to Deendayal Upadhyay*, Deendayal Research Institute, 1978. Pp 43-48. URL: https://deendayalupadhyay.org/destination_book.html

14 Deendayal Upadhyay, "Integral Humanism," Lecture -4, April 25 1965.

15 Ibid.

16 Ibid.

17 Singh, Keshava Prasad, "Agreement on Fundamentals," in P. Parameswaram ed. *Gandhi, Lohia and Deendayal*, Deendayal Research Institute, 1978. Pp 24-47.

18 Ibid.

19 Thengdi, D. B, *His Legacy: Our Mission*, Jaya Bharath Publications, 1973. Pp. 15.

20 Ibid.

21 Thengdi D. B., "Marx and Deendayal: The Two Approaches," *Manthan*, Vol. 3. No. 4. March 1981. Pp. 5-12.

22 Ibid.

23 Ibid.

24 Ibid.

25 Thengdi, D. B. "Integral Humanism" in *Destination: Nation's Tribute to Deendayal Upadhyay*, Deendayal Research Institute, 1978. Pp 51-55. URL: https://deendayalupadhyay.org/destination_book.html

26 Ibid.

27 Deendayal Upadhyay, "The Third Plan X-Rayed," *Organiser*, 21 August, 1961. URL: https://deendayalupadhyay.org/thirdplan.html

28 Ibid.

29 Deendayal Upadhyay, "Economics of Synthesis," *Manthan*, Vol. 3, No. 4, 1981.

30 Ibid.

31 Deendayal Upadhyay, "Integral Humanism," Lecture -2, April 23 1965.

32 Andersen Walter K., 1978.

33 Deendayal Upadhyay, "The Third Plan X-Rayed."

34 Deendayal Upadhyay, Lecture -4

35 Ibid.

36 Deendayal Upadhyay, "Aspects of Economics," *Selected Thoughts*. URL: https://deendayalupadhyay.org/economics.html

37 Deendayal Upadhyay, Lecture -4.

38 Deendayal Upadhyay, Lecture -3, April 24, 1965.

39 Ibid.

40 Ibid.

41 Ibid.

42 Ibid.

43 Ibid.

44 Vajpayee, Atal Bihari, "From Funeral Oration," Feb 18, 1968. URL: https://deendayalupadhyay.org/accept.html

45 Deendayal Upadhyay, "Who is a suitable Candidate," *Organiser*.

December 4, 1961. URL: https://deendayalupadhyay.org/vote_1.html

46 Ibid.

47 Deendayal Upadhyay, "Candidate, Party and Ideology all Count," *Organiser*. December 11, 1961. URL: https://deendayalupadhyay.org/vote_2.html

48 Deendayal Upadhyay, "Ford Foundation and Cow Slaughter," November 30, 1959. Compiled in *Political Diary*, Jaico Publishing House. 1968. pp. 152-154

49 Deendayal Upadhyay, "The Battle for the Cow Is the Battle for Freedom and Democracy," *Organiser*. December 15, 1958. URL: https://deendayalupadhyay.org/cow.html

50 Deendayal Upadhyay, Lecture -4

51 Ibid.

52 Deendayal Upadhyay, "Growing Dependence on the State," August 4, 1959. Compiled in *Political Diary*, Jaico Publishing House. 1968. pp. 155-157

53 Ibid. 157

54 Ibid. 157

Chapter Ten

Integral Humanism and Sustainable Development Goals

Shameem C C.

Integral Humanism, as articulated by Deendayal Upadhyay, presents a holistic framework that integrates spiritual, cultural, and material dimensions of development, making it highly relevant to the Sustainable Development Goals (SDGs) established by the United Nations. Both frameworks emphasize the importance of social equity and environmental sustainability, advocating for a balanced approach to development that respects human dignity and promotes justice for all individuals, regardless of their background[1]. The SDGs, comprising 17 goals[2] aimed at addressing global challenges such as poverty and climate change, align closely with the principles of Integral Humanism, which seeks to harmonize economic progress with ethical governance and social justice.[3] Furthermore, the concept of holistic development, which encompasses economic, social, environmental, and spiritual well-being, reinforces the need for comprehensive strategies that support sustainable progress.[4] Ultimately, the incorporation of Integral Humanism into the pursuit of the SDGs can foster a more inclusive and sustainable future, ensuring that development efforts are not only economically viable but also socially equitable and environmentally responsible.[5] This synergy is crucial for addressing the pressing challenges of our time.

Pandit Deendayal Upadhyay was an Indian philosopher, social thinker, and political activist who was a pivotal figure in Indian political thought, known for his philosophy of Integral Humanism, which emphasizes the unity of individual and collective existence. His ideology, termed 'Ekatma Manavavad', advocates for a holistic approach to life, integrating moral and ethical dimensions beyond mere religious affiliations. Upadhyay's contributions were instrumental in the formation of the Bharatiya Jana Sangh, which later evolved into the Bharatiya Janata Party (BJP), reflecting his vision of a culturally rooted nationalism. He is best known for his concept of "Integral Humanism," which became the guiding philosophy of the Jana Sangh and later influenced the ideology of the BJP. He emphasized the importance of national identity and cultural consciousness, arguing that true freedom is meaningful only when grounded in a shared cultural heritage. His advocacy for Sanatan culture highlights the need for a comprehensive understanding of Indian identity, which he believed was essential for societal progress.

Integral Humanism, as propounded by Deendayal Upadhyay, is a socio-political and economic philosophy that seeks to harmonize individual and societal interests by emphasizing the integration of the spiritual, cultural, and material aspects of human life. Here are some key aspects of Upadhyay's views on Integral Humanism.

1. Holistic Approach

Integral Humanism promotes a holistic approach to life, considering the physical, mental, intellectual, and spiritual dimensions of human existence. Upadhyay believed in a balanced and integrated development of the individual and society.

2. Cultural Nationalism

Upadhyay emphasized the importance of India's cultural heritage and sought to build a political and social system rooted in Indian traditions. He argued for the preservation and promotion of cultural values as essential for the well-being of the nation.

3. Decentralization

Integral Humanism advocates for a decentralized political and economic structure. Upadhyay believed in the principle of "Antyodaya," which means the welfare of the last person in the society. He favoured local self-governance and economic policies that empower grassroots communities.

4. Dharma and Ethics

Upadhyay stressed the significance of Dharma (ethical and moral principles) in public life. He believed that political and economic systems should be guided by ethical values and principles derived from India's spiritual and cultural traditions.

5. Economic Self-Reliance

Integral Humanism promotes the idea of economic self-reliance. Upadhyay envisioned an economic system that reduces dependence on foreign powers and fosters self-sufficiency, with a focus on meeting the basic needs of the population.

6. Social Harmony

Upadhyay advocated for social harmony and the integration of various sections of society. He sought to bridge the gaps between different communities and promote a sense of unity and brotherhood.

Integral Humanism has had a lasting impact on the political thought and ideology of the Rashtriya Swayamsevak Sangh (RSS), the ideological parent of the BJP, and continues to influence political discourse in India. It is important to note that interpretations and applications of Integral Humanism may vary, and different individuals or groups may emphasize certain aspects over others based on their understanding and priorities.

In the case of environmental protection, the modern environmental movements have been influenced by Deendayal Upadhyay's ideologies. However, his philosophy of Integral Humanism, which encompasses a holistic view of human life and society, can be interpreted to have implications for environmental stewardship. The major aspects of Integral Humanism that related to environmental protection includes:

(*a*) *Balanced Development*

Integral Humanism advocates for balanced and harmonious development that considers not only economic progress but also cultural, spiritual, and environmental well-being. The emphasis on balance suggests a consideration for the sustainable use of natural resources.

(*b*) *Dharma and Ethical Values*

Upadhyay's philosophy emphasizes the importance of Dharma, which includes ethical and moral values. The principles of Dharma could be extended to environmental ethics, promoting responsible and ethical interactions with the environment to ensure its long-term health.

(*c*) *Local Self-Governance*

Upadhyay advocated for decentralized governance and local self-reliance. Local communities, when empowered, may be more attuned to the needs of their environment and could play a role in sustainable resource management.

(*d*) *Economic Self-Reliance*

While economic self-reliance primarily refers to reducing dependence on foreign powers, it could also be interpreted as promoting practices that are sustainable and environmentally friendly, avoiding over-reliance on resources that may lead to environmental degradation.

While Upadhyay's Integral Humanism does not explicitly address environmental protection, it provides a framework that values the interconnectedness of various aspects of life. Environmental protection aligns with the broader goal of ensuring the well-being of individuals and society in the long term.

Integral Humanism: From the Perspectives of Jacques Maritain

Jacques Maritain was a prominent French Catholic philosopher and political thinker. He made significant contributions to various fields, including philosophy, political theory, ethics, and theology. While Jacques Maritain is not specifically associated with the term "Integral Humanism" as popularized by Deendayal Upadhyay in the Indian context, Maritain's philosophy shares some common themes with Integral Humanism in the broader sense.

Key aspects of Jacques Maritain's philosophical views include:

1. Personalism

Maritain was a proponent of personalism, which emphasizes the dignity and value of the individual. He argued for a social and political order that respects the inherent worth and rights of each person.

2. Christian Philosophy

As a devout Catholic, Maritain integrated his Christian faith with his philosophical and political views. His work often explored the relationship between faith and reason, advocating for the compatibility of religious values with a just and humane society.

3. Natural Law

Maritain was a proponent of natural law theory, asserting that there are objective moral principles that can be known through reason and are applicable to all human beings. This perspective influenced his discussions on ethics and political philosophy.

4. Democratic Humanism

Maritain supported a form of democratic humanism that aimed at promoting human rights, individual freedoms, and the common good within a democratic framework. He argued for a society that values both individual liberties and social responsibilities.

5. Integral Humanism in a Broader Sense

While Maritain may not have explicitly used the term "Integral Humanism," his philosophical views encompass the idea of integrating various aspects of human life, including spiritual, moral, and social dimensions. His vision of society emphasized the development of the whole person within a framework of ethical and spiritual principles.

It is important to note that Maritain's influence extended beyond political philosophy, and his contributions to the development of modern Catholic thought and Thomistic philosophy are widely recognized. While the term "Integral Humanism" is more closely associated with specific political and cultural movements in different parts of the world, Maritain's work has inspired discussions on the integration of human values in various contexts.

In the case of environmental protection, he addressed environmental issues in his writings. However, some aspects of his philosophical and ethical positions can be interpreted in relation to environmental protection.

(*a*) *Stewardship and Respect for Creation*

Maritain, influenced by Thomistic philosophy, emphasized the idea of human beings as stewards of creation. While he may not have explicitly discussed environmental concerns, the notion of stewardship implies a responsibility for the care and preservation of the natural world.

(*b*) *Natural Law*

Maritain's adherence to natural law theory, which posits the existence of objective moral principles derived from the nature of humanity, could be extended to environmental ethics. The principles of natural law might be invoked to argue for the moral responsibility of humans to protect and preserve the environment.

(*c*) *Human Dignity and Quality of Life*

Maritain's focus on human dignity and the common good may indirectly support environmental protection. A healthy environment is seen as contributing to the well-being and quality of life for individuals and communities.

(*d*) *Social Ethics*

Maritain's discussions on social ethics, justice, and the common good could be applied to issues related to environmental justice and ensuring that the benefits and burdens of environmental policies are distributed fairly among communities.

The UN Sustainable Development Goals on Environmental Protection

The United Nations (UN) has been actively involved in promoting sustainable development and environmental protection through various initiatives and frameworks. The UN Sustainable Development Goals (SDGs), adopted in 2015, include several goals specifically focused on environmental sustainability. Here are some key aspects of the UN's efforts in this regard:

1. **Goal 13:** Climate Action: This goal emphasizes urgent action to combat climate change and its impacts. The UN encourages countries to strengthen resilience and adaptive capacity to climate-related disasters.

2. **Goal 14:** Life Below Water: This goal aims to conserve and sustainably use the oceans, seas, and marine resources. It addresses issues such as overfishing, marine pollution, and ocean acidification.

3. **Goal 15:** Life on Land: Focused on protecting, restoring, and promoting sustainable use of terrestrial ecosystems, this goal aims to combat desertification, halt biodiversity loss, and ensure the sustainable management of forests.

4. **UN Framework Convention on Climate Change (UNFCCC):** The UNFCCC is an international treaty aimed

at addressing climate change and its impacts. The annual Conference of the Parties (COP) meetings bring together nations to discuss and negotiate climate-related policies and actions.

5. **Paris Agreement:** Adopted in 2015 under the UNFCCC, the Paris Agreement is a landmark international accord that sets out efforts to limit global temperature increase, enhance climate resilience, and support developing countries in their climate-related endeavours.

6. **UN Environment Programme (UNEP):** UNEP plays a crucial role in coordinating global environmental efforts. It works on various issues, including climate change, biodiversity, chemicals and waste, and resource efficiency.

7. **International Environmental Governance:** The UN supports efforts to strengthen international environmental governance to effectively address environmental challenges. This includes promoting cooperation and coordination among countries.

8. **Capacity Building:** The UN assists countries, particularly developing ones, in building their capacity to address environmental issues. This includes providing technical assistance, knowledge sharing, and facilitating technology transfer.

9. **Partnerships:** The UN encourages collaboration between governments, businesses, civil society, and other stakeholders to achieve environmental sustainability. Partnerships are seen as essential for mobilizing resources and expertise.

10. **Monitoring and Reporting:** The UN emphasizes the importance of monitoring and reporting on progress toward environmental sustainability goals. This involves

collecting data, assessing trends, and identifying areas that require further attention and action.

By integrating environmental protection into broader sustainable development goals, the UN aims to address interconnected challenges and promote a balanced approach that considers social, economic, and environmental dimensions. The success of these efforts relies on the collective commitment and action of the global community.

Integral Ecology is a concept that integrates various dimensions of ecology, including environmental, social, economic, and cultural aspects. It emphasizes the interconnectedness and interdependence of all elements within an ecosystem, recognizing that ecological issues cannot be fully understood or addressed in isolation.

Integral Ecology: Prospects

The term "Integral Ecology" gained prominence through the work of philosopher and integral theorist Ken Wilber, who proposed an approach that combines different perspectives and levels of analysis. In the context of environmental issues, Integral Ecology encourages a holistic understanding that goes beyond a narrow focus on the physical environment. It includes:

1. Environmental Ecology

Examining the health and well-being of ecosystems, including the study of biodiversity, ecosystems, and the impact of human activities on the environment. Ecology enriches our world and is crucial for human wellbeing and prosperity. It provides new knowledge of the interdependence between people and nature that is vital for food production, maintaining clean air and water, and sustaining biodiversity in a changing climate. Governments and citizens around the world are increasingly aware of the consequences of atmospheric pollution and climate change. In large-scale experiments, plants and animals are exposed to carefully controlled atmospheres and different ecological conditions. Scientists use this information to understand how they respond to pollution levels, and make predictions about future climate change.

2. Social Ecology

Considering the social dimensions of ecological issues, such as the impact on communities, social justice, and the distribution of environmental benefits and burdens, it broadly focusses on multiple factors that might affect health. This broad approach to thinking of health, advanced in the 1947 Constitution of the World Health Organization, includes physical, mental, and social well-being. As described by Stokols, the core principles of social ecology include: Multidimensional structure of human environments—physical & social, natural & built features; objective-material as well as perceived-symbolic (or semiotic); virtual & place-based features. A social-ecological system consists of 'a bio-geo-physical' unit and its associated social actors and institutions. Social-ecological systems are complex and adaptive and delimited by spatial or functional boundaries surrounding ecosystems and their context.

3. Economic Ecology

Evaluating the economic systems and their impact on the environment, exploring sustainable and regenerative economic practices. Ecological Economics addresses the relationships between ecosystems and economic systems in the broadest sense. These relationships are the locus of many of our most pressing current problems (i.e. sustainability, acid rain, global warming, species extinction).

4. Cultural Ecology

Recognizing the role of culture in shaping attitudes and behaviours towards the environment, as well as the impact of ecological issues on cultural practices. Cultural ecology is the study of human adaptations to social and physical environments. Human adaptation refers to both biological and cultural processes that enable a population to survive and reproduce within a given or changing environment. It also focuses on how the overall environment, natural resources available, technology, and population density affect the rest of the culture and how a traditional system of beliefs and behaviour allows people to adapt to their environment. Interplay between any population and their environment is the subject of ecological studies. Cultural ecologists study how humans in their society and through specific cultures interact with the larger environment. In the case of human beings, much of the behaviour involved in interaction with the environment is learned behaviour that has become part of the learned skills, technology, and other cultural responses of a people in a society.

To sum up, Integral Ecology promotes an inclusive and comprehensive approach to address environmental challenges by integrating insights from various disciplines and perspectives. It calls for a collaborative effort that involves not only scientists and policymakers but also communities and individuals from diverse backgrounds. This integrative approach is seen as essential for developing effective and sustainable solutions to the complex environmental issues facing the planet. In this context Deendayal Upadhyay's concept on Integral humanism emphasizes on man, nature, and spiritual harmony on this earth. In this scenario his views on environmental protection have supported the concept of integral ecology as essential for developing effective and sustainable solutions to the complex environmental issues facing the earth.

Conclusion

The environmental protection is crucial for several reasons, encompassing ecological, social, economic, and health aspects in India. In this, environmental protection has evolved over time and contemporary environmental movements often draw on a range of philosophical, ethical, and cultural perspectives to advocate for sustainable practices and the preservation of ecosystems in our country. Deendayal Upadhyay's philosophy and concepts are relevant in Indian context especially on environmental protection. His principles of Dharma could be extended to environmental ethics, promoting responsible and ethical interactions with the environment to ensure its long-term health.

Upadhyay's views on sustainable environment development exhibits the concept of integral ecology through harmonising relationship between man, nature and the Universe. This was the one of major idea behind the UN Sustainable Development Goals to protect environment for next generations. Upadhyay also advocated for decentralized governance and self-reliance. Local communities, when empowered, may be more attuned to the needs of their environment and could play a role in sustainable resource management. His idea on economic self-reliance primarily refers to reducing dependence on foreign powers, it could also be interpreted as promoting practices that are sustainable and environmentally friendly, avoiding over-reliance on resources that may lead to environmental degradation.

While Jacques Maritain did not explicitly delve into contemporary environmental issues, his philosophical framework, rooted in Catholic social thought and Thomistic philosophy, provides a basis for ethical reflection on humanity's relationship with the natural world. Interpreting his principles in the context of environmental concerns aligns with broader ethical discussions about the responsible and sustainable use of natural resources.

To conclude, Deendayal Upadhyay's integral humanism and the Sustainable Development Goals (SDGs) are concepts that addresses different aspects of human development in the modern world, but share common ground on their focus on improving the well-being of individuals and societies. His views on integral humanism necessitated harmonious relationship between man, nature, and the Universe which remains an essential and fundamental part of UN Sustainable Development goal within the purview of environmental protection and sustainable development.

References

1. Deendayal Upadhyay (Sixth edition), *Integral Humanism*. (New Delhi, Hindi Sahitya Sadan, 2014).
2. Deendayal Upadhyay. *Integral Humanism: An Analysis of Some Basic Elements*. (New Delhi, Prabhat Prakashan Publishers, 2018).
3. Veerabhadram Bhukya, *Ideology and Vision of Pandit Deendayal Upadhyay's Way Forward for the Emergence of Bhartiya Swadeshi Consciousness*, (New Delhi: International Journal of Science and Research (IJSR), Volume 12 Issue 7, 2023).
4. Hukma Ram Suthar, *Analysis of political views of Pandit Deendayal Upadhyay*, (New Delhi: Research Review International Journal of Multidisciplinary, Vol, 8, Issue No.5, 2023).
5. Jacques Maritain. *Integral Humanism, Freedom in the Modern World, and A Letter on Independence*, Revised Edition (Collected Works of Jacques Maritain). (Notre Dame: USA, University of Notre Dame Press Publishers, 1996).

6. Jacques Maritain. *Integral Humanism.* (Notre Dame: USA, University of Notre Dame Press Publishers, 1973).

7. Ram Madhav. *The Hindutva Paradigm: Integral Humanism and Quest for a Non-Western Worldview.* (Chennai, Westland Book Publication, 2021).

8. Sdghub. *The Global Goals Yearbook.* Global Goals Yearbook 2020 - SDG Business Hub (sdghub.com). (New York, Sdghub, 2020).

Endnotes

1 Integral Humanism is a philosophical framework developed by Deendayal Upadhyay that emphasizes the holistic development of individuals and society, integrating spiritual, cultural, and material dimensions. It is relevant to the Sustainable Development Goals (SDGs) as it advocates for a balanced approach to development that respects human dignity and promotes social equity.

2 Social equity is the fair distribution of resources and opportunities among all individuals, regardless of their background. It is a core principle of both Integral Humanism and the SDGs, emphasizing the need for inclusive policies that address disparities and promote justice.

3 The Sustainable Development Goals are a set of 17 global goals established by the United Nations in 2015, aimed at addressing various global challenges such as poverty, inequality, climate change, and environmental degradation. Understanding the SDGs is crucial for implementing Integral Humanism, as both frameworks seek to promote holistic and sustainable development.

4 Holistic development refers to an approach that considers the complete well-being of individuals and communities, encompassing economic, social, environmental, and spiritual aspects. This concept aligns with both Integral Humanism and the SDGs, as it promotes comprehensive strategies for sustainable progress.

5 Environmental sustainability focuses on maintaining the health of ecosystems and natural resources for future generations. This concept is integral to the SDGs and resonates with Integral Humanism's emphasis on respecting nature and promoting responsible stewardship of the environment.

Chapter Eleven

Social Welfare and Individual Dignity: A Dialogue Across Cultures

Pratibha Poonia

Integral Humanism, as articulated by Deendayal Upadhyay, and Jacques Maritain's philosophy share some similarities but also have significant differences. Both philosophies emphasise the holistic development of individuals within society, but approach this from different perspectives. Integral Humanism, as propounded by Deendayal Upadhyay, is a socio-political philosophy rooted in the principles of Indian culture and spirituality. It emphasises the idea of "Antyodaya" or the upliftment of the last person in society, focusing on social justice and welfare. Integral Humanism promotes the concept of "Integral Development", which involves the harmonious growth of individuals in all aspects—physical, mental, emotional, and spiritual– within the framework of a cohesive society. It advocates for a decentralised approach to governance, giving importance to self-governance at the grassroots level, and fostering a society based on self-reliance and cooperation. Maritain's philosophy, often associated with personalism, focuses on the dignity and freedom of the individual within society. He emphasises the importance of human rights, freedom of conscience, and the pursuit of the common good through a balance of individual rights and societal responsibilities. Maritain's personalism also incorporates elements of natural law theory and Thomistic philosophy, emphasising the inherent dignity of every human being and their capacity for moral and spiritual growth. Unlike Integral Humanism, Maritain's philosophy is not explicitly rooted in a particular cultural or spiritual tradition but draws from various philosophical and theological sources.

Both Upadhyay's and Maritain's philosophy emphasise the importance of the individual within society and advocate for the common good. Deendayal's 'Integral Humanism' is deeply rooted in Indian cultural and spiritual traditions, whereas Maritain's philosophy is more broadly based on Western philosophical and theological thought. Deendayal Upadhyay places a strong emphasis on self-reliance, decentralisation, and social justice within a cultural context, while Maritain's personalism focuses more on individual rights, freedom, and the pursuit of the common good within a framework of natural law and human dignity.

This paper is based on the objective analyses of the philosophy of Integral Humanism by Deendayal Upadhyay and Jacques Maritain. While both Upadhyay's and Maritain's philosophy share common themes of individual dignity and social welfare, they differ in their cultural foundations, philosophical underpinnings, and emphasis on specific aspects of societal organisation and development.

Integral Humanism of Deendayal Upadhyay

Integral Humanism, as conceptualised by Deendayal Upadhyay, stands as a profound socio-political philosophy rooted in the ethos of Indian culture and values. With its comprehensive approach towards individual and societal development, Integral Humanism emerged as a beacon of thought, offering a holistic framework to address the complex challenges of modern society. In this exposition, we shall delve into the core tenets and principles of Integral Humanism, examining its philosophical underpinnings, socio-political implications, and enduring relevance in contemporary times.

Deendayal Upadhyay, a visionary Indian philosopher, politician, and social thinker, articulated the principles of Integral Humanism in the mid 20th century. Upadhyay envisioned a society where the dignity and welfare of every individual are upheld, and where socio-economic progress is harmonised with spiritual and cultural values. At the heart of Integral Humanism lies the belief in the inherent divinity and worth of every human being, emphasising the holistic development of individuals in all spheres of life. The fundamental basis of Indian civilization and Dharma created the philosophical underpinnings of integral humanism. Upadhyay has effectively dismantled the social and political ideologies of both capitalism and communism by emphasising their innate contempt for the humanitarian parts of human existence and their rightful focus on the economic side. Thus, the core tenets of integral humanism are the unity of the individual, the community, the world, and the supreme authority. According to Upadhyay, every country has its own core cultural and societal beliefs, known as Riti, and every society has some quirks, known as Virat. Every person has distinct responsibilities and a wide range of tasks. Combining these diverse facets of human existence into an ongoing interaction is the essence of integral humanism[1].

Integral Humanism proposes a synthesis of the material, intellectual, and spiritual dimensions of human existence, rejecting the narrow dichotomies prevalent in contemporary thought. It advocates for a balanced approach to socio-economic development, one that integrates material prosperity with ethical considerations and spiritual values. Upadhyay argued that true progress encompasses not only material wealth but also moral and spiritual growth, fostering a harmonious and sustainable society.

Integral Humanism emphasises the principle of "Antyodaya", which translates to the upliftment of the last person in society. This principle underscores the importance of prioritising the needs of the most marginalised and vulnerable sections of society, ensuring their inclusion and empowerment in the developmental process. Upadhyay envisioned a decentralised model of governance where decision-making power is distributed at the grassroots level, enabling active participation and empowerment of local communities.

Integral Humanism advocates for a self-reliant and sustainable economic model, rooted in the principles of "Sarvodaya" (the welfare of all) and "Swadeshi" (self-reliance). Upadhyay envisioned an economic system that promotes indigenous industries, empowers local artisans and farmers, and fosters equitable distribution of resources. He emphasised the importance of striking a balance between economic growth and social justice, rejecting both unbridled capitalism and centralised socialism.

Integral Humanism places a strong emphasis on the preservation and promotion of cultural and spiritual heritage, recognizing the intrinsic value of India's rich cultural diversity. Upadhyay believed that cultural and spiritual values provide the moral foundation for a cohesive and harmonious society, fostering a sense of identity and belonging among its citizens. He advocated for the integration of traditional wisdom with modern knowledge, envisioning a society that draws strength from its cultural roots while embracing progress and innovation.

Integral Humanism espouses the principle of "Dharma", which encompasses ethical and moral values that guide human conduct and behaviour. Upadhyay emphasised the importance of ethical governance and leadership, rooted in integrity, compassion, and selflessness. He called for a political system that prioritises the common good over narrow self-interest, promoting transparency, accountability, and participatory democracy.

Integral Humanism rejects the narrow materialism and consumerism prevalent in modern society, advocating for a more balanced and sustainable lifestyle that prioritises spiritual fulfilment and human relationships over material possessions. Upadhyay emphasised the importance of simple living and high thinking, encouraging individuals to cultivate inner virtues and qualities that lead to personal fulfilment and societal harmony.

Lenin said that if we want to know a subject, we have to look around the subject and inspect all the links and intermediate conditions. We, the common man, can never be able to fully explore all sides of it, but if we are aware of it, then the possibility of error may decrease. From this statement, it proves that the centre of an event is an objective analysis of the actual situation. When it comes to deciding on a subject, that subject should be well analysed. This type of method is also followed in modern science. This is exactly what Pandit Deendayal Upadhyay has said in his integral humanism[2].

In this exploration, we will delve into the core characteristics of Integral Humanism, elucidating its philosophical foundations, key principles, and practical implications for society.

Holistic Development: At the heart of Integral Humanism lies the principle of holistic development, which emphasises the nurturing of all facets of human existence–physical, mental, emotional, and spiritual. Upadhyay argued that true progress cannot be measured solely in terms of material wealth or economic growth but must also encompass moral, ethical, and spiritual well-being. Integral Humanism seeks to create conditions conducive to the holistic development of individuals, fostering a sense of fulfilment and purpose in life.

Antyodaya: Integral Humanism places a strong emphasis on the principle of Antyodaya, which advocates for the upliftment and empowerment of the most marginalised and vulnerable sections of society. Upadhyay believed that the welfare of society should be measured by the well-being of its weakest members, and thus, policies and programmes should prioritise their needs. Antyodaya underscores the importance of social justice, inclusivity, and compassion in building a just and equitable society.

Decentralisation: Integral Humanism advocates for a decentralised model of governance, wherein decision-making power is distributed at the grassroots level. Upadhyay believed that decentralised governance fosters greater accountability, transparency, and responsiveness to local needs and aspirations. By empowering local communities to participate actively in decision-making processes, Integral Humanism seeks to promote participatory democracy and grassroots development.

Self-Reliance and Swadeshi: Integral Humanism promotes the idea of self-reliance and Swadeshi, advocating for an economic model that prioritises local industries, artisans, and farmers. Upadhyay emphasised the importance of reducing dependency on foreign goods and technologies, fostering indigenous innovation and entrepreneurship, and promoting sustainable development practices. Self-reliance and Swadeshi are integral to Integral Humanism's vision of economic empowerment and national resilience.

Cultural and Spiritual Heritage: Integral Humanism recognizes the intrinsic value of India's rich cultural and spiritual heritage and emphasises its preservation and promotion. Upadhyay believed that cultural and spiritual values provide the moral foundation for a cohesive and harmonious society, fostering a sense of identity, belonging, and solidarity among its citizens. Integral Humanism seeks to integrate traditional wisdom with modern knowledge, drawing inspiration from India's cultural heritage to address contemporary challenges.

Ethical Governance: Integral Humanism advocates for ethical governance rooted in integrity, compassion, and selflessness. Upadhyay emphasised the importance of leaders and policymakers upholding moral and ethical values in their conduct and decision-making processes. Ethical governance entails transparency, accountability, and a commitment to the common good, prioritising the welfare of society over narrow self-interests. Integral Humanism envisions a political system that promotes ethical leadership and participatory democracy.

Sustainable Lifestyle: Integral Humanism encourages a lifestyle characterised by simplicity and high thinking, emphasising the cultivation of inner virtues and qualities over material possessions. Upadhyay believed that true happiness and fulfilment are not derived from material wealth or consumerism, but from spiritual growth and meaningful human relationships. Integral Humanism calls for a balanced and sustainable lifestyle that prioritises spiritual fulfilment, intellectual pursuits, and social connections.

The core characteristics of Integral Humanism by Deendayal Upadhyay revolve around the principles of holistic development, social justice, decentralisation, self-reliance, cultural and spiritual heritage, ethical governance, and simplicity. These characteristics reflect Upadhyay's vision of a just, harmonious, and sustainable society, where the dignity and welfare of every individual are upheld, and where socio-economic progress is harmonised with ethical and spiritual values. Integral Humanism offers a compelling framework for addressing the complex challenges of modern society, guiding us towards a more inclusive, compassionate, and resilient future.

In conclusion, the Integral Humanism of Deendayal Upadhyay stands as a timeless philosophy that offers profound insights into the nature of human existence and society. Its emphasis on holistic development, ethical governance, and cultural preservation resonates strongly in today's rapidly changing world, offering a compelling vision for a more just, harmonious, and sustainable future. As we navigate the complexities of the modern world, the principles of Integral Humanism continue to inspire and guide us towards a more inclusive and compassionate society, where the dignity and welfare of every individual are upheld and cherished.

Integral Humanism of Jacques Maritain

Integral Humanism, as articulated by Jacques Maritain, is a philosophical and socio-political framework that seeks to affirm the dignity and worth of every individual while promoting the common good and social solidarity. Maritain, a prominent 20th century French philosopher, developed Integral Humanism as a response to the challenges posed by modernity, including the erosion of traditional values, the rise of totalitarian ideologies, and the fragmentation of society. In this exploration, we will delve into the core principles and key characteristics of Integral Humanism by Jacques Maritain, examining its philosophical underpinnings, ethical foundations, and implications for contemporary society.

For Maritain, a man is an individual and a person, which translates to individuality and personality in the future. He was opposed to both fascism and communism altogether and was actively engaged in opposing both. Maritain also criticised the theory of economic determinism. The aim for Maritain was to formulate a society that keeps flourishing.

Maritain was influenced by Aristotle and Thomas Aquinas, and was called a "Christianised Aristotle." He draws from Aristotle about the importance of individuals and persons of society and the state. The state and society are no ends in themselves if they are independent of these two strands, individual and person.

The idea he drew from Aquinas was about the absolute devotion to any noble truth or idea, no matter where it came from. He combined faith with reason because, according to Aquinas, there can be no conflict between true reason and true faith. Hence, it made him a strong opponent of atheism. Maritain was also the first Western philosopher who dedicated pages and pages of work to Satyagraha led by Gandhi.

Of all the neo-Thomists who would genuinely transport us back to the mediaeval School, Jacques Maritain is arguably the most eminent and significant. From the onset, the title he chose appears to be a misuse of words. In its most common and original use, the word "humanism" refers to an endeavour to understand man and the cosmos to the fullest extent possible—that is, to what the ancients called "philosophy," or the love of wisdom. However, Maritain requests that we give the revered moniker to what is really a relatively limited specialism in mediaeval metaphysics. Despite being promised "true humanism," we find ourselves disappointed to find little more than a reworked version of an antiquated religion.[3]

The core tenets of philosophy of Integral Humanism by Maritain are as discussed below:

Human Dignity: Integral Humanism, as conceived by Maritain, places a strong emphasis on the inherent dignity and worth of every human being. Maritain believed that human dignity is grounded in the spiritual nature of humanity, and is not contingent upon external factors such as social status or material wealth. Integral Humanism asserts that every individual possesses inherent rights and freedoms that must be respected and protected by society and the state.

Personalism: Integral Humanism is rooted in the philosophical tradition of personalism, which emphasises the unique value and significance of each person as an individual. Maritain argued that human beings are not mere objects or means to an end but are ends in themselves, possessing intrinsic worth and moral agency. Personalism rejects the reduction of individuals to mere cogs in a social or economic machine and advocates for the recognition of each person's dignity, autonomy, and rights.

Common Good: Integral Humanism affirms the importance of the common good, which Maritain described as the sum total of conditions necessary for human flourishing and fulfilment. Maritain believed that individuals are interconnected and interdependent, and therefore, the well-being of each person is intimately tied to the well-being of the community as a whole. Integral Humanism calls for a society where the pursuit of individual interests is balanced with a commitment to the greater good of all members of society.

Social Solidarity: Integral Humanism promotes the principle of social solidarity, which emphasises the bonds of mutual respect, cooperation, and support among members of society. Maritain argued that human beings are by nature social beings who thrive in communities characterised by solidarity and mutual aid. Integral Humanism calls for the cultivation of a sense of shared responsibility for the welfare of others, especially the most vulnerable and marginalised members of society.

Subsidiarity: Integral Humanism advocates for the principle of subsidiarity, which holds that decision-making authority should be delegated to the lowest level of organisation capable of addressing a particular issue effectively. Maritain believed that centralization of power and authority can lead to the erosion of individual freedom and autonomy. Subsidiarity calls for a decentralised approach to governance, where local communities and associations are empowered to take responsibility for their own affairs, thus fostering greater participation, accountability, and responsiveness.

Cultural Pluralism: Integral Humanism recognizes and respects the diversity of cultures, traditions, and worldviews within society. Maritain argued that cultural pluralism enriches society by providing a variety of perspectives, values, and forms of expression. Integral Humanism calls for a society where different cultural and religious communities coexist peacefully, engaging in dialogue and mutual respect while preserving their distinct identities and traditions.

Integral Education: Integral Humanism emphasises the importance of education in nurturing the whole person–intellectually, morally, and spiritually. Maritain believed that education should not only impart knowledge and skills but also cultivate virtues such as critical thinking, empathy, and social responsibility. Integral education seeks to develop individuals who are capable of contributing positively to society, upholding ethical principles, and promoting the common good.

Maritain's commitment to theology is a pillar of his educational philosophy and theology. He espouses the theology and philosophy of Thomas Aquinas. Thomas Aquinas' grand synthesis of Aristotle's realism defines the human as an intelligent being possessing a material body and spiritual soul. The purpose of human existence as a being in the presence of God in heaven lacks a religious orientation to be an essential element in Western culture, but without the guidance of a final teleos[4].

In summary, Integral Humanism by Jacques Maritain is a philosophical and socio-political framework that affirms the dignity and worth of every individual while promoting the common good and social solidarity. It emphasises principles such as human dignity and rights, personalism, the common good, social solidarity, subsidiarity, cultural pluralism, and integral education. Integral Humanism offers a compelling vision for a just, inclusive, and harmonious society, where individuals are respected as ends in themselves and where the well-being of all members of society is upheld and nurtured.

Integral Humanism of Upadhyay and Maritain: A Comparative Analysis

Integral Humanism, as elucidated by Deendayal Upadhyay and Jacques Maritain, offers distinctive philosophical frameworks that share common principles while diverging in their emphasis and application. In this comparative study, we will explore the key similarities and differences between Integral Humanism by Deendayal Upadhyay and Jacques Maritain, examining their philosophical underpinnings, socio-political implications, and practical relevance.

Talking about philosophical foundations of both Upadhyay and Maritain, former's Integral Humanism is deeply rooted in Indian cultural and spiritual traditions, emphasising the holistic development of individuals and society through the integration of material, intellectual, and spiritual dimensions, whereas latter's Integral Humanism draws inspiration from

Christian personalism and natural law theory, asserting the inherent dignity and worth of every human being while promoting the common good and social solidarity. Both are deeply rooted in their religious traditions. Maritain and Upadhyay believe that true religion is supernatural. Further, they believe in a non-dogmatic interpretation of their religion. Dharma for them is a form of natural law, not some theocratic state system. Without the religious energies of the soul, the universe would be drained, believed Upadhyay and Maritain.

Coming to human dignity and rights, both Upadhyay and Maritain affirm the inherent dignity and worth of every individual, grounding human rights in the spiritual nature of humanity. While Upadhyay emphasises the divinity of the individual within the context of Indian spirituality, Maritain grounds human dignity in Christian personalism and natural law theory.

Talking about the common good and social solidarity, both Upadhyay and Maritain advocate for the importance of the common good and social solidarity in Integral Humanism. Upadhyay emphasises the principle of Antyodaya (upliftment of the last person) and the decentralisation of governance to promote social solidarity and inclusive development. Maritain emphasises the principle of subsidiarity, which calls for decision-making authority to be delegated to the lowest level of organisation capable of addressing a particular issue effectively, fostering greater participation, accountability, and responsiveness. Neither of them was party men. Both Upadhyay and Maritain were against extreme statism and theocracy. They were what we can call true conservatives (a true conservative is the one who never inclines to the left or to the right but is ready for most of their radical movements).

When discussing cultural pluralism, both Upadhyay and Maritain recognize and respect the diversity of cultures, traditions, and worldviews within society. Upadhyay emphasises the preservation and promotion of India's rich cultural and spiritual heritage within Integral Humanism whereas Maritain advocates for cultural pluralism as a means of enriching society and promoting dialogue and mutual respect among diverse cultural and religious communities.

In the case of ethical governance, both Upadhyay and Maritain advocate for ethical governance rooted in integrity, compassion, and selflessness. Upadhyay emphasises the importance of leaders and policymakers upholding moral and ethical values in their conduct and decision-making processes within a decentralised governance structure, whereas Maritain emphasises the importance of ethical leadership and the cultivation of virtues such as justice, solidarity, and respect for human rights within the framework of the common good.

In the end, about integral education, both Upadhyay and Maritain emphasise the importance of education in nurturing the whole person — intellectually, morally, and spiritually.

Upadhyay emphasises the role of education in fostering holistic development and cultivating virtues such as critical thinking, empathy, and social responsibility within the context of Indian cultural values, whereas Maritain emphasises the role of education in developing individuals who are capable of contributing positively to society, upholding ethical principles, and promoting the common good within the context of Christian personalism and natural law theory.

While Integral Humanism by Deendayal Upadhyay and Jacques Maritain share common principles such as human dignity, the common good, social solidarity, and ethical governance, they diverge in their philosophical foundations, emphasis, and application. One needs to understand that both Sanatana Dharma and Christianity do have some divergences, but what is more important is that both Upadhyay and Maritain bring convergence from the religious divergences when it comes to the matter of human condition.

Upadhyay's Integral Humanism is rooted in Indian cultural and spiritual traditions, emphasising holistic development and decentralised governance, while Maritain's Integral Humanism draws inspiration from Christian personalism and natural law theory, emphasising human dignity, the common good, and subsidiarity. Despite their differences, both frameworks offer valuable insights into the nature of human existence and society, guiding us towards a more just, inclusive, and harmonious future.

Conclusion

While Jacques Maritain derived his theory of "Integral Humanism" from "Christendom," Deendayal Upadhyay formed his idea of "Integral Humanism" from the concept of "Dharma". Notwithstanding their disparate cultural backgrounds, the two thinkers addressed issues that were strikingly similar and shared a dedication to the full development of people within the parameters of a fair and peaceful society.

Philosophers and politicians with a variety of cultural and ideological origins have expressed the political and philosophical ideas of integral humanism in their writings. A prominent figure in the Bharatiya tradition, Deendayal Upadhyay, popularised the idea of Integral Humanism in the post-independence Indian setting. His integral humanism, which has its roots in Indian cultural and spiritual traditions, stresses the fusion of ethical and spiritual principles with material advancement. Deendayal Upadhyay asserts that "an individual is made up of their body, mind, intelligence, and soul, all of which are integrated". Each component cannot be considered separately. According to Deendayal Upadhyay, the idea of integral humanism views life as an integrated totality.

Jacques Maritain and Deendayal Upadhyay's articulations of Integral Humanism can be compared to uncover the universality of some principles in spite of the cultural and theological variety of their respective contexts. In the quest for a just society, these thinkers provide insightful perspectives on the advancement of human dignity, moral leadership, and the fusion of material and spiritual aspects.

Endnotes

1 Parmila & Jyoti Singh. "Integral Humanism Philosophy of Deen Dayal Upadhyay", *International Journal of Multidisciplinary Sciences,* Vol. 3, no. 2 (2021), pp. 152-153.

2 Tushar Ranjan Bhowmick. "The Scope of Humanity", *IJCRT,* Vol. 5, no.1 (2017), p 258.

3 G. G. Coulton. "The Historical Background of Maritain's Humanism", *The Journal of History of Ideas,* vol. 5, no. 4 (1944), pp. 415-417

4 Gerald L. Guteck. "Jacques Maritain and John Dewey on Education: A Reconsideration", *Educational Horizons,* vol. 83, no. 4 (2005), pp.247-263.

Chapter Twelve

Integral Humanism in the Digital Age

Shweta

Silvan Tomkins, a psychologist, philosopher, and anthropologist, posits that the controversies between different worldviews and ideologies about humanism can be traced to a dilemma:

> "Is man the measure, an end in himself, an active, creative, thinking, desiring, loving force in nature? Or must man realize himself, attain his full stature only through struggle toward, participation in, conformity to a norm, a measure, an ideal essence basically prior to and independent of man?"[1]

Humanism elevates humanity's capabilities, virtues, and achievements, while normativism presents a gloomier, more Hobbesian vision. Humanistic worldviews bring attention to unconditional love, openness to affect, and satisfaction of desires, while normative worldviews highlight discipline, punishment, respect, control of effect, and restraint. They also emphasize observation, rigor, and error minimization as essential to the pursuit of knowledge and maintaining law and order. These worldviews have pivotal implications for understanding human behavior and societal goals.[2]

Various organizations have promoted humanistic principles and provided various definitions. Highlighting the rationality of human beings among living beings, it is stated that, "Hu-man beings are radically different from the non-human nature, that human beings are self-conscious and self–governed beings making a community of human individuals according to the rational principles."[3] The Encyclopedia Britannica states, without an understanding of humanitas, debate of Humanism cannot be legitimate. The term Humanitas describes the ultimate development of human virtue in all its forms. The term also alluded to qualities like understanding, kindness, compassion, and mercy that are associated with the contemporary word humanity. Humanism is frequently classified as secular, religious, Renaissance, post-humanist, educational, Marxist, Vedantic, and integrated schools of thought.[4] Among these, Deendayal Upadhyay, who elaborated on Integral Humanism in the 1960s, was a member of the Indian intellectual tradition, defined it as:

> "Integral Humanism outlined the following key principles: Limited government intervention in business; promotion of private investment and entrepreneurship; and equal rewards for everybody. A plethora of little projects, mass manufacturing for mass consumption, a decentralized economy, and individual land ownership are encouraged, as is technological advancement, but mechanization should not supplant livelihoods. Nonviolence, peace principles, and Secular state having no linguistic, religious, racial, political, or other distinctions between majority and minority."[5]

Historical context of Integral Humanism

The concept of Humanism, an entirely human-centered viewpoint, has varied definitions, interpretations, and explanations. Humanism can be traced back from Western thought since the ancient era, as Protagoras, the Greek philosopher, gave the famous maxim, "Man is the measure of all things."[6] Since that time, the concept has been found in diverse philosophical and ethical traditions worldwide. According to Aristotle and followed by Aquinas, every creature is nothing but only a part of the whole perfection of the universe, such as one instrument in an orchestra is a part of the whole perfection of harmony. "Society is a whole composed of persons, which is to say that society is a whole composed of wholes."[7] He enables the reader to relate the existential world with absolute self-existence-God. He unfolds four principles of being that include identity, sufficient reason, finality, and causality.[8]

Meanwhile, Indian philosophical traditions incorporate Humanism with concepts like duty/righteousness and a holistic approach to human welfare. Integral humanism in India acts in accordance with the tradition of Advaita, which Adi Sankara developed. According to this, non-dualism delineated the unifying principle of each and every object within the universe, of which humankind was a part. Integral Humanism, claimed Upadhyay, was the quintessence and contribution of the Indian culture. Practically, Integral Humanism is a paraphrase of Mahatma Gandhi's prospect of a future India. Mahatma Gandhi and Upadhyay both pursued akin but a discrete path for India's future. They both discarded the materialism of socialism and capitalism, as well as the individualism of modern society, in favor of a holistic, Varna-dharma-based community; they both insisted on an infusion of religious and moral values in politics and pursued a culturally authentic mode of modernization that safeguard Hindu values. Furthermore, Integral Humanism circumscribes visions around two themes: one, morality in politics and swadeshi, and the other, small-scale industrialization in economies, though these two themes are Gandhian in general but are distinctly

Hindu nationalist. These visions revolve around the primary themes of harmony, the priority of cultural-national values, and discipline. The philosophy of integral Humanism, like Gandhism, opposed unbridled consumerism that accentuates the increase of material wealth through rapid industrialization since such an ideology construes social discrepancies and regional imbalances in economic growth and fails to alleviate poverty in the country and, hence, alien to Indian culture. The traditional culture stresses restraining one's desires and advocates spiritual contentment rather than a ruthless pursuit of material wealth. There is a need, according to Upadhyay, to strike a balance between Indian and Western thinking for the dynamic nature of society and the cultural heritage of the country.[9]

Indian humanism, however, is significantly different from that of Western humanism. It did not extend to enslaved people there and Christianity, which, in fact, preached its own Humanism. Yet, the philosophy of India is spiritual, and the Indian concept of Humanism is rooted in Vedas and Upanishads and, therefore, comprises values like Universality, Non-aggressiveness, and Humanism. Indian philosophy evolves and reflects spiritual life in three stages. The first stage is worship and adoration with hymns and songs, fasting, and pilgrimage to God outside. The second stage is inward contemplation, which will cause the feeling of the presence of God within itself. True religion begins only at this stage. When the heart becomes purer and purer through meditation, it will experience the pull of divinity within and be filled with joyous communion of the soul and God, which is the third stage. In the West, as V. P. Varma stated, "Humanism is regarded as a philosophy which champions the cause of man, his freedom, and individuality against a theological worldview." He further mentioned, "In the West, humanism is oriented to raising man as if, against the imperialism of God."[10]

Fundamental Principles of Integral Humanism: Deendayal Upadhyay

Integral Humanism is a socio-political-religious concept featuring the holistic development of individuals within the framework of society. It was brought into vogue by Deendayal Upadhyay, an Indian philosopher, political thinker, and leader of the Bharatiya Jana Sangha, the precursor to the Bharatiya Janata Party (BJP) in India. Integral Humanism of Upadhyay, also known as "Ekatma Manavavad," was conceived as an alternative socio-political and economic model for India, rooted in the country's cultural and spiritual heritage, highlights the holistic development of individuals and society, and advocates for a balance between material progress and spiritual growth, recognizing the importance of both individual rights and social responsibilities. It promotes the idea that every individual is unique and has inherent dignity; therefore, society should aim to foster the overall well-being of all its members.[11]

The central principle of Upadhyay's philosophy purely is "Antyodaya," which construes the upliftment of the last person in society. Integral Humanism upholds a governance model primarily based on "dharma," or righteousness, ensuring all citizens' justice, equality, and welfare; preserving and promoting cultural heritage and traditions as well as cultural unity and pride for national integration and social cohesion; advocating an indigenous approach that respects traditional Indian wisdom and modernity, with addition to the economic policies that aimed at self-sufficiency and equitable resource distribution.[12]

Upadhyay visualizes society as a living organism with a body, mind, intelligence, and soul using the lens of Integral Humanism. The progress of a human being and society involves the simultaneous development of all aspects. According to

Bharatiya Daishik Shastra, a society is a natural organism with limbs that humans cannot create or destroy. The reason for its creation and destruction is the same as the creation and destruction of the living world. The relationship between a society and its individuals is similar to that of an organism to its limbs or a tree to its branches, leaves, and flowers. This idea holds that society and the person are interdependent. A society without people is unimaginable, and a person is worthless without society. According to Indian philosophy, humans are born to meet material needs and achieve Wisdom (jnanam), the core of Indian culture. Deendayal Upadhyay also emphasized the concept of 'Samasti Dharma,' focusing on the relationship between infants, parents, siblings, friends, society, nation, and the universe. Upadhyay's Integral Humanism aims to promote holistic human welfare and national self-reliance in India. He brings attention to the concept of "Antyodaya" to uplift the last person in society and integrate life's spiritual, cultural, and material aspects. It encourages decentralized governance and economic self-reliance, stressing the principle of Dharma as a guiding force, and rejects capitalism and socialism in favor of a third way rooted in Indian ethos.[13]

Fundamental Principles of Integral Humanism: Jacques Maritain

French philosopher Jacques Maritain, prominent in Christian and Thomistic thought, pointed out Integral Humanism as the inherent dignity and worth of every human being, regardless of race, religion, or social status. Influenced by the Catholic faith and Thomistic philosophy, he rejected ideologies like communism and fascism, advocating for a society that respects and promotes individual flourishing. Maritain also recognized that humans are inherently social beings, and our fulfillment and development are closely connected and interrelated to our relationships with others and society. He endorsed the principle of subsidiarity, supporting local decision-making to safeguard individual autonomy and dignity. Maritain asserts that Integral Humanism is the harmony of body and soul, natural law, and a balanced approach that values personal and community.[14]

Jacques Maritain published his significant work Humanisme Intégral in 1936. Initially, Maritain focused on metaphysics and theology, which later on shifted to social and political issues, moral philosophy, and politics after Pius XI denunciated Charles Maurras' L'Action Francaise party in 1926, which led him to ten years of interest in political and philosophical issues, as presented in his further three publications which includes Primauté du spiritual (1927), Du Régime Temporel et de la Liberté (1933), and finally, Humanisme Intégral. Humanisme Intégral by Jacques Maritain is a philosophical and ethical framework emphasizing religion's and society's spiritual and temporal aspects. It differs from medieval Christendom but is based on reason and aligns with Catholic teachings. Maritain's work covers historical skies, civilization, Christendom, theocentric humanism, pluralism, and the temporal mission of the Christian. It offers a holistic view of society, rooted in principles of dignity, solidarity, and the common good, offering an alternative to modern dehumanizing ideologies.[15]

Marx's humanism is rooted in Feuerbach's conceptions and atheism, a Manichaean type of humanism that rejects religious aspects of the human heritage. On the other hand, Christian humanism acknowledges God's existence and the divine government's movement, acknowledging historical forces that have served God despite themselves.[16] Catholic social doctrine emphasizes the dignity of human beings and the primacy of the common good as foundational pillars of social thought and action. In the eye of God, each human person has unique and endless worth, as "God created each human person in His image, in the image of God, he created humankind, male and female. He created them" (Genesis, 1: 27). God created humankind in His image, wanted them to participate in His glory and happiness, and to defend the dignity of the human person and the primacy of the common good. It is essential to understand what constitutes a human person. Maritain further distinguishes between individual and person, stating that the whole human being, soul and body, is a person. The crisis from modern to present times challenges man's natural community and ordination to the transcendent as the source of ultimate value. To reconcile the common good and personal good, turning God into a shared good and loving one's neighbor as oneself is necessary.[17]

According to Jacques Maritain, Materialistic "humanism" leads to contempt and destruction of all actual human beings. True Humanism is God-centered, re-establishing the creature in the Creator. The love that forms the foundation of Humanism leads those who respond to the summons to realize the sufferings of the Savior into the darkest night of sacrifice and crucifixion. Thomism is a philosophical approach that links theory and practice, guiding us towards the heaven of Wisdom. It requires Wisdom to exert its dominion even at the boundaries of action, where Wisdom and Science must give way to Prudence. Moral science aims to direct action, but many moralists, even Christian moralists, design beautiful frescoes of universal principles. They often resort to speculative metaphysics or empirical Prudence from experts in the "lesser evil" and "realists" of Success and Gain. Father Vann's words about politicians can be applied to moralists, as he recognizes that moral philosophy is practical and that ethics cannot abdicate in the presence of action; this highlights the importance of balancing the principles of religion with practical application in moral philosophy.[18]

As described by Jacques Maritain, Integral Humanism values the inherent dignity of every human being and rejects ideologies that treat them as mere means to an end. It promotes human flourishing, focusing on material well-being, virtue cultivation, truth pursuit, and beauty. Integral Humanism is rooted in the Christian understanding of human nature as created in the image of God and acknowledges natural law as a foundation for moral and social order. Maritain's philosophy advocates for the harmonious development of all dimensions of life, commits to democracy, human rights, and social justice, as per Christian ethics, and rejects individualism and collectivism.[19]

Integration of Technology and Human Flourishing

Technology is as old as human evolution. It is the core of human development and has a prime focus on understanding human life, society, and human consciousness.[20] Science and technology influence the dimensions of society, including law, politics, economics and business, public health and safety, national security, education, and culture, affecting labor, communication, healthcare, privacy, autonomy, data security, and environmental sustainability. However, technology is a double-edged sword that promises to advance health and wealth on one side and potentially destructive applications on the other. It is surrounded by both hype and fear as it contributed to and challenged the Western philosophical development perspective and modified cultural values, attitudes, beliefs, and practices. Therefore, science and technology are immersed in human conditions and the vision and aspirations for the future.[21] Further, one of the writers, Carl F. Stover, observed-

"A source of great authority over nature, the modern scientific technology promises to be both the hope of man's future and the instrument of his enslavement or destruction. If we are to avoid the disasters it lays open to us and take advantage of the opportunities it presents, we... must understand what modern technology is, what it means, and what must be done with it if it is to serve man well."[22]

Maritain argues that human equality is the foundation for justice in a free society but does not simply eliminate relative inequality. He identifies three main aspects of anthropocentric Humanism:

- An inversion of the order of ends,
- A powerful imperialism about the forces of matter and
- A progressive movement back of man by matter.

The first aspect involves an inversion of God's transcendence, where God became a decorative God for human beings, leading to a change in our end. Instead of focusing on eternal life, we seek dominance over matter. The second aspect is a powerful imperialism about the forces of matter, where God becomes an idea, engulfed in the dialectical progress of self-asserting ideas and the evolving world. The third aspect involves a progressive movement back of man by matter, where man must subordinate himself to inhuman and technical necessities. It leads to a struggle between freedom by technique and freedom by asceticism. Instead of guiding us by reason and grace, anthropocentric Humanism promotes an anti-ascetical morality that is essentially technological. The modern man believed in liberty without mastery of self or moral responsibility, as free will was incompatible with scientific determinism. The law of the machine, the law of matter, will apply itself to us, enslaving us. Without changing our hearts and transforming ourselves, we become consumers of goods provided by science and technology, leading to increased misery.[23]

Deendayal Upadhyay, on the other side, believed technology should uplift and empower individuals rather than exploit or dehumanize them. His Integral Humanism advocates for a balanced approach to development, where spiritual, cultural, and ethical considerations accompany technological progress. It stresses the importance of preserving traditional values and social cohesion amidst rapid technological change, promoting a holistic vision of human welfare that transcends material prosperity. Deendayal believes that nature is the wealth of human beings for their livelihood, and if material wealth exceeds natural limits, people will deviate from ethical behavior. He prioritizes that consumption should consider necessities and comforts, not luxuries, and that circumspection should govern the allotment of natural resources in the economy. Deendayal believes natural resources are limited and should be used responsibly, considering long-term needs and the natural cycle of ever-changing change. He believes that man is destroying nature by destroying its resources for his own existence, and the speed of destruction by man is not compensated by the speed of renewing resources in nature. According to Indian thoughts, individuals should be loving, cooperative, service-oriented, tolerant, and disciplined, which are essential human activity analysis and progress principles.[24]

Contemporary Relevance and Ethical imperatives in Technological Advancement

The underlying social and political philosophy of Integral Humanism invokes significant but radical changes in our present regime of culture to employ analogical terminology of hylomorphism, a substantial transformation. This transformation does not need only the instauration of new social structures and of a new social life regime that replaces capitalism, but also, and consubstantially, a rising of the forces of faith, intelligence, and love springing from the interior depths of the soul, advancement in the understanding of the world of spiritual realities. Only under such circumstances can a man be able to penetrate more deeply into the depths of his nature without destroying or deforming it.[25]

According to the IHEU's (International Humanist and Ethical Union) by law,

> "Humanism is a democratic and ethical life stance, which affirms that human beings have the right and responsibility to give meaning and shape to their own lives. It stands for the building of a more humane society through an ethic based on human and other natural values in the spirit of reason and free inquiry through human capabilities. It is not theistic, and it does not accept supernatural views of reality."[26]

Social ethics is currently facing an identity crisis caused by a loss of self-confidence in the Western tradition of Humanism, where disillusionment with welfare state programmes is prevalent. The currently shaky identity is rooted in the central concern for human well-being and the hope for their development. The modern belief that knowledge can lead to mastery of nature, social life, and history is being challenged, as pursuing such mastery often appears destructive. Suchlike Descartes' "self" was a demigod seeking power over nature and society, suggesting that achieving clarity about values becomes "implementation." However, advances in understanding reveal that we have little control over societal events and the natural environment, leading to a crisis of faith as we lose the belief that we can shape social life according to our values. Troeltsch's view of ethics suggests it is an adjustment to the world's situation, aiming to achieve what is practically possible. He argued that the Kingdom of God is within us and cannot be definitively expressed in social interaction and institutions. Social ethical reflection has evolved since Troeltsch's writing, with movements like Marxism, structural-functional sociology, neo-classical economics, neo-liberalism, communitarianism, and ideal-discourse theory. However, contemporary stances towards these variations are characterized by a dour mood, nihilism, and the "sullenness" of the postmodern mentality. This mood is the antithesis of modern self-confidence, which suggests that humans can bring the conditions of their social existence under human reason, placing social life at the service of a more humane existence. This contemporary self-distrust has both theoretical and practical dimensions. Today, strong currents challenge the capacity of reason to attain genuine knowledge in various fields, including religion, humanities, and sciences. Postmodern thought extends the critique of reason beyond metaphysics and theology. The diversity of disciplinary methods and cultural pluralism discourage efforts to integrate multiple forms of knowledge.[27]

Intellectual specialization establishes disciplines to insights beyond their field of inquiry, which leads thinkers to conclude that intellectual life can only aspire to fragments of meaning that are purely human constructs rather than vistas of what is accurate or true. It challenges normative Humanism, whether Christian or secular. The postmodern intellectual epoch is marked by suspicion toward all meanings, traditions, ideologies, and scientific theories that claim total explanatory power. Science has been used for genocidal slaughter at Auschwitz and Dresden, while psychological theories have awakened a form of self-consciousness that threatens narcissism. Economic-political ideologies promised to liberate workers but ultimately expired in the face of a velvet revolution led by poets, shipbuilders, and priests. The retrieval of just and limited war traditions has led to a shift from civilian-only warfare to nearly 90% civilian casualties. Religious visions have contributed to conflict and terror against the innocent in Iran, the West Bank, Gaza, Belfast, and other places.[28]

Therefore, "Addressing societal and ethical issues is the right thing to do and the necessary thing to do. It is the right thing to do because, as ethically responsible leaders, we must ensure that technology advances human well-being and does not detract from it. It is the necessary thing to do because it is essential for speeding technology adoption, broadening the economic and societal benefits, and accelerating and increasing our return on investment," As stated by Philip J. Bond, former undersecretary for technology at the U.S. Department of Commerce (2003).[29]

According to Deendayal Upadhyay, balance is the key to success in both the material and spiritual worlds. His integral Humanism can overcome many of India's current challenges. Some of India's most significant issues, such as sanitation, corruption, poor education, bonded labor, religious violence, unemployment, and others, require tailor-made solutions. Amidst poverty which affects a substantial portion of the world's population, the concept of Integral Humanism encourages diversity and a tailor-made solution to varied situations, which is an appropriate model that might serve the goal.[30]

Synthesis and Final Remark

Deendayal Upadhyay's Integral Humanism and Jacques Maritain's philosophy offer a framework for ethical decision-making in technology-driven societies. They both emphasize the importance of ensuring technological advancements serve human needs and promote human flourishing, prioritizing individual rights like privacy, autonomy, and dignity. Ethical governance in technology-driven societies should prioritize inclusivity and democratic participation, consider diverse perspectives in decision-making processes, and help bridge the digital divide and promote the common good by promoting equitable access to technology, digital literacy programmes, and empowerment of marginalized communities through digital education and skills training. It also addresses concerns about job displacement, algorithmic bias, and the ethical implications of AI and automation.[31] Integral Humanism advocates for holistic development and dignity of labour, guiding discussions and policies to ensure these technologies serve society's well-being and prioritizing human values like fairness, accountability, and transparency. Both perspectives acknowledge the interconnectedness of humanity with the natural world, emphasizing responsible stewardship of natural resources and mitigating the environmental impact of technological innovations. Promoting the common good reduces inequalities, fosters social cohesion, and promotes inclusive economic development. By integrating these perspectives, ethical decision-making and policy formulation can be guided by principles prioritizing human dignity, holistic development, ethical governance, environmental sustainability, and promoting the common good. Integral Humanism principles—such as human dignity, solidarity, and subsidiarity—serve as the foundation for ethical decision-making in the design, development, and use of digital technologies.[32]

Deendayal Upadhyay and Jacques Maritain, who contributed to the development of Integral Humanism, share similar philosophical approaches to Human Welfare, such as promoting a holistic approach to human life; valuing individual freedom and social responsibility; rejecting ideologies that reduce humans to material progress; supporting governance systems based on moral values and principles of justice, solidarity, and the common good; criticizing materialistic ideologies prioritizing economic prosperity and technological advancement; reinforcing policies addressing poverty, inequality, and marginalization; advocating for preserving and promoting cultural and spiritual heritage.

However, there are significant differences between Upadhyay and Maritain's underlying philosophies. Upadhyay's Integral Humanism is deeply rooted in India's cultural and spiritual heritage, highlighting ancient wisdom traditions and spiritual values. In contrast, Maritain's Integral Humanism is more influenced by Western Christian philosophy, drawing on principles of Thomistic thought and natural law. Upadhyay's Integral Humanism promotes the preservation and promotion of India's cultural identity and heritage; on the other hand, Maritain's Integral Humanism is Universalist, focusing on human dignity, rights, and the common good. Upadhyay's Integral Humanism advocates for decentralized governance and economic self-reliance, while Maritain's does not. Upadhyay critiques Western ideologies and models of development, arguing they are incompatible with India's cultural ethos, while Maritain reinterprets Western philosophical traditions in light of Christian principles. Upadhyay and Maritain both focus on social justice. The approaches of the two aim to promote human flourishing and address modernity's challenges but contrast with cultural foundations, nationalism vs. universalism, and critiques of Western development models.

The philosophy of Integral Humanism values and respects the inherent worth of every individual, regardless of factors like race, religion, nationality, or socioeconomic status. It addresses the needs of the whole person, including physical, emotional, intellectual, and spiritual, and upholds human development in all dimensions. It also brings attention to the interconnectedness of individuals within communities and the importance of promoting the common good, fostering conditions for individual flourishing, and reaching their full potential. It calls for the reconfiguration of traditional values with nationalism, democracy, socialism, and world peace to remove mutual conflicts and achieve life goals. It also calls for revitalizing ancient culture, removing traditions like untouchability that hinder progressive nation-building and threaten national unity.

The duo wanted to create a more humane system, a system that should reflect Chiti,[33] promoting sympathy, oneness, and affection towards one's brethren. We shall create a Bharat with the help of universal knowledge and our heritage, which will outshine its past glories and enable manifold immanent potentialities in every citizen to achieve a state higher than that of a complete human being, a state in which Nar (Man) becomes Narayan (God), which is the eternal and continuous divine form of our culture.[34]

Deendayal Upadhyay emphasizes the importance of introducing an educational system that fosters socially obliged and service-oriented generations, leading to an all-inclusive development of individuals, society, and nation. He believes that remedies from one country should not be applied to others and accentuate the eternal connection between humans and nature. In general, the concepts of Vedantic Humanism and Integral Humanism will be depicted in the Shanti Mantra that is:

> "Sarve bhavanthu sukhina
> Sarvesantu niramaya
> Sarve bhadrani pashyantu
> Maakaschit dukha bhaag bhavet."

The mantra implies, "May all be happy; may all be free from disabilities; may all look to the good of others; and may none suffer from sorrow."[35]

Endnotes

1 Silvan S. Tomkins, "Left and Right: A Basic Dimension of Ideology and Personality," ed. White RW. (New York: Atherton Press, 1963), pp. 391-392.

2 Artur Nilsson, "Humanism and Normativism facet scales and short scales," *Lund Psychological Reports,* vol. 15, no. 1 (January 1, 2015), p. 2. https://doi.org/10.13140/2.1.4324.9447.

3 Harold John Blackham. *Humanism*, (Penguin Press: 1968), p. 13.

4 S. Umadevi. "Humanism in Indian Philosophy – Contributions of Swami Vivekananda and Deendayal Upadhyay- an Analysis." *The Indian Journal of Political Science,* vol. 76, no. 3 (July-September 2015), p. 271. https://www.jstor.org/stable/26534828

5 Kanishk Kant, Misra, and Deepak Singh. *"Integral Humanism and the Modern World." 2020. Juni Khyat,* vol. 10 no. 2, p. 136. http://www.junikhyatjournal.in/no_1_jan_20/17.pdf.

6 S. B. P. Sinha. *Perspectives of Philosophy*, (Authors press, 2005), p. 209.

7 Jacques Maritain, Joseph W. Evans, and Leo R. Ward. *The Social and Political Philosophy of Jacques Maritain*, 1955, p. 85.

8 Quang Van Tran, "From Human Dignity to the Common Good: A Study of Jacques Maritain's Integral Humanism," 2022, p. abstraction. https://dlib.bc.edu/islandora/object/bc-ir:109444/datastream.

9 Ratnesh. "Pt Deen Dayal Upadhyay and Integral Humanism." My *Voice*, March 8, 2020. https://myvoice.opindia.com/2020/03/pt-deen-dayal-Upadhyaya-and-integral-humanism.

10 Vishwanath Prasad Varma. *The Political Philosophy of Mahatma Gandhi and Sarvodaya*. Internet Archive, 1959, p. 72.

11 Vasant Raj Pandit and Deendayal Research Institute, *INTEGRAL HUMANISM*, 2002, https://deendayalUpadhyay.org/images/book/Booklet%20on%20IntegralHumanism.pdf.

12 Ibid.

13 S. Umadevi. "Humanism in Indian Philosophy – Contributions of Swami Vivekananda and Deendayal Upadhyay- an Analysis." *The Indian Journal of Political Science,* vol. 76, no. 3 (July-September 2015), p. 273. https://www.jstor.org/stable/26534828

14 "Jacques Maritain (Stanford Encyclopedia of Philosophy)," May 1, 2019. https://plato.stanford.edu/entries/maritain/.

15 Jacques Maritain. *Integral Humanism: Temporal and Spiritual Problems of a New Christendom*. (New York: Scribner, 1968), pp. v-viii.

16 Ibid., pp. 91-92.

17 Quang Van Tran, "From Human Dignity to the Common Good: A Study of Jacques Maritain's Integral Humanism," 2022, p. abstraction. https://dlib.bc.edu/islandora/object/bc-ir:109444/datastream.

18 Jacques Maritain. "Men and Morals." *New Blackfriars*, vol. 19, no. 223 (October 1, 1938), pp. 720-721. http://www.jstor.org/stable/43811283.

19 Ibid., pp. 722-23.

20 Rocci Luppicini, *Technoethics and the Evolving Knowledge Society: Ethical Issues in Technological Design, Research, Development, and Innovation: Ethical Issues in Technological Design, Research, Development, and Innovation* (IGI Global, 2010), p. 48.

21 Gabor L. Hornyak, H.F. Tibbals, Joydeep Dutta, and John J. Moore. *Introduction to Nanoscience and Nanotechnology*. (CRC Press, 2008), p. 61.

22 Eli Ginzberg. *Technology and Social Change*. (The USA: Columbia University Press, 1964), p. 1.

23 Quang Van Tran, "From Human Dignity to the Common Good: A Study of Jacques Maritain's Integral Humanism," 2022, pp. 144-46. https://dlib.bc.edu/islandora/object/bc-ir:109444/datastream

24 S. Umadevi. "Humanism in Indian Philosophy – Contributions of Swami Vivekananda and Deendayal Upadhyay- an Analysis." *The Indian Journal of Political Science*, vol. 76, no. 3 (July-September 2015), p. 274. https://www.jstor.org/stable/26534828

25 Jacques Maritain. *Integral Humanism: Temporal and Spiritual Problems of a New Christendom*. (New York: Scribner, 1968), p. 89.

26 S. Umadevi. "Humanism in Indian Philosophy – Contributions of Swami Vivekananda and Deendayal Upadhyay- an Analysis." *The Indian Journal of Political Science,* vol. 76, no. 3 (July-September 2015), p. 271. https://www.jstor.org/stable/26534828

27 D. J. Hollenbach. "Social Ethics under the Sign of the Cross." *the Annual of the Society of Christian Ethics,* vol. 16, (January 1, 1996), pp. 3–18. https://doi.org/10.5840/asce1996162.

28 Ibid.,

29 Gabor L. Hornyak, H.F. Tibbals, Joydeep Dutta, and John J. Moore. *Introduction to Nanoscience and Nanotechnology.* (CRC Press, 2008), p. 61.

30 Kanishk Kant, Misra, and Deepak Singh. *"Integral Humanism and the Modern World." 2020. Juni Khyat,* vol. 10 no. 2, p. 137. http://www.junikhyatjournal.in/no_1_jan_20/17.pdf.

31 Mario Bunge. "Towards a Technoethics." *the Monist,* vol. 60, no. 1 (January 1, 1977). pp. 96–107. https://doi.org/10.5840/monist197760134.

32 Craig Hanks, *Technology and Values - Essential Readings with Philosophy of Technology SET* (United Kingdom: Wiley-Blackwell, 2010), pp. 99-113.

33 Chiti is a Nation's soul. The power that energizes and activates the Nation is called Virat, which in turn is aroused, organized, and canalized by Chiti. The place of Virat in the life of a Nation is similar to that of Prana in the body. Just as Prana infuses strength in various organs of the body, refreshes the intellect, and keeps body and soul together, so in a Nation with a strong Virat alone can democracy succeed and the government is effective. Then, the diversity of our Nation does not prove to be an obstacle to our national unity. The differences in language, occupation, etc., are present everywhere. However, when the Virat is awake, diversity does not lead to conflict, and people co-operate with one another like the various limbs of the human body or like the members of a family.

34 Vasant Raj Pandit and Deendayal Research Institute, *INTEGRAL HUMANISM*, 2002, https://deendayalupadhyay.org/images/book/Booklet%20on%20IntegralHumanism.pdf.

35. S. Umadevi. "Humanism in Indian Philosophy – Contributions of Swami Vivekananda and Deendayal Upadhyay- an Analysis." *The Indian Journal of Political Science,* vol. 76, no. 3 (July-September 2015), p. 276. https://www.jstor.org/stable/26534828

Political Aspects of Integral Humanism

Chapter Thirteen

Ekatma Manav Darshan: Conceptualising an Alternative Paradigm of Sovereignty

Yashowardhan Tiwari

Sovereignty and its contours play a central role in defining the relations between the nation-state and its citizens. It also gives a certain structure and direction to social relations and affects the trajectory of a nation. The quest for defining, explaining, and attempting to widen or restrain the powers associated with sovereignty seems to be both a perpetual and an unsolvable one. The conceptions of morality, be it private, public, or constitutional, have also been intricately connected with the wielding of sovereign powers. India emerged as a modern nation-state post-Independence, and so the question of sovereignty was bound to capture the imagination of political thinkers and leaders of our fledgling nation-state. The modern nation-state and its position as the sovereign were a new phenomenon for India, and so political actors attempted to grapple with it in a variety of ways. One such response from the Indian political scenario emerged in the form of Pandit Deendayal Upadhyay's *Ekatma Manav Darshan*, a political philosophy broadly sketched as a civilizationally-rooted response to the question of sovereignty. It was also a political-spiritual programme to be followed by the Bharatiya Jana Sangh and, through it, by the Indian society at large. According to Deendayal Upadhyay, India, that is Bharat, was capable of coming up with an indigenous response to the largely imposed Western notions of sovereignty and was thus consequently equally capable of chalking out a different path for the evolution of its nation-state. The path carved out by Deendayal was that of Dharma. He realized that the problem with the modern Indian nation-state was not just that it was based on a Western framework, but also that it was totally sapped out of any Dharmic moorings. Deendayal had a brilliant solution to this national crisis—he placed Dharma at the position of the sovereign, thus ensuring its percolation throughout the institutional framework of the nation and the state. Dharma, in his political philosophy, which closely resembled the essence of Indic civilizational ethos, was placed at this exalted position as an assurance of a future Bhartiya nation-state exuding the Dharmic ethos. This paper tries to put into focus this crucial aspect of *Ekatma Manav Darshan* as the core idea of Pandit Deendayal Upadhyay's vision of Bharat as a nation-state. It also attempts to argue that this radical departure made by Deendayal from the prevalent Western notions of sovereignty offers immense potential to develop an ethical, culturally-rooted framework of a nation-state. It has the possibility of establishing a statehood model that is aware of, and is positively responsive to the Indic civilizational ethos, and perseveres towards actively working for social inclusion of the marginalized sections of society. Dharma as the sovereign does not reduce the state to a dry welfare model. It furthers the overall economic and spiritual upliftment of the entire society in an integrated manner and works towards providing the marginalized sections with a dignified life. In the Dharmic vision, dignity of an individual cannot be guaranteed without one's spiritual upliftment. Dharma, catapulted to the apex of the nation-state institutional hierarchy, takes up the mantle of being the guiding light for the economic, social, cultural, and spiritual upliftment of the masses.

Sovereignty in the Western Political Traditions

Sovereignty has been a constantly transforming yet consistent theme in the language of Western/Eurocentric political traditions. With the advent of modernity, Western intellectual thought has been preoccupied with the concept. It could even be argued that the laying out of sovereignty as a well-defined concept was one of the foundational moments of the advent of modernity. The centrality of sovereignty to Western political thought has been explained as such:

> "Ever since Bodin and Hobbes, the concept of sovereignty has been a foundational, a worldview-conceiving political concept. What makes it thus, is its bonding capacity. This concept creates an inside and an outside, it encompasses political ideas of order, toward the inside (security, peace, hierarchy) and outside (equality of states, prohibition on intervention, etc.), it drafts assumptions about the essence of law (commando theory of law), the basic configuration of public power, and relates all these ideas to each other. Due to its extraordinary status, many thinkers have discussed anew the concept, as a result of historic turning points such as the French revolution or the two world wars, and have tried to reconcile it with the situation that arose."[1]

Sovereignty needs to be understood as a "quintessentially political concept"[2] that governs socio-legal relations between the state and its subjects. It has to be understood as a "representation of the autonomy of the political, and as providing the foundational concept of the discipline of public law"[3]. Martin Loughlin has argued that:

> "Sovereignty has been devised for the purpose of giving expression to the distinctively political bond between a group of people and its mode of governance. Sovereignty comes into existence through a process in which a group of people within a defined territory is molded into an orderly cohesion through the establishment of a governing authority that can be differentiated from society and which is able to exercise an absolute political power. This concept of sovereignty is bound up with the emergence of the modern state and the establishment of an institutionalized form of government which is able to impose itself on a society as an instrument of power. And the principal method by which this sovereign is expressed is through the medium of the law. Sovereignty and law are inextricably linked."[4]

As part of laying out his ten tenets of sovereignty, the first tenet that Martin formulates is that "sovereignty is a facet of the modern state"[5]. The construction of the sovereign as a through and through modern project was realized in stages:

> "Royalty was first obliged to acquire the *plenitudo potestatis,* the supreme power, and this necessitated the destruction of all authorities that sought to challenge the power of the royal will. By breaking the political power of the feudal magnates, an internal coherence of governing authority was established. It might be noted here that the situation in England was unusual since, after the conquest, Norman statecraft ensured that, although the chief barons

became major landlords, they did not assume the tasks of government; the conditions thus favoured the growth of a unified and highly centralized polity. Elsewhere in western Europe, the struggle was longer drawn...An especially important aspect of achieving these modernizing objectives was the deployment of law as an instrument of royal power... The project of forging a modern state required the promotion of a conception of law as an instrument of command. For this purpose, jurists drew heavily on such Roman law maxims as *quod principi placuit legis habet vigorem* (what pleases the prince has the force of law), which provided the intellectual force of such contemporary expressions as *si veut le roi, si veut la loi; car tel est notre plaisir* (what the king wills, the law wills; for such is our pleasure) ... Sovereignty thus emerged as an aspect of the formation of the modern state. Michael Oakeshott has indicated that the modern state was a 'free' or 'sovereign' association in respect of three main characteristics: first, because its government was 'not subject to any superior external authority'; secondly, 'in virtue of being an association in terms of law'; and thirdly, because its government possessed 'the authority and the procedures to emancipate itself continuously from its legal past', in the sense that 'there was no law so ancient and so entrenched that it could not be amended or repealed'. Put slightly differently, it might be said that sovereignty gives expression to three basic features of the modern state: inherent coherence, external independence, and supremacy of the law."[6]

It is clearly established that not only did sovereignty come into being as a political concept intrinsically tied with the modern state, but that it was meant to be a central aspect of the modern state's nature of existence throughout the period of its conceptual evolution. In such a situation, it is very difficult to imagine its existence independent of the modern state. It is also difficult to conceptualize any other form of sovereignty where the sovereign powers are not vested in the state itself, that too in a centralized manner, and instead the powers are shifted and handed over to an altogether different authority or institution. To put it bluntly, it is clearly very difficult to imagine the manifestation of sovereignty outside the structure of the modern state. One could possibly state that with the rise of electoral democracies and constitutional regimes, sovereignty has moved out of its conventional positions and has helped set up new hierarchies in national political structures around the world. For instance, sovereign powers are seen to be vested in the constitutional text itself in the case of some constitutional democracies. However, this statement would have to factor in the point that electoral democracies and/or constitutional regimes also ultimately function within the political structures associated with the modern state. Democratic constitutional regimes do pose a challenge to the idea of sovereign powers conventionally operating within the state structures, as they claim that sovereignty ultimately resides with the people. It is the citizens of such regimes who are the ultimate holders, keepers, and prime beneficiaries of sovereign powers. But on a close examination of the functioning of such regimes, one realises that it is again through the state structures that the citizens choose to express and wield their sovereign powers. The constitutions also govern such states in the name of the people, and it is the people to which the allegiance of these documents lies. Constitutions derive their legitimacy from the people, as they are presented as texts that have been prepared for the governance of the people by the people themselves. As it has been described:

"A central feature of this new era of government was the establishment of the altogether novel idea of the constitution. Political constitutions were no longer to be conceived as some ideal expression of a nation's culture, manners, and traditional forms of rule. A constitution in the modern sense was to be a document drafted in the name of the people to establish and regulate the powers of the main institutions of government, to specify the relationship between government and citizen, and to take effect as fundamental law.

Since the late eighteenth century, these documentary constitutions have been adopted throughout the world at critical moments in a nation's history. During the twentieth century, a lingering conservative distrust of 'paper constitutions' and mere constitutional machinery gave way to a general acceptance of the need to draft constitutions that fixed the basic terms of a nation's political compact. And in the last 30 years or so, the distrust many on the left had often exhibited about the way written constitutions might be used to halt the continuing social revolution has apparently waned. The claim that constitutions specify the authoritative ground rules of politics is today more widely accepted than at any other point in modern political history. Whether the matter involves an assertion of a nation's right to self-determination, a challenge to the legitimacy of an exercise of governing power, a plea to be treated with equal dignity and respect, or even a basic struggle for justice in distribution, the political demand is now invariably cast in the form of a constitutional claim. In this sense, we live today in a constitutional age."[7]

When the people tend to use methods beyond the domain of the constitution, they are either suppressed or negotiated with in the name of the constitution, or there is a complete overthrow of the constitutional regime. During the period when the regime is being overthrown, the people are seen exercising their sovereign powers directly in the form of a revolutionary movement, but it presents a peculiar situation as the people are at odds with the regime and so sovereignty does not rest with either of them. When the dust settles down, a new regime might come up again in the name of the people. The period of transition from one regime to another is surely a period of crisis with no proper location of sovereignty. Then one may note that sovereignty remains tied with the state structures even in such situations, and it has been an uphill task (often resulting in failure) to replace or dislocate sovereignty from its bonds and association with the modern state. A realization of the gravity of this statement is necessary to understand the all-powerful nature of the modern state and the problems resulting from it. The modern state has often functioned in an oppressive manner against its own people and has unleashed its brute force against the masses. The modern state creates a peculiar problem because the oppression that is meted out by the state functionaries or structures is also done with the assistance of its sovereign powers and in the name of the people. Oppression, marginalization and social exclusion faced by various pockets of society due to state actions go against the grain of such political structures, which are meant to represent and ensure the social well-being of people. Here arises a need to put restraints on the modern state's sovereign powers and limit its authority over the lives of its subjects. It becomes crucial here to explore the possibility of conducting a radical re-assessment of sovereignty and divesting the modern nation-state of its all-powerful position and authority as the sovereign. Pandit Deendayal Upadhyay's political philosophy of *Ekatma Manav Darshan* presents itself as a significant alternative to the Western political traditions. Its relevance is immediate in the contemporary era as an indigenous alternative to be seriously considered for the better future of Bharat's polity.

Dharma as Deendayal Upadhyay's Sovereign

Pandit Deendayal Upadhyay conceptualizes a theory of sovereignty that would sound too radical to Western political thought. He essentially divests the state of its status as the locus of sovereignty and strips it off its sovereign powers. Dharma emerges as the new manifestation of sovereignty, and locating a central site of the sovereign becomes a futile exercise. The sovereign powers get decentralized, yet they have an ever-lingering, overarching presence throughout the nation and its constituents. What is more, the sovereign no longer appears as an all-powerful alien entity attempting to dominate the people under its tutelage. Rather, it emerges as a consciousness shared by Bharat and its people and is in apt synchronization with Bhartiya culture and civilization.

Pandit Deendayal Upadhyay considers the state to be just one of the several institutions created for the smooth working of the society. He imagines society as a nation with a soul, which he refers to as 'Chiti' and regards the state as a structure created in service of the nation's needs and requirements. He explains Chiti as follows:

> "A human being is born with a soul. Human personality, soul, and character are all distinct from one another. Personality results from a cumulative effect of all the actions, thoughts, and impressions of an individual. But the soul is unaffected by this history. Similarly, national culture is continuously

modified and enlarged by the historic reasons and circumstances. Culture does include all those things which, by association, endeavors, and the history of the society, have come to be held as good and commendable, but these are not added on to Chiti. Chiti is fundamental and is central to the nation from its very beginning. Chiti determines the direction in which the nation is to advance culturally. Whatever is in accordance with Chiti is included in culture."[8]

The state, for Deendayal, cannot be the end goal of any society's evolution. He also does not pitch an argument for the need of a stateless society. The state, according to him, is meant to be just one of the many wheels that keep running a society. In a sense, he moves away from the Western political theories, which portray the nation and the state as intricately connected and inseparable. He reconfigures the idea of the modern nation-state by separating the two entities, and also inducing a hierarchy and keeping the nation above the state. The state is meant to be one of the limbs of the nation and is given a limited role in national life. He states that:

"The state is one of the several institutions, an important one, but it is not above all others. One of the major reasons for the problems of the present-day world is that almost everyone thinks of the state as synonymous with society. At least in practice, they consider the state as the sole representative of society. Other institutions have declined in their effectiveness while the state has become dominant to such an extent that all the powers are gradually being centralized in the state. We had not considered the state to be the sole representative of the nation. Our national life continued uninterrupted even after the state went into the hands of foreigners.

> The Persian nation came to an end with their loss of independence. In our country, there were foreign rulers now and then in various parts of the country. At some point, the Pathans seized the throne of Delhi, and then the Turks, the Mughals, and the British too established their rule. Despite all this, our national life went on, because the state was not its center. If we had considered the state as the center, we would have been finished as a nation long time ago. In some tales for children, it is described that an evil spirit resided in some parrot, and to kill the evil spirit, one had to kill that parrot. Those nations whose lives centered in the state were finished with the end of the state. On the other hand, where the state was not believed central to its life, the nation survived despite the transfer of political power."[9]

A direct question that arises from Deendayal's analysis is that if the state no longer occupies the central position in the nation and is just one of the several structures created by the nation, then who shall be handed over the task of leading the nation as an overarching sovereign? To answer this, Deendayal first explains how the state is meant to be subject to Dharma:

> "Thus, the fundamental law of human nature is the standard for deciding the propriety of behavior in various situations. We have termed this very law as 'Dharma'. The nearest equivalent English term for Dharma can be 'Innate law', which, however, does not express the full meaning of Dharma. Since 'Dharma' is supreme, our ideal of the State has been 'Dharma Rajya'. The king is supposed to protect Dharma. In olden times at the coronation ceremony the king used to recite three times — "There is no authority which can punish me." (Similar claim

> was made by kings in the western countries, i.e., it was said, "King can do no wrong", and hence there too, nobody could punish the king). Upon this, the Purohit used to strike the king on his back with a staff saying, "No, you are subject to the rule of Dharma. You are not sovereign." The king used to run around the sacred fire and the Purohit would follow him striking him with the staff. Thus, after completing three rounds, the ceremony would come to an end. Thereby the king was unambiguously told that he was not an unpunishable sovereign. Dharma was above him. That is, even he was subject to Dharma. Can the people do whatever they please? It may be contended that democracy means just that. The people can do what they please. But in our country, they are not free to act contrary to Dharma."[10]

Pandit Deendayal Upadhyay then moves on to theorize his idea of an indigenous, Indic notion of sovereignty:

> "In a Dharma Rajya, the state is not absolutely powerful. It is subject to Dharma. We have always vested sovereignty in Dharma. Presently there has arisen a controversy. Whether the Parliament is sovereign or the Supreme Court, and whether the Legislature is higher or the Judiciary. This is like a quarrel as to whether left hand is more important or right hand? Both are the limbs of the state, the Legislature as well as the Judiciary. Both have distinct functions to perform. In their individual sphere each is supreme. To consider either one above the other would be a mistake. Yet the legislators say, "We are higher." On the other hand, members of the Judiciary assert that they have a higher authority, since they interpret the laws which the Legislature makes. The

> Legislature claims to have given the powers to the Judiciary. If necessary, Legislature can change the Constitution. Hence it claims sovereignty. Now since powers are bestowed by the Constitution, they are talking of amendments to the Constitution. But I believe that even if by a majority the Constitution is amended, it will be against Dharma. In reality, both the Legislature and the Judiciary are on an equal plane. Neither the Legislature is higher nor the Judiciary. Dharma is higher than both. The Legislature will have to act according to Dharma and the Judiciary too will have to act according to Dharma. Dharma will specify the limits of both. The Legislature, the Judiciary or the people, none of these is supreme."

Further, Deendayal Upadhyay proceeds to define democracy in accordance with Dharma:

> "Let us understand very clearly that Dharma is not necessarily with the majority or with the people. Dharma is eternal. Therefore, it is not enough to say, while defining democracy, that it is the government of the people. It has to be a government for the good of the people. What constitutes the good of the people? It is Dharma alone which can decide. Therefore, a democratic government Jana Rajya, must also be rooted in Dharma, i.e., a Dharma Rajya. In the definition of Democracy viz. "government of the people, by the people and for the people", 'of' stands for independence, 'by' stands for democracy, and 'for' indicates Dharma. Therefore, the true democracy is only where there is freedom as well as Dharma. Dharma Rajya encompasses all these concepts."[11]

Pandit Deendayal Upadhyay's proposal to acknowledge Dharma as the sovereign clearly emerges as an alternative paradigm wherein the hierarchy of state as the ultimate power exercising authority is subordinated. It restrains and governs the powers of the state in accordance with Dharma. It presents a model similar to a constitutional democracy, drifting away from it in the sense that instead of the presence of a constitutional text as the primary governing authority, it's the cultural ethos of Bharatiya civilization embodied in the idea of Dharma that becomes the chief governing authority.

Dharma as the manifestation of sovereignty also introduces a radical shift in our imagination of the human rights discourse. The Western discourse of human rights essentially puts the onus of claiming an availability of rights on the individuals, as opposed to which Dharma directs the creation of a responsible state as well as responsible citizens. The state is duty-bound to make human rights available to all the citizens, and simultaneously the citizens also owe duties towards the state and the society at large. Dharma also facilitates the emergence of an Indic human rights discourse that would be culturally informed. Another crucial consequence of imagining Dharma as the sovereign is the decentralization of power, meaning that the state no longer serves as the sole locus of power, and that power gets diffused among the various stakeholders within and outside the parameters of the state's framework. Pandit Deendayal Upadhyay's ideation provides us potential inroads into theorizing an indigenous paradigm of sovereignty, with serious implications for the Western construct of a modern state and its relations with the common citizenry.

Dharma, Dignity, and Social Inclusion

Pandit Deendayal Upadhyay labours to chalk out a coherent economic programme on the basis of his idea of Dharma as the sovereign as a part of *Ekatma Manav Darshan*. His philosophy of Antyodaya, which surely builds upon Mahatma Gandhi's philosophy of Sarvodaya, is a direct product of his worldview with Dharma as the sovereign. He perceives all social welfare, inclusion, and upliftment programmes from the lens of Dharma, and makes a case for education for all, free medical treatment, and a guarantee of work.[12] His philosophy seeks to prepare an integral whole at both the individual and societal levels. He lays down the following objectives for Bhartiya economy to realize social upliftment and cultural rootedness: "an assurance of minimum standard of living to every individual and preparedness for the defence of the nation"; "further increase above this minimum standard of living whereby the individual and the nation acquires the means to contribute to the world progress on the basis of its own Chiti"; "to provide meaningful employment to every able bodied citizen, by which the above two objectives can be realized and to avoid waste and extravagance in utilizing natural resources"; "to develop machines suited to Bhartiya conditions (Bhartiya Technology), taking note of the availability and nature of the various factors of production (Seven M's of Vishveshvaraya)"; "this system must help, and not disregard the human being, the individual. It must protect the cultural and other values of life. This is a requirement which cannot be violated except at a risk of great peril"; "the ownership, state, private, or any other form, of various industries must be added on a pragmatic and practical basis."[13]

Deendayal Upadhyay's lectures on *Ekatma Manav Darshan* should not be seen as merely outlining a political philosophy. His theory of Integral Humanism should be treated as laying down a roadmap for the future of Bharat. His political philosophy develops a framework rooted in the indigenous concept of Dharma, thus giving us an indigenous theory for political praxis and institutional organization. It also paves the way for social inclusion of the oppressed and the marginalized, whose exclusion revolts against the core tenets of Dharmic ethos. The future of Bharat in accordance with his philosophy shall be a future shaped in accordance with Dharma, because Dharma is meant to be the guiding light for all the people as well as social and political institutions. Deendayal opens an arena for the exploration of how Bharat can be shaped as a civilizational state. He also ensures that Dharma as the sovereign shall look out for those who have been the downtrodden people of Bharat. Their treatment as per Dharma, and the evolution of their individual souls seeped in Dharmic ideas shall restore their dignity. Overall social, cultural, and spiritual well-being of the people, wearing their civilizational identities on their sleeves, and leading a Dharmic life is what would make the lives of people dignified. What constitutes Dharma, eventually, shall have to be deliberated upon by the people of Bharat, informed by the cultural traditions of the land.

Conclusion

Pandit Deendayal Upadhyay, a theorist and political philosopher par excellence, carves out a niche to be explored further on the subject of statehood and sovereignty. His argument of Dharma, instead of the modern nation-state, being the sovereign has a resonance with Indic civilizational ethos. It is a radical departure from Western conceptions of sovereignty, and promises to be a great subject for further deliberation. Dharma as the manifestation of the sovereign could be seen as a possible remedy to the problem of the modern nation-state as an oppressive institution. Dharma ought to be adhered to by all the societal institutions and state structures, which would develop and uplift the lives of all the citizens, especially the downtrodden, for the realization of Antyodaya.

Endnotes

1 Christian Volk, 'The Problem of Sovereignty in Globalized Times', *Law, Culture and Humanities*, 2019, p. 2, accessed at https://journals.sagepub.com/doi/pdf/10.1177/1743872119828010.

2 Martin Loughlin, "Ten Tenets of Sovereignty", in Neil Walker (ed.), *Sovereignty in Transition* (Oxford: Bloomsbury, 2006), p. 56.

3 *Id.*

4 *Ibid*, pp. 56-7.

5 *Id*, p. 57.

6 *Ibid*, pp. 58-9.

7 Martin Loughlin, 'The Constitutional Imagination', *The Modern Law Review*, vol. 78, no. 1, 2015, p. 2.

8 Pandit Deendayal Upadhyay, *Integral Humanism*, (5th edn., Noida, Jagriti Prakashan, 1992), p. 41.

9 *Ibid*, p. 47.

10 *Ibid*, pp. 54-5.

11 *Ibid*, p. 60.

12 *Ibid*, pp. 68-9.

13 *Ibid*, p. 77.

Chapter Fourteen

Effects of Deendayal Upadhyay's Thought on Modi's Governance

Nidhi Singh

The life of Deendayal Upadhyay was committed to the cause of the country and the people. He was a deep thinker, an ardent orator, a kind man, and a fervent patriot. Deendayal Upadhyay was born on September 25, 1916. He lost his father, Bhagwati Prasad, when he was less than three years old, and his mother before he was eight. He was then brought up by his maternal uncle. He won several prizes and scholarships. At Sanatan Dharma College in Kanpur, he joined the Rashtriya Swayamsevak Sangh (R.S.S.). He had the necessary credentials to be a teacher, but he had little interest in the field. From 1942 on, he committed himself to working full time in the RSS. In 1951, the Bhartiya Jana Sangh was created by Syama Prasad Mookerjee, and Deendayal was named as its first general secretary for the state of Uttar Pradesh. Deendayal's knowledge and attention to detail greatly pleased Dr. Syama Prasad Mookerjee, who made the well-known comment, "If I had two Deendayals, I could transform the political face of India.[1]"

Deendayal Upadhyay incessantly emphasised on the positive aspects of Indian culture, such as its spirit of nationalism, patriotism, spirituality, humanism, and universalism. He refused to suggest western ideas and foreign ideologies as solutions to the nation's many issues. He was a thinker and an activist, an idealist and a realist, a visionary and a hawk, who had given his theory of Integral Humanism to suit the condition of his own country[2]. He had the wisdom and ability to recognise the threat posed by the nation's enemies and traitors. Thus, he was not kidding when he said that the country needed a strong leader like Chandragupta Maurya and Chanakya, who defended India's political and territorial sovereignty by standing up to external and internal influences. He advocated for a system of administration that would help the country achieve self-sufficiency, instill in its citizens a sense of patriotism and nationalism, and elevate it in the eyes of the international community. He asserted that Indian civilizational values, culture, and philosophy, not Western "isms" like Socialism, Communism, Marxism, Liberalism, etc., could provide solutions to this country's problems at a time when many leaders of his time were looking to the West and trying to understand what the West stood for and what could be taken from the Western ideas for India.

Socio-Political Ideas

Upadhyay advocated for a decentralised government that would allow each person to implement their ideas for significant change, as an alternative to absolutism[3]. Integral Humanism's major range is the synthesis of the material and the spiritual, such as the combination of both an individual and a group. His well-known remarks have helped people comprehend and witness the "Oneness" of thought and action.

According to Upadhyay, the concept of integration can be observed and understood in a variety of contexts, from planetary orbit to metamorphosis. He promoted self-reliance in the economy and the idea that the village should be the primary factor in all government activities. Although he has nothing against modern technology, he believes that it should be applied to the needs of India, especially for the wellbeing of all Indians.

Following John Locke's philosophy, he firmly dispersed the notion of opposing the government anytime it acts against public interest. National interest should take precedence over all of the people's interests, and is a sign of both individual and societal consciousness. He said that one should weigh one's conscience. Upadhyay's concept of Integral Humanism is regarded as the Jana Sangh's political and economic platform. Yet it is a scheme for the general emancipation of society.[4]

He has articulated Adam Smith's "laissez faire" as greater governance and less government. According to him, measuring government by quantity may not be appropriate; only quality will do. He promoted competition with decentralised governance when discussing federalism.

His beliefs in Bharatiyata, Dharma, Rama Rajya, and Antyodaya shall always be true in making Bharat Vishwa Guru[5]. He provided us with the blueprint for independence in a democratic economic system with his "Education for Everyone" and "*Har Hath Ko Kam, Har Khet Ko Paani*" visions. Deendayal Upadhyay argued against a system that limits employment opportunities and in favour of a society that is free of social inequality and is decentralised in terms of both authority and wealth. Sadly, as a nation, we never attempted to look for the answers to our issues and difficulties in his vision, based on Indian culture providing freedom, equality, and justice to everyone.[6]

What Drives the BJP to Support Upadhyay?

The two arguments given by the BJP and government to support Upadhyay's deification are as follows. First, it is asserted that Upadhyay lived a humble life and shunned flamboyance, in contrast to other notable BJP leaders like Mookerjee and Atal Bihari Vajpayee. Second, Upadhyay is exalted for having experimented with a new political philosophy and an alternative economic perspective. Although for the administration led by a prime minister known for his sartorial sense, including the much-discussed pinstripe suit with his name woven into the fabric, choosing to emphasize the simplicity of the man opens it up to criticism and accusations of double standards. But more importantly, it is important to assess his originality, profundity, and ongoing significance.

Deendayal Upadhyay's Integral Humanism is the term used to describe the philosophical concepts that the Jan Sangh leader advocated in the early 1960s. Conceptual boundaries of integral Humanism have their roots in the old Indian cultural ethos and heritage. The fundamental tenets of Indian civilization and Dharma shaped the philosophical underpinnings of integral humanism. Upadhyay has effectively dismantled the social and political doctrines of capitalism and communism by highlighting their innate contempt for the humanitarian aspects of personal existence and their unwarranted focus on the financial side. Thus, the core tenet of integral humanism is the unity of the individual, the community, the universe, and the supreme authority. According to Upadhyay, every country has a fundamental notion that has cultural and societal significance.

The ideas of Deendayal Upadhyay are still relevant now and will always remain. In the 1965 Indo-Pak war, India was forced to rely on the arms of other countries. At that time, he had stated that we needed to create an India that was self-sufficient not just in agriculture but also in defence and armament. According to Prime Minister Modi, who was speaking at Samarpan Diwas on the occasion of the death anniversary of Deendayal Upadhyay, "the self-reliant India" campaign is now being used to help the poor, farmers, labourers, and middle class in villages to build their future. He also noted that Deendayal Upadhyay's vision for the local economy was evidence of how useful and all-encompassing his ideas were even at the time. Today, the nation is achieving his ambition thanks to the motto "Voice for Local," he remarked.

The nation demonstrated the Antyodaya spirit and compassion towards the impoverished during the Covid-19 era. The nation has used the force of self-reliance to spread medicines over the globe, demonstrating the validity of the Integral Humanism Philosophy. He added that the life-improving reforms occurring in the infrastructure sector will give India a new, modern image, and that every Indian will be proud of the India of today as the country's stature is fast increasing.

Yogi Adityanath, the Chief Minister of Uttar Pradesh, claimed that Deendayal Upadhyay's vision for the welfare and advancement of those in the lowest social strata is being fulfilled by the BJP's double-engine government, which is being headed by Prime Minister Narendra Modi. Adityanath claimed that the BJP's "Seva Hi Sangathan" campaign, which suggests that selfless service to one's country and people is the highest value, was inspired by great thinkers like Deendayal Upadhyay. Political parties are unable to care about the welfare of people in the absence of such thinking, and this realisation among the political class inspires confidence in the nation's population.

In addition to having his name associated with numerous plans and initiatives, his collected works are also being distributed to government-run schools in the states where the BJP is in control. Many public institutions, government programmes, and most recently a railroad station, have been renamed ever since the BJP came to power, such as Mughalsarai Junction has been renamed to Deendayal Upadhyay Junction. In addition to the aforementioned, he has numerous hospitals, colleges, and NGOs named after him. The Deendayal Upadhyay Antyodaya Yojana, a comprehensive programme of the central government, aims to provide chances for livelihood for the disadvantaged in urban and rural areas through skill development and other ways.

He was also a strong supporter of organic farming, being aware that natural farming will not only boost farmers' incomes but also make agriculture more robust and sustainable. He said that the cornerstone of India's economic strategy should be swadeshi and small-scale industries, which should be characterised by harmony, the priority of cultural and national values, and discipline. Although he was not opposed to accepting technologies from around the world, he wanted to make the items we needed right here in India so that our reliance on other nations would be kept to a minimum.[7]

Inconsistencies Between Upadhyay's Viewpoint and Modi's Strategy

Upadhyay, like M.S. Golwalkar, did not think that democracy was the best form of government; rather, he believed that it was the "least evil" option. He believed that India's federal structure was inappropriate and that a centralised government would be more suitable. Nevertheless, Upadhyay failed to explain how a "unitary constitution" would "decentralise our budgetary and other resources."

"The Two Plans: Promises, Performance and Prospects" from 1958 and "Integral Humanism" from 1965 are

Upadhyay's two most famous works. Among the two, the BJP has put greater emphasis on the latter. Although there are currently a number of dissonances between it and the party's prevailing culture, it has served for more than 50 years as the Jana Sangh and BJP's official philosophy. The earliest attempt to define Hindu political ideology after independence was "Integral Humanism." Upadhyay rejected the idea that India is a pluralistic country, and asserted that the country has a "chiti"-based soul. Chiti determines the course of the nation's cultural development. He said "Everything that is in line with Chiti is a part of culture". Together with chiti, Upadhyay advanced the idea of "virat", or the force that gives the country energy.

Between Upadhyay's philosophy and Modi's approach to development and administration, there are numerous inconsistencies. For instance, the long-deceased leader believed that it was "wrong to accept industrialization as our ultimate objective" and did not view huge dams as "temples of modern India." Also, he opposed modernity, mechanisation, and government initiatives to boost the economy. He had romantic affections for an ideal India where man and machine worked at slower speeds and did not share Nehru's excitement for modernising the Indian economy. Upadhyay, a proponent of independent business, asserted that "large-scale industrialization undermines individual entrepreneurship," implying that the scope of his vision was limited to small-scale companies.[8]

Effect of Deendayal's Ideology on the NDA's Foriegn Policy

In addition to domestic issues, Deendayal Upadhyay was very concerned about India's foreign policy. His goal was to give India's foreign policy a solid ideological foundation. He also argued that India's rich cultural and spiritual values should be promoted abroad. His writings and talks revealed an unfamiliar 'India-centric' policy that prioritised the 'India-First' strategy. In order to advance the nation's security and prosperity, he urged "adopting an alternative foreign strategy to that of Russia, America, or China."

It should be noted that the current NDA government, led by Prime Minister Modi, gave Pt. Upadhyay's recommendations for foreign policy wings for the first time. Since 2014, the principles for which Pt. Upadhyay stood are being translated and put into practise through extensive policy initiatives and programmes referred to as "Soft power diplomacy." This soft power diplomacy tries to highlight India's democratic ethos and credentials while also promoting India's cultural and spiritual values, which include promoting yoga and Buddhism, and reuniting with Indian diasporas around the world. As a result, India's "India-Centric" and "India-first" policy has been a defining feature of its soft power diplomacy in recent years, and the government has been working hard to promote it.

The Bharatiya Janata Party's stance on India's relationship with China aligns with Deendayal Upadhyay's views on foreign policy by emphasizing Bharat's cultural and civilizational values, engaging in greater dialogue, promoting shared prosperity, ensuring regional and global security, and strengthening cultural and civilizational linkages with countries around the world. The BJP's approach to India's relationship with China reflects its ideological moorings and Prime Minister Modi's unique political credibility, balancing strategic interests with economic considerations.

Sushma Swaraj, former minister of external affairs for India, made the observation at a talk that "integral humanism" must be leveraged by New Delhi through its foreign policy to expand its cultural footprint in other countries of the world."

She quoted Deendayal Upadhyay and said, "Maintaining a national culture could lead to economic and political progress as well as promote respect for our country in the international community". Deendayal Upadhyay acknowledged the soft power of culture. According to Upadhyay, understanding India's spirit requires viewing it through the lens of culture rather than politics or the economy. In a similar manner Upadhyay has been also praised as a "philosopher-politician" who had foreseen the influence of culture on India's international relations. Deendayal Upadhyay was a politician and philosopher in early independent India. He was an advocate of integrated humanism and saw the importance of cultural relationships in creating strong diplomatic, geopolitical, and economic ties between nations.

According to him, India's cultural and spiritual power, which makes up its soul, is its true strength. Its authority should be reflected in every element of national life, including international relations. So, it was the stated goal of the foreign policy to promote the positive attributes and ideals of this nation abroad. He firmly thought that both modern India's scientific temperament and its spiritual-cultural values should be given a key role in the country's foreign policy if India was to hold a place of pride and preeminence in the world. As only then could India's cultural and spiritual magnificence be known to the rest of the world, Upadhyay was dedicated to witnessing the growth of India's cultural footprints in distant lands.

Even though he died more than 50 years ago, the nationalist philosophy and its influence on Indian foreign policy are still quite apparent today. His opinions on a wide range of foreign policy topics clearly demonstrate his nationalistic enthusiasm. His critical comments and insights on the pressing challenges of his time are just as pertinent today as they were back then.

For instance, his repeated warnings to the Nehru administration about the dangers posed by Pakistan and China continue to serve as a caution to the current administration. Even more than fifty years after his passing, his conviction that India's attempts to win China over to its side through diplomatic and political means would result in the de-hyphenation of Pakistan-China relations and decrease the Pakistani threat to India remains uncomfortably accurate. When it comes to China and Pakistan, the NDA administrations' foreign policies—during the Vajpayee administration (March 1998–May 2004) and the Modi administration since 2014—have typically been on high alert.[9]

Conclusion

As a prominent leader of the Jana Sangh, Upadhyay worked tirelessly to promote cultural nationalism and Hindu unity while also advocating for social justice and economic self-reliance. He was known for his organizational skills and played a crucial role in building the party's grassroots support base. In many ways, Deendayal Upadhyay's revitalization of an indigenous philosophy that was superior to the established order of things was groundbreaking. The Indian government launched the Deendayal Upadhyay Gramin Kaushalya Yojana as a result of his efforts to find local solutions to local problems and emphasise natural methods of doing things where resources for skill development have been made available to the nation's rural children. Such government policies and programmes are in line with integral humanism since they aim to improve the individual as a whole and add value to his life by creating an ecosystem for learning and personal growth. The political philosophy of Deendayal Upadhyay has come to life under the JAM (Jan dhan, Aadhar, and Mobile) trinity, as evidenced by the massive scaling up of financial inclusion for the socially and economically disadvantaged that has taken place in recent years.

A strong nation and a healthy society require a minimal level of probity in everyday life. Without probity, no society is capable of providing for its citizens. The people must be trustworthy, and this must be frequently observed. Honesty cannot be a prized possession. The ideals of Deendayal Upadhyay were lived by him. The degree of integrity in his life is of immense importance to the BJP workers and everyone who read about him.

Endnotes

1 Upadhyay, Deendayal. *Integral humanism*. Bharatiya Janata Party, 1965.

2 Upadhyay, Deendayal. *Integral humanism*. Bharatiya Janata Party, 1965.

3 Raj, Roop. "Socio-Economic Thought of Pandit Deen Dayal Upadhyay." *International Journal of Research in Social Sciences* 11, no. 06 (2021).

4 Deb, Pranay. "Exploring Different Facets of Integral Humanism of Pandit Deen Dayal Upadhyay." *AMBEDKAR COLLEGE*: 34.

5 Yadav, Bhupender, and Ila Patnaik. *The Rise of the BJP: The Making of the World's Largest Political Party*. Penguin Random House India Private Limited, 2022.

6 Ganguly Anirban. "Both Visionary and Pragmatic" The Pioneer, Sept 14, 2016. URL: https://www.dailypioneer.com/2016/columnists/both-visionary-and-pragmatic.html

7 "PM Modi recalls Deen Dayal Upadhyay's contribution towards building self-reliant India" The Times of India, Feb 11, 2021. https://timesofindia.indiatimes.com/india/pm-modi-recalls-deen-dayal-upadhyayscontribution-towards-building-self-reliant-india/articleshow/80837792.cms

8 Mukhopadhyay Nilanjan. "Past continuous: What lies behind

BJP's Deification of Deen Dayal Upadhyay", The Wire, Sep 26, 2017.

9 Prof. Gupta Sanjay "The ideological footprints of Pt. Deen Dayal Upadhyay on India's Foreign Policy and its Contemporary Relevance", Journal of Acharya Narendra Dev Research Institute, vol-27 (Jan 2019-June 2019).

Chapter Fifteen

Unfolding the Idea of Humanism and Integral Humanism

Ranjana Singh

A study of the idea of 'Integral Humanism' by two thinkers at two different times and space zones would make readers wonder if any of them inspired the other. Probably, one may think the latter got inspiration from the former. John Abraham, in his article, underwent this arduous work of finding a connection between the two (their economic views to be precise) to find that Pandit Deendayal Upadhyay indeed can be said to have driven from Maritain's thought—though without any specific evidence and logic[1]. If one was to believe Abraham, one may jump on to conclude that Upadhyay's work was an Indianized version of Maritain's, copied and converted. Another scholar, Koenraad Elst, contends that the practice of separating 'ism' (some scholars have suggested a change in the terminology in an attempt to distance from Western influence) from humanism and replacing it with 'vada' or 'darshan' is making no change to Deendayal Upadhyay's philosophy. He claims that even the idea of 'chiti' propounded by Upadhyay is not new (not new as it was always present in the Indian Philosophy from where Deendayal took the idea). Elst rather states that the idea of 'chiti' is exactly what 18^{th-} century German romantic nationalist Johann Gottfried Herder called *'folkszilla'* meaning 'nation's soul'[2]. This Paper is an attempt to compare the Integral Humanism of both philosophers to explore similarities and differences between them.

Understanding Humanism: Waves of Humanism

Perez Zagorin gave a brief narration of various humanistic trends to contend that before the 15th and 16th centuries, all humanism sought to produce Christian gentlemen who were well-educated, morally upright, skilled communicators and writers, capable of providing advice and serving in the administrations of cities, princes, and kings, and with the graces to appear well at the court[3]. Let us see all of them to get a clear picture.

When political philosophers thought about an ideal state, ideal government, global order, etc., they also took cognizance of human nature, aspirations, attitudes, and emotions as the determining factor. The practice of reaffirming the value and power of the individual, which was earlier guided by religious institutions, can be called Humanism. Classical Humanism originated in Greece in the Platonic and Aristotelian eras of the 4th and 5th century B.C.E. The origins of humanism as a multifaceted cultural-educational programme aimed at the construction of the maximum excellence of which man was capable may be traced back to the Sophists. The Middle Ages saw the emergence of Medieval Humanism, also referred to as 'Scholasticism'. Philosophers like St. Augustine and St. Thomas Aquinas were the key proponents. Scholasticism was an attempt to reconcile faith with reason and Aristotle's logic with Christian theology. After the dominance of rationalism in the previous ages, the aim was to balance reason with human dignity, the grandeur of the universe, and the importance of divinity.

The 14th and 15th centuries viewed the rise of the Renaissance (cultural revivalism) Humanism or Modern Humanism, also sometimes called Secular Humanism. The philosophers of the age advocated for Democracy and science in place of theology for human excellence. Noted philosophers include Petrarch, Leonardo Bruni, Niccolo Machiavelli, etc. This period led to the end of scholasticism (rationalism) as ancient texts got translated and circulated, giving rise to subjects like poetry, ethics, history, grammar, etc. It was neither irreligious nor anti-Christian but centered on human free will and political activeness. By the age of Enlightenment in the 17th and 18th centuries, humanism was associated with religious disbelieve and indifference. Science and reason replaced superstitions as the basis of human dignity and progress.

The collapse of humanism began in the 19th century, when humans were no longer considered noble and moral. Hopes of progress in human dignity began to fade. Noted philosophers of this period were Nietzsche, Deleuze, Stiegler, Haraway, etc. Nietzsche through his idea of '*will to power*' gave rise to the new wave of humanism (without wanting himself to be called a humanist) known as post-humanism[4]. They believed that setting up some essentialities, commonalities, and characteristics for the most unique character 'human' is against the nature of humans. Humans are ever-evolving (discussed later in the paper), no two humans can be said to be similar in attitudes, beliefs, or appearances except for physiology (that too with variations). Yet, attempting to generalize them is a major fault of the philosophers they believe. Nietzsche argues that for a human to be truly a human, one has to rise above the horizon (the set rules, responsibilities & disciplines) of the civilized world. Stiegler compared humans with the non-human world and believed that humans are not a creation of God but rather are self-created as well as a creation of the non-human world. According to him, the capacities, attitudes, and nature of humans have been influenced by the 'tools' present and designed by humans comprising the non-human world. And with the changes in the non-human world (like technological advancements), human abilities and nature tend to change too.

Lastly, the most recent development in the history of humanism is the Age of Anti-Humanism. Jean Paul Satre's claim that existentialism is a form of humanism reflects the assumption about humans. That there is no God to guide human action and perfection. Martin Heidegger criticized the centrality of humans and their aim to dominate the universe as the supreme being by discarding the term 'humanism'. Michael Foucault was the most celebrated anti-humanist when he declared the "death of man" in *'The Order of the Things'*. Anti-humanists, in short, denied the metaphysical and transcendental nature of human beings.

Certain practitioners of natural sciences also contributed to humanism, like Sigmund Freud, Abraham Maslow, etc. Maslow in his *'Hierarchy of Needs'* talks about the fulfillment of five needs in chronological order, starting with physical needs and ending with the need for *'self-actualization'*. By self-actualization he meant if the person is not doing what he is suited for, we may frequently—if not always—expect that new unhappiness and restlessness will emerge shortly after all of these requirements are met. If one is to be happy in the end, a musician must create music, an artist must paint, and a poet must write. A guy has to be what he can be. It alludes to his aspiration for self-fulfillment, or more specifically, to his propensity to actualize his potential. One way to describe this inclination would be the desire to become everything that one is capable of becoming or to become more and more of who they are. The antecedent satisfying of the wants of biology, security, love, and esteem, is necessary for the obvious manifestation of these needs[5].

Alma Acevedo cites that according to Maritain, "no other conception of humanism is more disappointing than Aristotle's." Maritain criticized the ambiguous nature of good and happiness as defined by Aristotle. It pushes humans towards egoism. Referring to his ethics, Maritain considers his description of happiness and good 'incomplete' and 'ineffective' as they fail to know the existential reality of humans. To him, human *'will'* is infinite, undefined, and unspecific, making humans dynamic. The search for happiness in humans without an end makes them selfish and egoistic. Maritain criticized the 'universality' (a notion against nature) of the Kantian philosophy that provides no space for individuality and subjectivity. To him, human ends and goods can be merged in uniformity with nature and not against it[6].

Unfolding the idea of 'Integral Humanism'

Jacques Maritain:

Based on realistic metaphysics, Jacques Maritain distinguished humans as 'persons' and 'individuals'. He diverted from the preceding humanistic tradition by not considering humans as a 'subject' (Rene, Descartes, Immanuel Kant) or as an 'individual' (Adam Smith, Friedrich Hayek, Abraham Maslow) but as a 'person'. Maritain based his philosophy of Integral Humanism on the criticism of non-personalistic humanists. Personalistic Humanism for Maritain was not an abstract humanity as advocated by August Comte but something concrete—men and women in flesh and blood.

He did not refer to ideas abstract in nature like 'humanity' in his philosophy. He contends that non-personalistic humanists could provide only an incomplete account of human beings based on either rationalism or empiricism. Therefore, there is a need for an integrated discourse on understanding higher needs, drives, and motives in humans. He has blamed humanists for addressing the limitations and strengths alone of human beings (distinguishing them) instead of exploring their potential, which tends to unite humans in commonalities.

Defining *'Personalism'*

The human *person* 'combines objectivity and subjectivity, causal activity and openness, unicity and relation, sense of self and imagination,' according to personalism, which is understood not only as a 'standpoint, a technique, and a need' but also as a philosophical school that 'emphasizes the value, distinctiveness, and indestructibility of the person, as well as the person's essentially interpersonal or communitarian dimension.' Personalism, thus, is about human intentions and consciousness rooted in 'human dignity' and community life. Believer of Thomistic philosophical realism, Maritainian personalism promotes the 'sanctification of the secular' for people to attain their full potential as human beings rather than contesting the secular (temporal) and holy orders. Truths are not something revealed by God (as theologians believe) but rather are self-evident to human understanding[7]. According to Maritain, humans gain knowledge not through senses (empiricism) or anything a disembodied self can know; rather, it is through what he called "relationality" that humans know about the world. By "relationality," he means communication within the soul and between souls[8].

Maritain discussed humans as *individuals* so far as their material composition is considered, showing a common human nature. Whereas, the spiritual soul's nourishment provided to the human composition is known as 'personality'. It is not the reduction of humans to *individuals* defining its *existence but* rather the *personality (essence)* that characterizes Maritain Humanism. It is to ensure the existence that humans are seen as individual fragments of society. Thus, to Maritain, every human is both—an individual as well as a person. *Person* accounts for both rational and irrational tendencies of human beings in their understanding of the world. Person thus, differentiates humans based on 'nature, origin, and end'. The person is free, unlike the individual.

The integration and inalienability of humans are rooted in human rights and dignity derived from natural laws, which are indeed indivisible. According to Maritain humans comprise *'person'* (essence) and *'individual'* (existence), both realms are interdependent which he tried to explain by the principle of 'relationality.' Two realms of Maritain's human are integral and inalienable, human and humanism cannot be understood and defined otherwise, probably therefore, it is called 'Integral Humanism.'

The same natural law that enshrines human rights, virtues, and dignity sets some limitations on their exercise too. It is through self-discipline suggested by natural law to freely and rationally prioritize greater human goods that make humans fully human. The common good is prior to personal good, the latter is inherent in the former. Morally repugnant conduct destroys a person's identity since it 'gives preponderance to the individual component of our being.' In them, the originality of the human being takes precedence over personality. These 'free' decisions are contrary to the truth since they are not in line with reality. Only when human identity is, so to speak, integrated into personality does it become good.

The true end of the human person is the attainment of the 'common good' not limited to materialism but moral, spiritual, and intellectual growth. It is to attain this true end that materially deficient *individual* humans need society to complement them. For *personality* too, interaction with other souls is essential, for which society is a means. The common good of the society then is the 'end of politics' where people live in harmony[9].

It can be concluded that Maritain's Integral Humanism suggested 'how humans can become truly human'. It would not be wrong to call his idea of humanism 'True Humanism' as the first English translation of *humanism integral* suggested in 1938.[10] Maritain thus, tried to address the loopholes in the non-personalistic approach by combining both the commonalities (dignity, rights) and peculiarities (drives, aspirations) of human beings. The conception of 'true humanism' fits in reality.

Pandit Deendayal Upadhyay:

When the world was debating over capitalism vs socialism, Deendayal Upadhyay discarded both to propound the philosophy of Integral Humanism (*Ekatma manavaad*). An idea emanating from Indian thought, culture, and philosophy rooted in cooperation instead of competition. The objective was to show a path for Indians introduced to an independent state and society after 200 years of servitude. Swaraj can be attained only after knowing *'swa'* that is self. And thus, in the attempt to define Nationalism, humanism found primacy.

It can be said that his Integral Humanism was not limited to just humans but society, state, and the cosmos as well. He discarded capitalism and socialism, which take humans as an 'economic unit' and 'political and labour unit'. Deendayal Upadhyay took humans as the smallest unit for the construction of 'Rashtra'. The individual leads to family, society, nation, and state eventually. As he described the evolution in chronological order of a yagyachakra comprising- *vyakti, samishti, srishthi,* and *paramishthi* have to be in cooperation and coordination with each other for the proper functioning of any nation[11]. To him, a human is not just a collection of flesh and blood but body, mind, soul, and intellect.

Deendayal Upadhyay coined certain terms to explain his philosophy of Integral Humanism that can have no exact and accurate translation in English. It is pertinent to understand the constituting parts of his philosophy explained through *chiti, virat, purusharatha, arthayaam, and antyodaya.*

Chiti— meaning the soul of the nation. Deendayal Upadhyay believed that different nations have different 'Chiti'. Due to the difference of 'Chiti', one nation considers itself dependent when it is under the rule of another nation, thus there is always a rule of man over man. This 'Chiti' is expressed in the culture, literature, and religion of a group of people due to their residence in a particular country. The unity of 'Chiti' creates a common tradition, history, and civilization. Therefore, the basic reason for the unity of any nation is not the unity of culture, civilization, religion, language, etc. but the expressed unity of minds. The body nourishes every organ for its existence, this holism is due to the presence of the soul. Similarly, the complete unity of a nation through the nourishment of virat (the collection of humans) is only possible due to the presence of chiti (the soul of the nation). The light of 'Chiti' leads to the rise of a nation, and the destruction of 'Chiti' leads to the downfall of the nation. If the self-realization of the soul of the nation does not take place, but the soul remains attacked and immersed in the same way, or if the mind of another nation influences one's mind, then instead of progress in the ethnic life, there is only degradation.

In this way, if the national 'Chiti' does not become strong in the struggle between 'Chitis', then in the end the life of the nation gets destroyed and its place is taken by another nation. Chiti thus leads to Swaraj[12].

Virat— is the material composition or fuel of the nation, comprising the collective whole of all humans. Virat is the body of the nation, of which chiti is the soul. For the overall growth of the body, people who are divided by varna (Brahmán, Kshatriya, Vaishya, Shudra) and religion must integrate.

Purusharatha— the code of conduct or set of four cardinal duties (*dharma, artha, kaam, moksha*) to be performed by humans.[13] For a human to live a perfect life, one must perform the four duties in the manner and nature as prescribed. Dharma is supreme among all, any other virtue gained without dharma would be considered immoral. Dharma is not religion; it is righteous and moral conduct and duties. One must perform the dharma of a son, brother, father, citizen, and member of the cosmos[14]. In the performance of his moral and righteous duties, one must earn (and not accumulate) wealth (artha) for the survival of self and family. Through wealth, one must lead a happy and pleasurable life (kaam). It is the happiness attained through right means and morality that one can attain salvation (moksha) in life.

Arthayaam— which means that both the absence and prominence of 'arth' lead to disintegration and degradation of 'dharma' and thus humanism. Deendayal Upadhyay believed in survival with the least resources for the sustainable growth of humans and the nation.

Antyodaya— upliftment and development of the last person in the queue. While the Western world believed in notions like 'survival of the fittest', 'victory of the mightiest' and 'accumulation of as much as wealth at the cost of others'

Indian philosophy believed feeding the weakest person through resources a relatively powerful could earn.

Deendayal Upadhyay took motivation from Indian philosophy; the way Swami Shankaracharya talked about *Advait (non-duality)* between humans and the cosmos, he propounded *advait* concerning the 'socio-economic-political-spiritual' aspects of a human being, and so, called his philosophy of humanism integrated. He did not limit it to humans only but rather took society as a set of which humans are a subset. The Nation for that matter, is a bigger set of which society is a subset. He believed that the whole is more important than the individual, dharma is the supreme virtue in a self-governing society.

He wanted the Indian state to be a decentralized state, wherein the ruling government must not take regulation of the economy into its hands, and education too must not be provided by the state. Both domains can be collectively dealt with by society. The state must take over issues that individuals and society cannot deal with, like global issues, and issues of conflicting interests.

In conclusion, it can be said that Pt. Deendayal Upadhyay clarified in his Integral Humanism philosophy that the study is not limited to the individual, society, nation, or world. Still, beyond this, there is a feeling of unity in the environment, nature, creation, and God who is the controller of this entire world. There is a direct relationship between them. Even a slight imbalance can cause widespread problems.

Comparative Analysis of Jacques Maritain and Deendayal Upadhyay's Views

1. Both Jacques Maritain and Deendayal Upadhyay based their idea of Integral Humanism on criticism of the status

quo, but in different time frames, the 1930s and 1960s, respectively. Capitalism, Socialism, and Totalitarianism, causing a change in human life and attitudes, made both think of an alternative way of life, making them sound similar. Apart from the world order, Maritain's philosophy tends to rest more on the criticism of the preceding non-personalistic humanists of the Western world. Although often called a 'Thomist' and 'Aristotelian', Maritain tends to distance from them more than being a follower. On the other hand, Deendayal Upadhyay's philosophy instead finds inspiration and motivation from the preceding scholars of the Indian philosophy (Shankaracharya, Vivekananda, Ghosh, Gandhi, etc.).

2. The basic difference between Maritain and Upadhyay lies in how 'Human' is perceived by both, which originates in their respective theological roots and civilizational underpinnings, and similarly so in the philosophical solution they propounded. To uplift the degraded status of humans, Upadhyay suggested returning to the past beliefs and practices of the Indian civilization. Maritain's suggestion cannot completely be called a return to the Christian way of life but rather a "return to nature," if to borrow Rousseau's idea, as he finds a guarantee of human rights and dignity in Natural law.

3. Both criticize extremism between collectivism/communitarianism and individuality/Individualism. They do not find a contradiction in both extremes; rather, they are part and parcel of each other, and complementary. They did not talk about any 'golden mean' but a harmonious combination of both. Deendayal Upadhyay's Integral Humanism is not limited to humans alone but also includes society, nation, and state. Maritain considers society as a 'means' of fulfilling the material

limitations of the human *individual* as well as of making communication between human *persons* possible. Suggesting an instrumental use of society in his Integral Humanism, while society is an indivisible constituent of Deendayal Upadhyay's Integral Humanism, Jacques Maritain talked about the integration of the 'individual' and the 'person', spiritual and material, rational and irrational. Deendayal Upadhyay contends that there is an integration between the socio-economic-political-spiritual aspects of a human, society, nation, world, and cosmos. Humans cannot be developed fully if these parts are disintegrated or uncompliant. Maritain's Integral Humanism considers achieving the 'common good' as the true end of the human person, while the end for Deendayal Upadhyay's Integral Humanism is the creation of a nation-state. Thus, it can be said that their Integral Humanism differed in the nature of origin, inherent nature, composition, as well as end.

4. In his philosophy of Integral Humanism, Maritain aimed at the actualization of the full potential of the human being, and 'how humans can be more human'. He tried to shape the perception of humans as a combination of both 'person' and 'individual'. Deendayal Upadhyay's Integral Humanism, on the other hand, can be said to be related to the chronological progression of humans, an evolution. More than defining how humans should be perceived, he focused on 'Human development' instead, which is sustainable and inclusive. Thus, Maritain, in his statement *'existence cannot be separated from essence'* explained what 'true humanism' is - Deendayal Upadhyay prioritized 'antyodaya' and 'arthayaam' providing a roadmap to the sustainable development of humans, thereby of society, nation, and state.

5. Both talked about the 'spirituality' of humans. While Western spirituality is related to religiosity, Indian spirituality talks about the metaphysical and transcendental interconnection of 'atma' (soul) and 'paramatma' (the creator of the cosmos). Maritain, placed importance on natural law as an antidote for a secular society and the present crisis of a pluralist society.[15] He can be considered inclined toward secularism while Deendayal Upadhyay is towards culturalism (not religiosity).
6. Both Maritain and Upadhyay appear to be similar in their suggestion of the ideal state. Maritain suggested a pluralistic democracy with subsidiary rights to humans for the development of human will, intellect, and virtues on the initiatives of free self-governing citizens. Similarly, Deendayal Upadhyay also advocated a decentralized state, and division of roles between the state, society, and individual.

Relevance of 'Integral Humanism' in the 21st Century

Today we are living in a digital world. Humans have made gadgets and tools as a part of their being. The tendency to consider 'humans' as a homogenous, single-fitting category is in itself erroneous. Beginning from the pre-human era, humans were composed of just males and females, who were different physically, emotionally, and socially. By the Middle Ages, 'transgenders' as a category was known, and by the early 21st century, 'Lesbian Gay Bisexual Transgender' (LGBT) emerged, followed by subsequent awareness of 'Queer' (LGBTQ), 'LGBTQ+', 'Asexual and Intersex' (LGBTQAI+) and so on. The conception of what physically comprises humans alone is not yet known, fully leaving aside their drives and sentiments. How can a philosophy describing humans be adequate and appropriate? After the development of what we call Industrialization 4.0, giving rise to 'Artificial Intelligence' (AI) and the Internet of Things (IoT), even machines can be considered as persons. Machines can understand, replicate, and predict humans; not even humans could do this throughout their existence[16]. Certain applications require humans to prove they are humans, for example, Captcha and choosing blocks. Yet, the world is still predominated by humans, we can say with certainty, as anything can be created by humans in the non-human world except the 'soul' in a living body. It is the soul that has to be perfected and reawakened to ensure the distinctive existence of humans. And there comes the relevance of the 'Integral Humanism' of both Deendayal Upadhyay and Jacques Maritain. It is believed that there is a need for uplifting 'humanity' when we talk about humanism. The ability to sympathize and empathize, with not just other humans but with all beings, love and gratitude for nature, and the ability to transpose are what the author believes must be instilled in contemporary humans.

Pt. Deendayal Upadhyay can be considered similar to that of Gosh, Gandhi, Roy, and Vivekanand. He was not the only leader to promote the foundation of the nation-state on the grounds of Indian philosophy and civilization, all other contemporary leaders too wanted the same, leaving Nehru. He believed that a form of government, ideology, and policy suiting one nation does not mean it would suit others too. Claims of his influence by Jacques Maritain find no grounds except that they talk about a perfect human as Maslow and Nietzsche talk too. They are similar only in using the same terminologies and criticizing the same world order. If we take Maritain as a circle and Upadhyay as a straight line passing nearby, they meet at just one point, like a tangent; the point can be named 'Integral Humanism.' Yet, even the point is not indivisible but only in name.

Moreover, it is hard to believe one taking inspiration or aping someone who criticized the Western world. Upadhyay's Integral Humanism seems to be relevant to today's world crises as it addresses the inclusive and sustainable development of humans and the world. Maritain's humanism also finds relevance as it demands valuing humans' unobservable and unquantifiable qualities too. But his thought seems to be incomplete as he could not deal with the nuances of conflict among individuals, the authority of society over individuals, and the division of roles between nation and society. Upadhyay passed away just four years after proposing the idea. Similarly, Maritain too appears to be utopian when talking about the harmonious coexistence of humans in the absence of active intervention of the state, as he says "end of politics". Later on, eventually, the human rights he talked about in the United Nations Human Rights Council (UNHRC) cannot be safeguarded without the will and intention of the nation-states to do so.

Endnotes

1 John Abraham. "In Search of Dharma: Integral Humanism and the Political Economy of Hindu Nationalism," *South Asia: Journal of South Asian Studies,* vol.42, no.1 (2019), p. 18. https://www.tandfonline.com/doi/full/10.1080/00856401.2019.1557362 (Accessed February 12, 2024).

2 Koenraad Elst. Integral Humanism. YouTube, Center for Indic Studies, 2019. https://youtu.be/_Q6MtkG3UPo?si=0Ogc3FmF9eWX4af1 (Accessed February 20, 2024).

3 Perez Zagorin. "On Humanism Past & Present," *Daedalus,* vol. 132, no. 4 (2003), pp. 87-88. http://www.jstor.org/stable/20027887 (Accessed February 18, 2024).

4 Abraham Maslow. "A Theory of Human Motivation," *Psychological Review,* Vol. 50, no. 4 (1943), pp. 373-384. https://psychclassics.yorku.ca/Maslow/motivation.htm (Accessed

February 28, 2024).

5 "Posthumanism Explained — Nietzsche, Deleuze, Stiegler, Haraway," YouTube, November 28, 2019, PlasticPills. https://youtu.be/GmJLsfUnGjY?si=SIRfHPeYy9viyTes (Accessed February 18, 2024).

6 Alma Acevedo. "Personalist Business Ethics and Humanistic Management: Insights from Jacques Maritain." *Journal of Business Ethics*, vol. 105, no. 2 (2012), p. 210. http://www.jstor.org/stable/41413255 (Accessed February 13, 2024).

7 Acevedo, Alma (2012). op. cit., pp. 202-205.

8 Acevedo, Alma (2012). op. cit., p. 208.

9 Acevedo, Alma (2012). op. cit., p. 207.

10 Acevedo, Alma (2012). op. cit., p. 208.

11 RSTV Special. Deendayal Upadhyay centenary celebrations. YouTube, Sansad TV, 2017. https://youtu.be/IiQ8OMhe0kE?si=1EEgCRWyB6gAqL8z (Accessed February 20, 2024).

12 Deendayal Upadhyay. *Rashtra Chintan* (New Delhi: Bhartiya Janata Party, 2017). pp. 111-112. http://library.bjp.org/jspui/handle/123456789/439 (Accessed February 16, 2024).

13 Vinod Mishra. *Ekatam Manavvad Darshan* (New Delhi: Bhartiya Janta Party, 2017). p. 65. http://library.bjp.org/jspui/handle/123456789/436 (Accessed February 16, 2024).

14 Mishra, Vinod (2017). op. cit., p. 77.

15 Trần, Quảng Văn. "From Human Dignity to the Common Good. A Study of Jacques Maritain's Integral Humanism" (PhD diss., Boston College, 2022), p. 3.

16 Pranav Kumar and Ranjana Singh. "Waves of Globalization," in Vandana Mishra and Swadesh Singh (eds.) *Aatmanirbharta: Revisiting the Idea & Practices* (New Delhi: Ane Books Pvt. Ltd., 2021), p. 68.

Chapter Sixteen

"Integral Humanism" East and West: The Remarkably Congruent Philosophical Anthropologies and Social Theories of Deendayal Upadhyay and Jacques Maritain

Timothy Samuel Shah

It is a great pleasure, privilege, and honor to contribute to this volume, which emerged from an illuminating and inspiring conference that took place at Banaras Hindu University in Varanasi, India in March 2024 on "Integral Humanism: Perspectives of Deendayal Upadhyay and Jacques Maritain."[1]

If I am not mistaken, the conference and the ensuing volume are absolutely unique and unprecedented. They represent the first scholarly effort to provide a comparative assessment of two extraordinary thinkers — Pandit Deendayal Upadhyay and Jacques Maritain — and their profound and influential philosophies of integral humanism. I therefore heartily congratulate all of the organizers of both the conference and this present volume. For the meeting of hearts and minds that we experienced in Varanasi, and which is memorialized in this collection of essays, is of much more than merely academic significance. Rather, our shared effort to recover and re-enliven the ideas of Deendayal Upadhyay and Jacques Maritain represents a noble attempt, so necessary in a world marked by enormous polarization and violent conflict between opposing identities, to promote a true confluence of civilizations rather than a clash of civilizations — a "*sangam*", we might say, of great civilizations and the moral and spiritual goods they carry.

I earned a doctorate in political science at Harvard University many years ago, more years ago than I care to admit. And my advisor in the political science subfield of comparative politics was Samuel P. Huntington. Writing in the journal *Foreign Affairs* in 1993, Huntington famously expounded the thesis that world politics in the coming decades would be dominated by conflict and clash between civilizations.

In short, Huntington argued that the forces of globalization would not in fact create one world family or one "happy family" of nations and cultures, radically contrary to what many believed at the time and believe even today. Instead, he argued that economic globalization would actually drive people to be in greater tension with each other. The deep anthropological premise of this argument was his firm belief — borne of his political realism and clear-eyed study of humanity as it is rather than as we might like it to be — that it is an inescapably human quality to hate "the other." Indeed, he observed, it is often the case that the more we learn about other peoples and communities, the more we learn to despise and distrust them because we come to discover that they are fundamentally different from ourselves. We discover that we disagree with them on important questions of religion, morality, and politics. We discover that they do not share our basic values. And when we encounter people who do not share our values, what is our response? Naturally, if not inevitably, our response is one of diffidence, fear, anger, and hatred.

In a sense, without using the term, Huntington prophetically foresaw three decades ago the phenomenon of late-modern polarization that has surprised and alarmed so many political observers around the world in recent years, in which the experience of sharing discursive space with diverse others, through globalization and more and more sophisticated communications technologies, does not necessarily unify peoples and nations across cultural and religious divides, but often drives or exacerbates an acute sense of disagreement and conflict both within and across the world's societies.

If one premise of Huntington's perspective was what one might call an anthropological pessimism (which, by the way, he probably learned from mid-twentieth century exponents of political realism such as Reinhold Niebuhr and Hans Morgenthau), another premise was a kind of cultural essentialism. As Fouad Ajami critically and memorably commented at the time, Huntington sketched his cartography of global civilizations using a very sharp pencil. In his essentialization of civilizational differences, he tended to argue that the West is monolithically defined by a certain set of values, Hindu civilization is characterized by a certain very different set of values, and likewise Islamic, Sinic (Chinese), and Japanese civilization. Though a valuable and indeed necessary corrective to an excessively naive and optimistic liberal cosmopolitanism that was pervasive as the US-Soviet Cold War came to an end in the early 1990s, Huntington's civilizational perspective is indeed overly severe and was incapable on its own terms of showing how the cooperation and understanding between civilizations he advocated in the closing pages of his 1996 book-length treatment of civilizations and world politics, *The Clash of Civilizations and the Remaking of World Order*, could actually materialize.

I believe that our discussions about integral humanism "East and West" may be a powerful intellectual antidote to the profound civilizational, cultural, and political polarization that rightly worried and preoccupied my great mentor and teacher Samuel Huntington in the 1990s. Indeed, the intellectual enterprise represented by our gathering here in Varanasi — and the volume of essays that emerged therefrom — may be one of the greatest and most potent antidotes to this phenomenon I have ever encountered. If it truly exists and if it could truly be demonstrated that it exists, a profound and substantial inter-civilizational confluence of ideas and values concerning the nature and destiny of the human person — i.e. around a robust philosophy of integral humanism — represents an essential and powerful corrective to the famous Huntington thesis about the dangers and near-inevitability of a global clash of civilizations.

In a sense, then, what I would like to focus on is the critical question: Can there truly be a confluence rather than a clash between the integral humanism of Deendayal Upadhyay and the integral humanism of Jacques Maritain, as well as between the great civilizations, Hindu and Christian, they represent? Perhaps you will not be surprised by now to learn that my answer to this crucial question is very much in the affirmative. Such a robust confluence very much exists — despite what Huntingtonian realists and many Hindus and Christians themselves might think — and its specific dimensions, furthermore, can be demonstrated and described in some detail.

At the very outset, I would like to highlight one clear convergence between Deendayal Upadhyay and Jacques Maritain. In the *Bhagavad Gita*, Chapter 3, Shloka 21, we read:

यद्यदाचरति श्रेष्ठस्तत्तदेवेतरो जनः ।
स सत्प्रमाणं कुरुते लोकस्तदनुवर्तते ।। २१ ।।

yad yad ācarati śreṣṭhas
tattadevetaro janaḥ
sa yat pramāṇaṁ kurute
lokas tad anuvartate

Whatever action a great man performs, common men follow. And whatever standards he sets by exemplary acts, all the world pursues.

In what is a purely empirical observation, the *Gita* notes that the path a great man follows is intrinsically and widely attractive; it naturally becomes a guide to the whole of humanity.

By that standard, if we define a great man as one who inspires others to follow his path purely by the force of his example and teaching — even when he wields no power and commands no armies — few men of the last 100 years have been greater than Deendayal Upadhyay and Jacques Maritain. Yet too few today appreciate how influential they were. The former, though he never held political office, set a new cultural and political course for hundreds of millions of Hindus, laying the philosophical foundations for what would arguably become the world's most successful cultural-nationalist movement, Hindu nationalism, and the world's most powerful political party, the Bharatiya Janata Party. The latter developed a new template for the relationship between Church and society that would decisively shape the theology and practice of the Roman Catholic Church, the world's largest Christian communion. Jacques Maritain's influence on the trajectory of Catholic Christianity was so immense that Pope Paul VI — who presided over most of the Second Vatican

Council, which reflected Maritain's spirit in numerous ways—proudly declared his debt to the French philosopher by saying, "I am a disciple, he is my teacher."

The massive extent to which millions followed the teaching and example of these great men is all the more astonishing given the fact that they were remarkably quiet and retiring personalities. Of course, Pandit Deendayal Upadhyay was more a man of action than was Jacques Maritain, who was by vocation and temperament a scholar, philosopher, and contemplative. Though it is undoubtedly true that Maritain was indeed primarily a thinker and writer, not least by inclination and preference, he was also in many ways a man of action. He fought vociferously against the polarization within the Catholic Church as a consequence of the Spanish Civil War. He fought against right-wing Catholics who blindly followed General Francisco Franco and Franco's brand of fascism. He courageously condemned Catholics who were consumed with anti-Semitic hatred. In the 1930s, he foresaw in a clear-eyed manner the horrible crimes against humanity Hitler would commit. Furthermore, he was active not only in opposing fascism but also in working with the United States Government to rescue Jewish and anti-fascist dissident intellectuals across Europe and securing refuge for them in America. Maritain, notably, was equally active in opposing Communist totalitarianism.

However, based on my own humble and inexpert efforts over the last few years to immerse myself in the writings of Deendayal Upadhyay and Jacques Maritain, it has seemed to me that a further major commonality binds these two men. In both of them, alongside their intense public activism and public influence, one senses extremely philosophical minds. As Dr. Ram Madhav described these men as visionaries — indeed, as "saintly visionaries" — is accurate and penetrating. These were not men animated by an ambition to dominate others or indeed to exercise any coercive power over others. Rather, one senses that these were saintly individuals who sought to understand and obey the eternal laws of the universe. They were men who wanted to diffuse a wider knowledge of these laws — i.e. the basic principles of the cosmos — for the benefit of all humanity. They were not concerned primarily with the exercise of power. They were certainly not concerned to lay hold of the levers of political influence for their own benefit or that of their particular tribe.

Instead, Deendayal Upadhyay and Jacques Maritain selflessly worked so that their societies, and the world as a whole, would flourish through a more faithful adherence to objective and transcendent moral principles — principles that Maritain termed the law of nature, rooted in the constant features of human nature and ultimately reflecting the Eternal Law of God, and that Upadhyay also often termed "natural laws" or the "fundamental law[s] of human nature" or the "fundamental principles of *Dharma,*" which he considered "eternal and universal."[2] In this sense, it is not just that Deendayal Upadhyay and Jacques Maritain espoused philosophies of integral humanism; they *were* integral humanists insofar as they lived lives integrally dedicated to the service of humanity as a whole in all of its dimensions, both material and spiritual.

To sustain the thesis that a substantial convergence obtains between the integral humanism of Deendayal Upadhyay and that of Jacques Maritain, it is essential to underscore a point I have only touched on just now. Between the eternal law and natural law as understood in Western Christian philosophy, on one hand, and *Dharma* as understood in the Hindu tradition, on the other, I believe there are certain strong convergences. In particular, I believe that there are some significant commonalities between the Thomistic understanding of the eternal and divine law that was at the heart of Jacques Maritain's thought and a Hindu understanding of *Dharma* that was at the foundation of Deendayal Upadhyay's spiritual and philosophical outlook.

Let me not be misunderstood, however. I am not denying that there may also be important *divergences* between Thomistic natural law as understood and invoked by Maritain and Hindu *dharma* as understood and invoked by Upadhyay. Nor am I suggesting that what convergences may exist are necessarily more numerous and more significant than those divergences that may exist. However, what I am suggesting — particularly as a premise for deeper research and for further Hindu-Catholic discussion and dialogue — is that the convergences appear to be numerous enough and strong enough to warrant the belief (or the hope) that there may well be at least some significant moral and philosophical agreement or overlap between the integral humanism of Jacques Maritain, which is grounded in natural law as a participation in, and reflection of, the eternal law of God, and the integral humanism of Deendayal Upadhyay, which is likewise rooted in *Dharma* and its "eternal and universal" principles.[3]

For the sake of realizing the fundamental, constant, and eternal principles in which both Deendayal Upadhyay and Jacques Maritain believed most profoundly — rather than for the sake of conserving any existing social order for its own sake — both men struggled and suffered, thought and wrote. They worked selflessly in the hope that these eternal principles would be put into practice. Because they both fought to bring society into alignment with transcendent standards rather than merely defend the status quo, including the economic and political status quo, it would be more accurate to regard both thinkers as radical progressives rather than as right-wing conservatives — despite the way the Left tends to characterize both Hindutva and Catholic Social Teaching.

In what remains of my reflections, I would like to make a few brief points in support of my conviction that there is a robust and substantial convergence between the integral humanism of Deendayal Upadhyay and that of Jacques Maritain.

The first point I would like to make is one I have already implied — namely, that these two individuals were not isolated geniuses who came out of nowhere. Each of them, in many ways, was very much a product and exemplar of his civilization and religious tradition. One could go so far as to argue that even if Deendayal Upadhyay had never existed, even if Jacques Maritain had never existed, one would still have seen — and in fact one already did see — the flowering of forms of integral humanism in both India and the West. In that sense, neither Jacques Maritain nor Deendayal Upadhyay created "integral humanism" in the way that Leonardo da Vinci painted the *Mona Lisa* or Shakespeare composed *Hamlet*. Dr. Ram Madhav Ji already mentioned the significance of Swami Vivekananda. You could mention many other neo-Hindu revivalist thinkers who were determined to creatively adapt the deepest principles of Hinduism to the conditions and challenges of modernity. And they were already remarkably successful in doing so. Deendayal Upadhyay's achievement was thus not to create or invent "integral humanism" from whole cloth. His genius was to synthesize, collect, and categorize what his tradition was already teaching in an analytical and systematic way, and apply this teaching to the political conditions of post-independence India. Clearly, Upadhyay was not an isolated genius. He was rather a learned and creative representative of India's great civilization and its philosophical and religious traditions.

Much the same can be said about Jacques Maritain who was devoted and indebted to the great Christian philosophical and theological tradition. Famously, of course, he was particularly devoted to St. Thomas Aquinas, one of the greatest thinkers in the history of Christianity. Maritain was well-known for saying as a young man: "Woe to me if I do not Thomistize!" (*Vae mihi si non Thomistizavero!*) You could say that he was a disciple or yogi of St. Thomas in the sense that he was absolutely devoted to both the thought and the spirituality of Aquinas. It was as a young man that Maritain discovered the philosophy of Thomas Aquinas, and for the rest of his life he was deeply devoted to interpreting and strengthening the great cumulative intellectual tradition — Thomism — that developed over the centuries upon the foundations of the medieval theologian's wide-ranging and systematic thought.

What is characteristic of the tradition of St. Thomas Aquinas? St. Thomas, who lived in the 13th century, was famous for his absolute devotion to the truth of the Catholic faith as taught in the Sacred Scriptures, but also absolutely devoted to respecting and honoring any authentic truth, genuine insight, or noble idea, regardless of its source. This is why he avidly studied the pre-Christian Greek philosopher Aristotle and Arab Islamic philosophers such as al-Fārābī, Avicenna, and Averroes. He spent enormous time and energy studying non-Christian thinkers because he was convinced that God's truth can come from any direction, from any source. In a sense, therefore, he created a tradition that was one great dialogue — a dialogical and inclusive tradition that was, and remains, open to wisdom and truth from anywhere.

So, when Maritain became a Thomist, he became a kind of philosophical inclusivist who — precisely as a Catholic and a Thomist — was committed to open and respectful dialogue with other points of view. As a consequence, one remarkable fact about Maritain that is extremely important to emphasize is that he may have been one of the first Western thinkers — and perhaps the very first major thinker — to have discovered the importance of Mahatma Gandhi. In Maritain's remarkable essay, *Freedom in the Modern World*, which he drafted and published shortly after 1930, he provides a lengthy and admiring analysis of Mahatma Gandhi's *Satyagraha* philosophy and programme of non-violent social action. The work even includes an entire appendix on *Satyagraha*. In this treatment, Maritain excoriates his fellow Western Christians for their failure to study Gandhi and derive essential lessons for social action and transformation, including the necessity of employing "pure means" in pursuit of political goals. This exemplifies the inclusivism of Maritain — an inclusivism, again, that does not merely reflect his own idiosyncrasies but the great dialogical quality of the Catholic Thomistic tradition.[1]

A second key point I would like to make is that the social philosophies of Deendayal Upadhyay and Jacques Maritain converged on a shared determination to fiercely criticize both the Right and the Left. And this convergence suggests that their distinct philosophies of integral humanism are animated by a very similar spirit. This may come as a surprise to certain people. As I noted earlier, many people might assume that Upadhyay and Maritain were both essentially conservative

1 Jacques Maritain systematically discusses Mahatma Gandhi and his *Satyagraha* philosophy and campaign — and the universal lessons they offer, including for Catholic Christians — in *Freedom in the Modern World,* including in a special Appendix entitled "The Doctrine of "*Satyagraha*" as set forth by M. K. Gandhi. See *Freedom in the Modern World* in *The Collected Works of Jacques Maritain,* Volume XI (Notre Dame: University of Notre Dame Press, 1996), pp. 89 – 91 and 112 – 115.

defenders of static religious traditions and an old hierarchical social order. Once again, however, what is clear is that the primary allegiance of both men was not to any narrow party or political position. Rather, the political North Star for each of them was an ensemble of transcendent principles on the basis of which they keenly felt both the duty and the right to critique a range of actual social and political arrangements and agendas, including those of the right and the left. Significantly, therefore, for each of them, integral humanism represented a principled "third way" between the unacceptable extremes of a static conservative traditionalism and an extreme left-wing radicalism.

We are no doubt already familiar with the ways in which Deendayal Upadhyay regularly critiqued the left. In his fierce opposition to collectivism and a command economy, he was critical of Nehruvian economic policy. And he was critical of a left-wing secularism that seeks to drain man and his politics of any spiritual foundation, orientation, meaning, or content, thus producing a "naked public square." To forget the necessarily spiritual nature and destiny of man is to produce only a thin and partial and purely material humanism rather than an integral humanism. Perhaps less well known, however, is the fact that on almost every page of his writings on integral humanism Upadhyay attacks various forms and expressions of extreme conservatism and traditionalism. He strongly critiques what one might call a politics of order at any cost. He critiques an excessive statism. He critiques the idea of a theocracy as alien to Hindu values. He attacks efforts to quash religious freedom and freedom of conscience, partly (though not always) in the context of contrasting the oppressive Islamic state of Pakistan with the far more religiously tolerant Indian polity. He critiques Hindu sectarianism and the narrowness of the Hindu Mahasabha. In other words, there is clearly a strong respect in which Deendayal Upadhyay is trying to define a third way between an extreme right-wing position and an extreme left-wing position.

Maritain's social and political philosophy can be described in remarkably similar terms. As far as left-wing ideologies were concerned, Maritain was vociferously critical of Communism from the time he was a young man, even though he was raised by Protestant parents in a milieu that was broadly anti-clerical and sympathetic to the Left and to socialism. Like Upadhyay, in addition, he was deeply opposed to secular liberalism's marginalization of religion in society and its simultaneous materialization of the nature and ends of the human person, perfectly exemplified by the one-dimensional philosophies of Hobbes and Rousseau — philosophies to which Maritain's fuller and richer philosophy of integral humanism is intended as a direct rejoinder. At the same time, he strongly critiqued the Right on a number of grounds. He blasted conservatives for their cruel indifference to the plight of the poor. He became increasingly critical of efforts to turn the state into an instrument of the Catholic Church and impose a kind of Catholic theocracy through coercive political means. As I already noted above, Maritain vociferously opposed Catholics who supported Franco's extreme right-wing Falange in the Spanish Civil War. For this principled stand, he was subject to vicious criticism and smear campaigns propagated by fellow Catholics — including within the Vatican — who claimed that he undermined both the theological integrity and the social and political interests of the Catholic Church.

In other words, a principled determination to stake out a "third way" — a serious alternative to the extremes of right and left — was characteristic of both of these great men. They were not party men. On the contrary, they wanted to transcend conventional partisanship. In some ways, their insistence on placing principle above party cost them, tangibly, in terms of friendships and influence. It made them less politically effective in a short-term conventional sense. But the depth and coherence of their philosophical positions made them extraordinarily influential and consequential in the long run.

Maritain actually describes his own position vis-à-vis the conventional ideological poles of right and left in a way that I think could apply just as well to the political philosophy and political positioning of Deendayal Upadhyay. In fact, Maritain explicitly says that by refusing to go along with the right or with the left, he is a true conservative, which he defines in the following way:

> Taken in its truest sense, to *conserve* means to *keep* all that is good in what has been acquired and achieved by human industry throughout the ages. To keep it, but to keep it *alive*; "conserve" it as God "conserves" His creation in being. In this sense, the word "conservative" is a noble word, and to be a "conservative" is a noble thing.
>
> A true conservative, then, is a man who is reverent towards the past, and yet is keenly aware of changing times and of the needs of the future. The true conservative is the greatest of innovators. He is prepared for the most radical of revolutions, for his task is to preserve the heritage of the past, a heritage which is not dead but alive. He will not try to juggle with history, piously invoking the past as a pretext for ignoring the present; he will not betray realities by a policy of sham, opportunism and alliances with elements and interests with which he should have nothing to do. He will not boast of being the champion of principles which he betrays in practice,

nor will he sacrifice essential ideals to immediate success.[2]

In this beautiful statement, Maritain encapsulates the spirit not only of his own philosophy of integral humanism, but also, I dare say, of the integral humanism of Deendayal Upadhyay as well.

Finally, I want to just make one additional point, which is that what we are accomplishing here is too important to stay here. Some of you may know that they used to air television ads in the United States about Las Vegas in order to encourage people to visit that famously decadent tourist destination sometimes known as "sin city." One particularly famous ad tried to entice people to visit Las Vegas with the slogan, "What happens in Vegas, stays in Vegas."

My hope is that what happens in this conference does not stay in this conference. The cultural and religious movements that have been shaped by the ideas of Deendayal Upadhyay and Jacques Maritain are too large and important for the ideas generated here at our gathering to remain confined to our gathering. There are well over a billion Hindus in the world, most of them of course living in India, which is now the most populous nation in the planet. There are approximately a billion Catholics in the world — roughly the same size as the world's Hindu population. Quite apart from size, these two communities are enormously important, dynamic, and multidimensional movements. Yet we must acknowledge that relations between these movements are not particularly strong, warm, or positive. In fact, they are marked by no small degree of mutual distrust, tension, and conflict. Furthermore, if I have to be perfectly honest, I would feel compelled to say that

---

2 Jacques Maritain, "'Right' and 'Left,'" *Blackfriars*, November 1937, Vol. 18, No. 212, pp. 807-812. The emphasis is in the original.

both sides must accept responsibility for this sub-optimal state of affairs. And I trust that most of us would agree that it is not just one side or the other that is the sole source of the tension and conflict.

It is precisely in the context of the tensions and conflicts between these two great movements and indeed two great civilizations that the deliberations of our conference on integral humanism in Deendayal Upadhyay and Jacques Maritain are of enormous real-world value and importance. If there are real tensions and divisions that complicate the relationship between the Hindu community and Catholic community, then the finding of our conference that there are at least some points of profound convergence and confluence between Deendayal Upadhyay and Jacques Maritain should be explored and discussed at greater length and well beyond the confines of our meeting here at Banaras Hindu University — as important a beginning as this conference truly is. Of course, further and wider study will inevitably reveal the existence not only of superficial differences but also of important and fundamental theological and philosophical divergences between Hinduism and Catholicism on a variety of important matters. We should not fool ourselves. To say the least, Catholicism and Hinduism are far from holding the same positions on such questions as God, salvation, and the destiny of human beings. Yet in terms of the nature of human persons as chiefly spiritual beings and not just material, in terms of their social teachings, in terms of their views of the temporal order and a proper balance between state and society that rejects both statism and a pure libertarianism, in terms of the sanctity of marriage and the importance of the family as the natural and fundamental group unit of society, in terms of a recognition of the importance of community and a rejection of excessive individualism, in terms of a rejection of theocracy and religious coercion and persecution — on all these social and political matters of enormous importance, there is remarkably profound agreement that state and society should respect the principles of a robust and truly integral humanism that honors the spiritual nature and lofty dignity of every human being.

On this solid basis, there is such a strong potential for greater mutual understanding and cooperation that it would be a terrible mistake if we allowed what happens here at this conference to stay at this conference. On the contrary, we are, I think, under a divine obligation to take further decisive steps beyond this gathering to ensure that we build on the remarkable convergence that exists between the integral humanism of the great Deendayal Upadhyay and the integral humanism of the great Jacques Maritain. If we can continue what was begun at Banaras Hindu University under the leadership of Ram Madhav Ji and the India Foundation and the outstanding scholars and students of BHU, then we may soon see a day when millions of Catholics and millions of Hindus can work more closely and systematically together to advance a shared agenda of integral humanism not only in Bharat but across the world, and thus provide a much-needed example of civilizational cooperation rather than civilizational clash for the entire world, and for the benefit of human beings everywhere.

Endnotes

1 The text is an edited and expanded version of remarks Timothy Shah delivered at the International Conference on "Integral Humanism: Perspectives of Deendayal Upadhyay and Jacques Maritain," March 4, 2024, Banaras Hindu University, Varanasi, India.

2 For Maritain, among numerous texts that could be cited, see his discussion under the section heading "Natural Law" (Chapter IV, section III) in his classic *Man and the State* (Washington, D.C.: Catholic University of America Press, 1998), pp. 84 – 94. This

text is based on the distinguished Walgreen Lectures originally delivered at the University of Chicago in 1949. For Upadhyay, see his lecture on "Harmony between the Individual and the Collectivity," originally delivered as part of a four-day lecture series in Pune, Maharashtra, from 22 – 25 April 1965, and later published in the volume *Integral Humanism* (Noida: Jagriti Prakashan, 1992), pp. 36 – 60.

3 In *The Abolition of Man,* the English Christian thinker C. S. Lewis compellingly described a possible convergence between Hindu ideas (and Eastern thought in general) and Christian ideas (and Western thought in general) concerning a transcendent order that is both ontological and moral as follows: "In early Hinduism that conduct in men which can be called good consists in conformity to, or almost participation in, the *Rta*—that great ritual or pattern of nature and supernature which is revealed alike in the cosmic order, the moral virtues, and the ceremonial of the temple. Righteousness, correctness, order, the *Rta*, is constantly identified with *satya* or truth, correspondence to reality. As Plato said that the Good was 'beyond existence' and Wordsworth that through virtue the stars were strong, so the Indian masters say that the gods themselves are born of the *Rta* and obey it." He continues: "The Chinese also speak of a great thing (the greatest thing) called the *Tao.* It is the reality beyond all predicates, the abyss that was before the Creator Himself. It is Nature, it is the Way, the Road. It is the Way in which the universe goes on, the Way in which things everlastingly emerge, stilly and tranquilly, into space and time. It is also the Way which every man should tread in imitation of that cosmic and supercosmic progression, conforming all activities to that great exemplar. 'In ritual', say the *Analects*, 'it is harmony with Nature that is prized.' The ancient Jews likewise praise the Law as being 'true'." Lewis concludes: "This conception in all its forms, Platonic, Aristotelian, Stoic, Christian, and Oriental alike, I shall henceforth refer to for brevity simply as 'the *Tao*'. Some of the accounts of it which I have quoted will seem, perhaps, to many of you merely quaint or even magical. *But what is common to them all is something we cannot neglect. It is the doctrine of objective value, the belief that certain attitudes are really true, and others really false, to the kind of thing the universe is and the kind of*

things we are" [emphasis added], in C. S. Lewis, *The Abolition of Man* (New York: Collier Books, Macmillan Publishing Company, 1947), pp. 27 – 29. For a supporting view, see M. S. Sundaram, "The Natural Law in the Hindu Tradition," *University of Notre Dame Natural Law Institute Proceedings,* Vol. 5 (1951), pp. 69 – 88. For a powerful argument that there are important divergences between natural law as understood in the Thomistic Catholic tradition and Dharma in the Hindu tradition, see Martin Ganeri, "Natural Law and Hinduism," in R. Wilcox and A. Carty, eds., *Natural Law and Comparative Law*, JCL Studies in Comparative Law 12 (London: Wildy, Simmonds and Hill Publishing, 2015), pp. 98–128. I am grateful to Gavin D'Costa for helping me refine and clarify (and indeed restrain) my comparative discussion of Thomistic natural law and Hindu *Dharma* in the above and preceding text.

Chapter Seventeen

The Vision of Global Peace in Integral Humanism of Deendayal Upadhyay

Divyapani Dwivedi

The current world order remains volatile and instability is growing across the world with the end of USA led unipolar world, assertiveness from Russia and muscles flexing by China. The great power politics has always impacted the world through various ways; geopolitical rivalry and confrontation among great powers cause tensions, conflicts and wars in different parts of the world. Although great powers do not collide with each other directly but they remain indulged into conflicts from behind the scenes. There are two major wars going on currently, first between Russia and Ukraine and another between Israel and Hamas. In both cases, there are elements of power politics as well as quest for cultural supremacy. To safeguard its security interests Russia invaded Ukraine, backed by the USA-led Western countries which aimed at weakening Russia by humiliating it in the battle field. But this war extended beyond military face off and elements of cultural supremacy and cultural conflict remained in the background even in between Russia and Ukraine which have been historically associated with the each other through shared culture, religion and language. Israel and Hamas are fighting over cultural supremacy too; Hamas is backed by Iran, the self-proclaimed leader of Shia Muslims which aspires to eradicate Jewish state. This objective itself led to war in between Israel and Iran-backed Hamas, a terrorist group when Hamas attacked Israel with the objective of inflicting serious damage to Jewish state and its citizens. These two examples showcase the situations, the world is dealing with currently. The world is marred by wars and conflicts emerging from geopolitical rivalries, cultural and religious supremacy and other eminent factors. The existing models of global peace have failed to bring the peace in the world. The world is going through uncertainty over suitable and effective model of global peace which could show the light of hope to the world. In such circumstances, the world looks for alternative model of global peace and this is where integral humanism of Pandit Deendayal Upadhyay becomes extremely relevant and much required.

Deendayal Upadhyay's integral humanism advocates peace in the world and while advocating global peace, it emphasizes on mutual cooperation and coexistence. Integral humanism of Pandit Deendayal Upadhyay argues that Bhartiya culture shows the world how to live with peace and if world aims at global peace, it needs to look towards Bharat and its culture which does not see an individual as separated and divided but an integrated entity. Deendayal Upadhyay argues that holistic view of Bharat's culture advocates integration rather than division and this is what needs to be pursued for peace and coexistence in the world.[1] Human beings are in completeness rather than in parts, Deendayal Upadhyay believed so and when human beings are taken into consideration as 'whole', it would result in peace and coexistence rather than destruction, conflict and violence.

Deendayal Upadhyay's integral humanism also focuses on pursuit of 'Dharma'. Dharma's pursuit by a man would check it from committing undoable acts, Dharma would motivate a man for good conduct and harmony in society. Since a man is not separated from various entities of the universe, he would look to have coordination, cooperation and connect with society, state and the world. Deendayal Upadhyay also talks about pursuit of 'Dharma Rajya', a state where Dharma is followed in all its actions and pursuit. When a state would pursue Dharma, it can be stated that a state would avoid involving into invasion, conflict and war, which results in deaths of civilians, bloodshed and crimes against children, women and elderly.

Locating Global Peace Through Various Models

Global peace has been addressed by various models in the world. The majority of the models and theories advocating peace and presenting a blueprint for the same are associated with international politics. Achieving global peace remains a challenging task, despite continuous efforts by various global bodies and forums, global peace has not been achieved. When it comes to understanding 'peace', there are various kinds of arguments which differ with region, culture, political system and even domain of study. Here, we need to understand global peace approaches under two categories, state-centric and human-centric.

Theories of international relations talk about peace in the world too; these theories primarily look into peace from the lens of state-to-state relations. International Relations theories view peace from state-centric approach. Liberalism and constructivism emphasize on peace in the world through certain state-to-state measures. Liberalism argues that world is primarily peaceful and harmonious.[2] Michael Doyle argued that if the world is based on democratic principles and democracy flourishes in the world, the conflicts and wars could reduce significantly.[3] Doyle's core argument that democratic countries do not wage war on other democratic countries, has not been fully accurate and conflicts and wars have taken place in between democratic countries too in last few decades. Keohane and Nye's emphasis on complex interdependence reduces the chances of wars but it does not limit a country's attitude completely and chances of conflicts remain.[4] Complex interdependence theory argued that if countries remain bounded by economic measures, they would not attack another country considering economic losses due to conflict and war. Complex interdependence theory is of limited importance due to excessive emphasis on trade and economic ties, it does not consider other prominent factors. If a country does not possess huge market and economic prosperity is limited, it could face the conflicts and wars due to no major economic impact on invading country. Another theory, liberal institutionalism advocates cooperation in the world despite accepting the anarchic order.[5] The theory which accepts anarchy cannot establish and maintain global peace. The cooperation on the basis of liberal institutions have repeatedly failed in the global order in recent decades. Alexander Wendt rejected existing realist and liberal theories of international relations and argued that it is collective sense of identity that plays pivotal role in agent's behaviour towards the global order. Wendt also argued that it is beliefs, values and ideas which determine a state's policy towards others and there is nothing beyond human understanding.[6] Constructivism does present a roadmap of looking beyond liberal and realist framework, and focuses on human-centric approach while dealing with state's external affairs. Despite constructivism's emphasis on human-centric approach, this theory fails to address various policy issues i.e. changes in leaderships, new trends in domestic politics and citizen's aspirations etc.

Talking of human-centric approaches, there are several models of peace given by many thinkers but Mahatma Gandhi's vision and practices of global peace comes very first. Gandhi believed in truth and non-violence, he practised the same throughout his life. Gandhi's advocacy of non-violence even in case of violence inflicted on someone, shows how much importance he gave to peaceful means and non-violence. Gandhi's agenda for the mankind remained entrenched in non-violence and human progress. Gandhi believed in discussion and persuasion to resolve human conflicts.[7] Johan Galtung argued about division of peace into two; positive and negative peace. Positive peace talked about absence of personal violence as well as structural violence while negative peace primarily highlighted absence of violence and conflict.[8] In Galtung's concept of peace, human being was considered an essential entity while analysing conflict, violence and peace. Jacques Maritain gave the concept of 'Integral Humanism' too. Maritain applied Christian values in his analysis of social and political issues, he also focused on individual in his concept of integral humanism. Maritain denounced violence against Jews during World War II through his writings. All these models, theories and concepts failed to resolve existing violence and ongoing conflicts and wars in the world, which led to search for alternative model of global peace.

An Overview of Integral Humanism

Integral humanism of Deendayal Upadhyay addresses various social, political, and economic problems existing in India. Deendayal Upadhyay emphasizes on need of realization of self in his first lecture while when he concludes his lecture on 'Integral Humanism', he already covered social, political and economic challenges and their solutions. Deendayal Upadhyay believes that Bharat faced challenges due to negligence of its national identity.[9] He argued that no country should forget its past, it remains an important element of a country's national identity. While talking about Bharat, he emphasized on need of looking towards Bharat's glorious past. Deendayal Upadhyay argued about pursuing Bhartiya culture and recommended not to be too much impressed by culture of Western countries which are much different in various ways from Bhartiya culture.

Deendayal Upadhyay argued that Bhartiya culture shows the path to the entire world. Bhartiya culture is inclusive and integrated, it rejects division.[10] 'Vashudhaiv Kutumkam' (the entire world is a family) has been mantra of Bharatiya culture for the entire world. Bharatiya culture has emphasized on peace, inclusion, growth and development since time immemorial. That is why Deendayal Upadhyay advocated that Bharatiya culture could show the path of peace and development to the entire world. Deendayal Upadhyay emphasized a lot on Bhartiya culture and values in his integral humanism. He argues that Bhartiya culture looks towards life as "an integrated whole".[11] In Bhartiya culture, there is no division and partition, every element of life is connected to other. Deendayal Upadhyay highlighted that in Western countries, problems arise due to partition of various elements of life while Bhartiya culture considers various elements as integrated, which helps in assimilation and cooperation in between various elements of life unlike Western societies and countries. Bhartiya culture has always endorsed unity in diversity and expression of unity in various form. Unity in diversity remains a prominent trait of Bhartiya culture.

While talking of human life, Deendayal Upadhyay emphasizes on four key components of human being; body, mind, intellect and soul. He argues that there is integration among these four components.[12] The concept of Purusharthas covers all the aspects of human life. Soul is truly important but

Bhartiya culture does not neglect human body but it places certain conditions on fulfilment of human needs. Dharma, Artha, Kaam and Moksha, these are four purusharthas which have been given much importance by Deendayal Upadhyay. Dharma remains the most important purushartha among these four purusharthas and by practising Dharma, a man should earn livelihood (Artha). Artha earned through Dharma only, leads a man to worldly pleasures (Kaam). After fulfilment of three purusharthas, Dharma, Artha and Kaam, a man should aim at attaining Moksha. Deendayal Upadhyay stated that Dharma is important not just to achieve Artha and Kaam but Dharma is important due to its role in living "civilized life".[13] Deendayal Upadhyay believes that a man is not just limited to body, mind, intellect and soul but he is part of bigger creations i.e. society, nation, state etc. While talking of a man's connect with various institutions, Deendayal Upadhyay defines 'nation' as a group of people living with a goal, an ideal, a mission and do consider a land as motherland.[14] When people come together with these elements, a nation is formed. He also talks about 'Chiti', soul of the nation, which remains unchanged ever since the beginning of the nation.

Integral humanism also talks of supremacy of Dharma and asserts that it is Dharma which sustains society and nation. Dharma is placed very highly in Bhartiya culture and it remains backbone of society and nation. Whenever rule of Dharma declines, chaos takes over the society, nation and state. Dharma refers to righteous acts conducted by each and everyone in the state including the state itself, overriding Dharma would dismantle the society and nation. Deendayal Upadhyay emphasizes on notion of 'Dharma Rajya', a state which follows Dharma (righteous and moral conduct) while dealing with its citizens. Integral humanism of Pandit Deendayal Upadhyay rejects Marxism and Capitalism as models of economic development. Deendayal Upadhyay believed that neither Marxism nor Capitalism can resolve the existing problems of economic development and growth. He supported swadeshi and decentralization for India's economic progress and prosperity.

Integral Humanism as a Model of Global Peace

Integral humanism of Deendayal Upadhyay truly shows a path of peace to the world. When countries in the world are prioritizing national interests over any other things and waging wars and indulging into conflicts, Deendayal Upadhyay advocates for pursuit of Dharma in statecraft. Deendayal Upadhyay supported mutual cooperation and peaceful existence. Through mutual cooperation only, various issues and deferring perceptions can be resolved and a consensus can be achieved which would eventually refrain participating parties from indulging into conflicts. Deendayal Upadhyay was against dividing human relations into either friends or foes category and talked of cooperation in the society and nation to strengthen the human-to-human bondings. Deendayal Upadhyay emphasized that if human relationship is based on conflict and enmity, and if the human history is analysed in this way, it would be very difficult to hope for global peace.[15] So, integral humanism argues that conflicts must be avoided and enmity should not be practised if individuals aim to have human relations; the similar concept can be applied on state-to-state relations. If countries expect to have harmonious, stable and peaceful world, they must avoid conflicts and wars and have meaningful dialogues over contesting viewpoints since wars and conflicts would only make things worse and normal ties among countries would not be possible let alone global peace. Integral humanism also supports peaceful coexistence and this mantra could be used by countries of the world to get rid of blind pursuit of national interests through conflicts and wars. The idea of peaceful coexistence should be pursued in the world to establish peace and harmony across the world. In the world of nuclear weapons and state-of-art weapon systems, the idea of peaceful coexistence becomes extremely relevant in the world since a small misadventure could lead to enormous destruction.

Deendayal Upadhyay gave huge importance to Dharma (righteous act) in his concept of integral humanism. Dharma has traditionally taken prominent place in Bhartiya culture and Hindu scriptures including Vedas and Upanishads. Traditionally, Dharma is considered to be the supreme authority in the matters of Bhartiya culture as well as nation and state. Pandit Deendayal Upadhyay follows the similar theory and gives utmost importance to Dharma in all matters of individual and state. Dharma is that guiding principle which prevents individual, society and nation from any kind of undoable acts and motivates to pursue righteousness. Pursuit of Dharma would not let a country do unjust, immoral and unethical conduct. Waging a war or indulging in conflict with another country leaves thousands dead and brutally injured in the battlefield from both the sides in addition to heinous acts conducted by both the sides against women, children and elderly people; this scenario goes against nature of Dharma. Pursuit of Dharma by the state would prohibit it from conflict, war and violence. The practice of Dharma by states in the world could prove very significant in addressing conflicts and wars.

Deendayal Upadhyay suggested the vision of 'Dharma Rajya'. Dharma is pursuit of righteous acts and duty while Rajya means state, so basically Dharma Rajya denotes to a state following righteous acts. Dharma Rajya would pursue righteous conducts for its citizens primarily but it would not neglect others. Deendayal Upadhyay believes that Dharma Rajya is good for all three; motherland, people and culture.[16]

In Dharma Rajya, the approach towards everything would be open and unbounded. Deendayal Upadhyay argues that welfare and prosperity of its citizens is the major objective of Dharma Rajya; if a single citizen remains unhappy due to unavailability of means of livelihood, it is against the nature of Dharma Rajya.[17] Dharma Rajya does not oppose religion neither it talks of secular state. Dharma Rajya accepts the role of region in pursuit of peace and happiness for an individual. For maintaining due conditions for religious practices by individuals, Dharma Rajya should attempt to do everything at its disposal. Individual remains at the very centre of Dharma Rajya, whatever policies, measures and decisions are introduced and put into action that must keep its citizen's welfare, happiness and prosperity in focus. Deendayal Upadhyay clearly argued that a state's horizon of welfare and progress should also consider human beings across the world and there should be coordination with individuals and states considering welfare of humanity.[18] He was of opinion that thinking about only ourselves should not be our objective, interests of our society, nation and country are important but our horizon should be beyond these limits and we should also focus on humanity and entire world. This vision is truly remarkable keeping in mind the geopolitical rivalries, wars and conflicts over lands and religions and unethical pursuit of national interests. The global peace can be established if all the states of the world pursue their Dharma (righteous acts) and avoid fighting useless wars over petty objectives for the welfare of humanity and the entire world.

Deendayal Upadhyay's argument that an individual is not mere a member of his family but also of society, nation, state and then whole mankind and universe, shows connect among people of the world; all human being in the world is integrated with the larger entity, universe and this integration should be understood by the leadership of the countries. Countries do have national interests to pursue and their pursuit of interests are for their citizens, since human beings are part of mankind and universe, there should be effective mechanism in place to address various points of difference. Even if, differences do persist, countries should avoid going for conflict keeping in mind, the impact of conflict on their citizens and whole mankind. This would really prove effective measure to stop any conflict and war from happening in the world since in today's time, a war not only impacts the countries directly involved in the war but also the entire region and the world because of some sort of economic integration due to globalization.

Conclusion

Deendayal Upadhyay's integral humanism truly highlights Bhartiya culture and its outlook towards various social, political and economic issues. Integral humanism of Deendayal Upadhyay advocates for integration; integration should be in human's connect with various institutions i.e. family, society, nation, country, entire mankind and universe. Deendayal Upadhyay does not see individual into fractions, his argument emanates from analysis of Bhartiya culture. He also emphasizes on mutual cooperation and coexistence in the society. Taking it into larger picture, the world could live with harmonious order and differing perceptions could be resolved through negotiations and considering humanity at the centre of all decisions.

Dharma remains very prominent entity in Deendayal Upadhyay's integral humanism. Dharma should be pursued by a state while indulging in welfare of its citizens as well as in statecraft. Dharma shows right path to the individual and those taking decisions and making policies for the individuals. Since, existence of human beings go beyond horizon of state, every state should consider welfare of humanity and the universe too. Waging wars and indulging in conflicts are against the very foundation of Dharma; the enormous loss of human beings and crimes committed during wars do not represent Dharma. States should establish Dharma Rajya, a state pursuing righteous acts. Dharma Rajya would prevent decision-makers from inflicting harm on citizens of another state, since it is against Dharma. India is a good example of that which has never invaded another country for religious purposes or territory. This model of Deendayal Upadhyay being relevant in today's context may be implemented as an alternative to existing models of global peace.

Endnotes

1 Deendayal Upadhyay. *Integral Humanism* (Chitrakoot: Deendayal Research Institute, 2002), p. 13.

2 Scott Burchill. "Liberalism", in Scott Burchill et al (Eds.) *Theories of International Relations* (New York: Palgrave Macmillan, 2005), 3rd edition, p. 58.

3 Michael W. Doyle. "Kant, Liberal Legacies, and Foreign Affairs," *Philosophy & Public Affairs*, vol. 13, no. 3 (1983), p. 217.

4 Robert Keohane and Joseph Nye. *Power and Interdependence* (New York: Longman, 2012), p. 24.

5 Burchill, Scott. op. cit., p. 64.

6 Alexander Wendt. "Anarchy is what state make of it: the social construction of power politics," *International Organization*, vol. 46 (March 1992), pp. 391-425. https://www.jstor.org/stable/pdf/2706858 (Accessed February 12, 2024).

7 Bhikhu Parekh. *Gandhi: A Very Short Introduction* (New York: Oxford University Press, 2001), p. 64.

8 Johan Galtung. "Violence, Peace, and Peace Research," *Journal of Peace Research*, vol. 6, no. 3 (1969), p. 183.

9 Upadhyay, Deendayal (2002). op. cit., p. 4.

10 Upadhyay, Deendayal (2002). op. cit., p. 13.

11 Deendayal Upadhyay. *Integral Humanism* (Noida: Jagriti Prakashan, 1968), p. 24.

12 Ibid., p. 30.

13 Ibid., p. 33.

14 Upadhyay, Deendayal (2002). op. cit., pp. 24-25.

15 Upadhyay, Deendayal (1968). op. cit., p. 27.

16 Deendayal Upadhyay. *Raastra Chintan* (Lucknow: Lokhit Prakashan, 2007), p. 117.

17 Ibid., pp. 117-118.

18 Ibid., p. 125.

Conclusion

Conclusion

The Legacy Continues: Deendayal Upadhyay and Jacques Maritain

Sonu Trivedi

The exploration of 'Integral Humanism' through the perspectives of Deendayal Upadhyay and Jacques Maritain presents a profound intersection of political thought, spirituality, and ethics. Both thinkers, despite emerging from vastly different cultural, religious, and historical contexts, converge on the idea of an integrated view of the humanism that transcends materialism, promoting the holistic development of individuals and societies. At the heart of their thought lies a fundamental commitment to the dignity of the human person.

Deendayal Upadhyay's 'Integral Humanism,' rooted in Indian philosophical traditions, particularly 'Dharma', emphasises the balanced development of the "body, mind, intellect, and soul - these four make up an individual which are all integrated. We cannot think of each part separately." For Upadhyay, the individual cannot be seen in isolation from the community or the cosmos. His vision integrates the individual into the larger social and spiritual fabric, focusing on the symbiotic relationship between the 'self' and 'society.' This integral approach seeks to harmonise the spiritual and material needs of human beings, countering the extremes of both capitalism and socialism.

Deendayal Upadhyay developed the seminal concept of 'Chiti' which describes the values that constitute the nation. According to him, "Chiti' is the soul of the nation." He emphasises the importance of cultural nationalism and the preservation of India's rich heritage in shaping a holistic human existence. Additionally, Deendayal Upadhyay's integral humanism promotes the idea of a decentralised and self-reliant economy, where local communities play a crucial role in decision-making and development. This vision aligns with the principles of 'Antyodaya' focusing on the upliftment of the last person in society. He argued that economic development should not be pursued at the expense of social and cultural values, emphasising the need for a balanced and harmonious approach.

Within the context of Western Philosophy, Jacques Maritain, a catholic philosopher and political theorist, contributed significantly to the development of integral humanism. Influenced by Thomistic philosophy, Maritain sought to reconcile the principles of classical philosophy with Christian theology. His 'Integral Humanism' places human dignity at its core, emphasising the intrinsic worth and rights of every individual. He understood, "humanism as inseparable from civilization or culture, these two words being themselves taken as synonymous." According to him, "culture or civilization is the expansion of not only whatever is needed for the material, but also above all moral development of speculative and practical (artistic and ethical) activities which is properly worthy of being called 'human development'." He further goes on to say that "civilization, thus develops between two poles: the economic pole on the one side dealing with the most urgent human necessities of the 'ethico-biological order', and the religious pole on the other side relating to the most urgent human necessities of the 'soul'". For him, "the true religion is essentially supernatural and, because it is supernatural, it is not of man, nor of the world, nor of a race, nor of a nation, nor of a civilization, nor of a culture—it is of the intimate life of God. It transcends every civilization and every culture; it is strictly universal."

Maritain's vision of 'Integral Humanism' incorporates a commitment to social justice and the common good constituting both material and moral aspect of life. He advocates for a society where political structures are aligned with ethical principles, fostering an environment where individuals can flourish spiritually, morally, and intellectually. His concept of integral humanism has had a great influence overall on the 'Christian Democratic' movements in Europe and Latin America.

Convergences and Divergences in Approach and Context

Although Upadhyay and Maritain came from vastly different religious traditions and cultural backgrounds, their shared concerns over the spiritual and ethical crises of their times create intriguing points of convergence. Both rejected the reduction of the human person to mere material or economic dimensions. They sought to offer a more comprehensive view of human life that integrated the material with the spiritual, the individual with the community, and freedom with responsibility.

However, the contributors of this volume have also pointed out the significant differences between the two thinkers. Upadhyay's vision was rooted in the philosophical traditions of ancient India, while Maritain's was deeply Christian, shaped by the Catholic intellectual tradition. Upadhyay's focus on 'Dharma' as the basis of social order contrasts with Maritain's emphasis on natural law and Christian personalism. These differences highlight the rich diversity within the broader concept of integral humanism, showing that it can be adapted to various cultural and religious contexts while maintaining its core commitment to human dignity and ethical responsibility.

While the two thinkers share a commitment to holistic human development, their approaches diverge in their cultural and philosophical foundations. Upadhyay's vision is deeply embedded in the Indian civilisational ethos, particularly the principles of 'Dharma,' which he seeks to reinterpret in a modern context. His focus on a decentralised polity, the self-reliance, and the integration of India's cultural values with modern governance reflects a unique response to the challenges of post-colonial India.

Maritain, on the other hand, emerges from the European catholic tradition, responding to the crises of modernity, secularism, and totalitarianism. His integral humanism is shaped by the need to reconcile religion and faith with democracy in a world increasingly governed by secular ideologies. While Upadhyay critiques western materialism, Maritain's thought grapples with reconciling individual liberty and human rights within a democratic, pluralistic framework that remains open to transcendence.

In today's rapidly transforming world, where cultural, economic, and political challenges continue to deepen, the concept of integral humanism offers a vital framework for addressing the needs of individuals and communities. Both Upadhyay and Maritain provide alternative visions to purely materialist or individualist philosophies that dominate much of contemporary thought. Upadhyay's emphasis on the balance between spiritual and material development resonates with contemporary calls for sustainable development and the need for a more ethical approach to modernisation. His advocacy for self-reliance and the decentralisation of political power voices the movements that critique the homogenising forces of this material world. Maritain's focus on human rights, democracy, and pluralism is equally relevant, especially in contexts where authoritarianism, inequality, and secularism are on the rise. His insistence on the spiritual dimension of the human person challenges purely secular ideologies, offering a model for integrating religious values into modern democratic governance without undermining individual freedoms or the plurality of society.

The Legacy Continues

As we reflect on the legacies of Upadhyay and Maritain, we find a robust foundation for addressing the challenges of the modern world which lies at an inflection point today engulfed by sectarian violence, humanitarian crises, social inequalities and the degradation of human values. Their calls for a balanced approach to development and the emphasis on ethical governance resonate powerfully today.

Integral Humanism envisions a society that prioritise human dignity and moral values, recognising the interconnectedness of all people. It challenges us to cultivate communities where compassion, respect, and mutual aid are not merely ideals but lived realities. In an era marked by polarisation and division, the teachings of Upadhyay and Maritain offer a way forward to dialogue, understanding, and cooperation across cultural and ideological boundaries.

This edited volume, which brings together the insights of eighteen contributors, serves not only as a reflection on the historical and philosophical impact of Deendayal Upadhyay and Jacques Maritain but also as an invitation to reimagine their contributions for the present and future. Both thinkers, while emerging from different cultural and ideological contexts crafted a vision of integral humanism that transcended the particularities of their origins. Their work speaks to the universal yearning for a society rooted in human dignity, ethical principles, and spiritual wholeness.

Throughout the preceding chapters, scholars have articulated various facets of integral humanism, illustrating how this philosophical framework can be applied to the challenges of modernity. It is evident that Upadhyay and Maritain, despite their different points of departure, shared a common goal: to offer a holistic alternative to the fragmentations of liberalism, materialism, and extreme ideologies that disregard the human person's spiritual dimension.

One of the central themes explored in this book is how Upadhyay's vision continues to resonate in the Indian context, especially as the nation grapples with various socio-cultural, economic and political challenges. His call for swadeshi, local autonomy, and self-reliance remains relevant in today's push for sustainable development along with decentralised and digital governance. The emphasis on cultural rootedness without falling into chauvinism provides a model for other post-colonial societies navigating their paths between tradition and modernity.

The contributors have also highlighted Upadhyay's profound understanding of the spiritual dimension of human life. By rejecting the reductive materialism of both capitalism and socialism, he presented a vision of development that encompasses the moral, ethical, and spiritual upliftment of society. In this, Upadhyay's integral humanism offers a critique of western economic paradigms and proposes a more inclusive, holistic approach to human development.

The essays on Maritain in this volume underline his importance in shaping the political thought of the 20th century, particularly in post-war Europe. As one of the architects of Christian democracy, Maritain's ideas informed the creation of political institutions that sought to balance the demands of individual liberty with the common good. His defense of human rights, grounded in the inviolable dignity of the person, remains a foundational contribution to contemporary human rights discourse.

Maritain's vision, like Upadhyay's, called for a rejection of the purely secular and materialist conception of man. He insisted on the necessity of metaphysical foundations for the proper understanding of the human being and society, urging that politics and culture must be permeated by moral values. This is where his legacy speaks profoundly to today's increasingly fragmented world, grounded in respect for the human person and the transcendent.

Conclusion

The contributors through this volume have demonstrated the continuing relevance of integral humanism in addressing the moral, social, and political challenges of our time. As we face the complexities of the 21st century, with its deepening inequalities, humanitarian crises, and the alienation brought on by rapid technological change, the insights of Upadhyay and Maritain offer invaluable guidance. The convergence of their thought on integral humanism reminds us that true human development cannot be reduced to economic growth or individual liberty alone; rather, it requires a harmonious integration of the material, social, and spiritual dimensions of life. The legacy of Deendayal Upadhyay and Jacques Maritain proposes to reconsider the role of spirituality and ethics in public life. Their integral humanism calls for a renewed commitment to building societies where human dignity is at the centre, where material progress does not come at the cost of spiritual degradation, and where the common good is pursued in harmony with individual freedom. It challenges us to envision a future where human beings are seen not merely as economic units or political actors, but as integral wholes—rooted in our cultural traditions and guided by ethical principles. It is in this balance that the promise of integral humanism lies—a vision that speaks to the deepest needs of both the individual and society in our time.

As this volume has shown, the dialogue between these two thinkers opens new roadmap for understanding human dignity and the role of society in fostering human development. In an era where sectarianism and fragmentation seem to dominate, the synthesis of these diverse perspectives offers a rich resource for building more integrated, humane, and compassionate societies. This book serves as a reminder that the wisdom of these two great thinkers can inspire us to forge new paths for human development, rooted in the belief that a truly integral society must care for both the material and spiritual requirements of its people.

Index

M

N

O

P

R

S

T

U

V

W

Y